The Long Wait

AND
OTHER
PSYCHOANALYTIC
NARRATIVES

M. MASUD R. KHAN

Summit Books

NEW YORK LONDON TORONTO SYDNEY TOKYO

SUMMIT BOOKS
SIMON & SCHUSTER BUILDING
ROCKEFELLER CENTER
1230 AVENUE OF THE AMERICAS
NEW YORK, NEW YORK 10020
COPYRIGHT © 1989 BY M. MASUD R. KHAN
ALL RIGHTS RESERVED
INCLUDING THE RIGHT OF REPRODUCTION
IN WHOLE OR IN PART IN ANY FORM.
ORIGINALLY PUBLISHED IN GREAT BRITAIN BY CHATTO & WINDUS LTD
UNDER THE TITLE *WHEN SPRING COMES:*
AWAKENINGS IN CLINICAL PSYCHOANALYSIS
SUMMIT BOOKS AND COLOPHON ARE TRADEMARKS
OF SIMON & SCHUSTER INC.
MANUFACTURED IN THE UNITED STATES OF AMERICA

1   3   5   7   9   10   8   6   4   2

LIBRARY OF CONGRESS CATALOGING-IN-PUBLICATION DATA

KHAN, M. MASUD R.
THE LONG WAIT AND OTHER PSYCHOANALYTIC
NARRATIVES / M. MASUD R. KHAN.
P.   CM.
BIBLIOGRAPHY: P.
INCLUDES INDEX.
ISBN 0-671-66621-5
1. PSYCHOANALYSIS—CASE STUDIES.   2. SEX (PSYCHOLOGY)—CASE STUDIES.
3. POWER (SOCIAL SCIENCES)—CASE STUDIES.   I. TITLE.
RC509.8.K47 1988
616.89'17—DC19   88-30798
                                             CIP

Contents

Foreword

When I started to collect these writings for publication, I had given them the title *Transgression: Passions, Pain and Solitude*. Now, preparing my texts for press some while later, I find that the dominant theme is rather that of 'awakening' – the acknowledgement and acceptance of those acts of transgression which invariably arise, in all areas of relating, from any attempt to satisfy needs, desires and demands.

Looking over the three books of monotheistic religions – the Old Testament, the Bible and the Holy Koran – one is struck by the fact that transgression is at the beginning of both individual character and collective cultures. Thinking about it further, one notices that, of course, there can be no transgression unless there is an *interdiction*. After all, having placed a human couple in Paradise, the Good Lord did forbid them to eat a particular fruit, and transgression followed. One also notices that transgression almost always is both in character and intent, power and sex. The first transgression, by Adam, resulted in a sexual happening. The consequence of that was the two sons, Abel and Cain. They struggled for power and Cain killed Abel. So, from the beginning of human life, according to these three scriptures, transgression, murder and sex make a curious trinity.

The major task each monotheistic religion sets itself is to make a person take responsibility for his transgression, which is only possible if he awakens to its nature, the need it satisfies in his character and the role it plays in his life. That sex and murder should play an important part in the lives of those who feature in my clinical writings (even though as fantasy rather than fact) is nothing out of the ordinary. These are the pervasive themes in all contemporary literature.

The primary task of any psychotherapeutic venture undertaken by two persons is to enable the one seeking help to awaken to the hidden or repressed forces in his or her nature, and their correlates in human conduct. Only through such an awakening, which can often be extremely painful, can a self become its own true person and function as such in the total matrix of his social environment. Religions, particularly the monotheistic ones, have always laid great emphasis on such self-realisation, and in St Augustine's own words we have very moving accounts of the travails which the early Christians had to undergo in order to find their true vocation in life amongst others.

A question which inevitably arises in connection with any form of counselling is why a two-person relationship is more conducive to awakening a person to the totality of his wishes and desires, needs and wants, overt or hidden, than solitary introspection, which is certainly more private. One reason is that *the other* is, by and large, a less censorious and inhibiting agent than a person's own vigilant self-awareness, unless, of course, a person is indulging in megalomaniac fantasies. Another reason is that conversing with *the other* is limited, both temporally and spatially, and so saves a person from the nightmare of perpetual chattering in the head. A third reason could be that the very sympathy and empathy of the listening person reassures the speaking person that his experiences are not absurdly and fantastically peculiar to himself; that, no matter how uncomfortable or bizarre they may be, they have a lot in common with the experience of other human beings and he is not a maniacal isolate.

Those familiar with my earlier books – *The Privacy of the Self* (1974), *Alienation in Perversions* (1979) and *Hidden Selves* (1983) – will notice a distinct change both in the type of clinical material presented here and in my manner of presenting it. In this book I am more intent upon stating candidly my role *vis-à-vis* a particular patient, and my own experience of the clinical relationship, than in any of the case histories narrated previously. Also, I had begun to realise that the patient's *style* of communicating is more him/her than most of their recounted 'acts'. Furthermore, we, as clinicians, know of a patient's 'acts' only from his spoken narratives; unless he or she is hospitalised, we rarely witness them. This is my reason for describing, often in some detail, how a patient conducts himself and dresses. Sartorial self-presentation tells a lot. I am aware that the emphasis I have placed on these factors has sometimes made for a less conceptualised rendering of case material than before, but I believe that as a result the reader will be

able to identify that much more closely with my patients, and their
needs, desires and demands.

A final point that I know will fare poorly with my Freudian
colleagues, yet it could receive some sympathetic attention from those
readers who have a wider humanistic culture. All of the patients who
appear in these pages had been reared by devoutly religious parents: of
Judaic, or Christian, or Muslim faith. They had transgressed against
their faith and beliefs through their sexual perversities of character and
the berserk antics of living which their neediness led them into. But the
faith one is born to, one can rarely shed. Carl Jung has acknowledged
this publicly and professionally, and Professor Doctor Sigmund Freud
only in correspondence, privately:

> I . . . would like to take it that if the child turns out to be a
> boy, he will develop into a stalwart Zionist.
>
> Freud to Sabina Spielrein
> 28 August 1913

M. MASUD R. KHAN
London
July 1987

I
Prisons

Then learn that mortal man must always look to his ending. And none
can be called happy until that day when he carries His happiness down
to the grave in peace.

SOPHOCLES *King Oedipus*

In such cases the repetition can be recognised in a discernible pattern
of events. We may say, as a pointer, that in the case of fate neurosis,
the subject has no access to an unconscious wish, which he thus first
encounters coming back at him, as it were, from the outside world
(whence the 'daemonic' aspect stressed by Freud).

J. LAPLANCHE AND J.-B. PONTALIS
The Language of Psycho-Analysis

PROLOGUE

Bill died last year, after a brief illness and heart failure. He was sixty-
nine years old; we had known each other for some thirty years – as
analyst and patient/person – although his three periods of analysis with
me occupied less than a third of that time. When I look back across
those years, it is very hard still to define what was the nature of the
bond between us. We respected each other and we cared. But the
relating never developed into a relationship proper: transference-wise
or inter-personally. Each kept his distance and allowed for the other's
autonomy and need not to be exposed or pried into. Only in the very
last years of his life did Bill personalise into having a self that could be
private as well as sharing. Since childhood he had had 'a profound
awareness of being fated to exist and observe'. But, he would add, he
had never dismayed or given up. What his true affliction was we never
really understood. But we learned from each other how to help Bill to
shift gradually from gamesmanship *with* himself and others, to living
from himself.

Bill first came to me for analysis in 1953, when he was thirty-nine years old. The referring psychiatrist had sent me a brief note, after a short consultative interview with Bill. His diagnosis was: a homosexual, who complains of a theoretical dislike of homosexuality. Ruminative, anxious and obsessional . . . Has had some analytic treatment before, in his country, with no worsening or improvement. Prognosis: poor.

As I start to write this account of Bill's last 'analysis' – in 1976, for a period of three months – I realise I have written about him three times already:

1. After sixteen months of analysis. The paper, published in Dutch in 1969, was titled 'The homosexual nursing of self and object' (1955).
2. After nearly five years of analysis, when Bill had returned to his country to take up research work. This paper was called 'Foreskin fetishism and its relation to ego-pathology in a male homosexual' (1965).
3. After Bill had come for a further year of analysis (1961–2). An account of some aspects of this, together with the 1965 paper, was first published in French as 'Le fétichisme comme negation du soi' (1970) and subsequently appeared in my book *Alienation in Perversions*.

For the new reader, I shall begin with a brief recapitulation of the salient features of Bill's life and 'analyses', and add a few details which I was previously unable to state.

Bill was born in England, the second of four children: he had an elder brother and a sister two-and-a-half years younger from his mother's first marriage, which ended when he was seven years old. His mother married again immediately, a rich man, and had another son. She left with her husband and children for another country when Bill was eight. The mother, from his earliest childhood, had made Bill both a witness and a confidant of her life with both her husbands, with each of which she had been passionately and vociferously unhappy. On her remarriage she had told Bill that all her three sons were from her second husband, and the daughter from another man; that her first husband was a dirty man, with nasty sexual habits – hence she had changed the boys' surname to that of her present husband.

Bill's parents came back to England when he was twenty, but he stayed in his country to complete his university education. He took a bachelor's degree in literature and political science, and another in law. But he never practised law. He was twenty-three years old then, and spent a year in a state of 'dull and insipid non-existence' (his words), only *fantasying* compulsively about beautiful young adolescent boys, with foreskin (cf Winnicott, 1971c), and masturbating, and feeling disgust afterwards. He had no real sexual experience with any boy during this time. Then he suddenly decided to leave his university town and become a labourer working in the mines. Just as he had made no friends at college, he lived an isolated, meagre existence in the mining town, shirking even making acquaintances and staying in a small bare room. He would later talk of this as perhaps the truest life he had led.

In 1940 he was called up for army service in the Second World War. He was taken prisoner by the Japanese in 1942, and spent a year in a P.O.W. camp in Singapore and two years in Japan. He was released and returned to his country in 1945. Once back, he again felt resourceless. He said little about his years in P.O.W. camps in the 'first two analyses'. It was only in the 'third analysis', as we shall see, that he grasped how he had survived the awesome and totally impetuous cruelty of the Japanese soldiers. Thousands had died in his camp.

He spent a year doing odd jobs, listlessly. Then he was offered a very good job in the foreign service in 1950. He accepted it and *panicked*. It was then that he first sought analytic treatment, with a distinguished female analyst (and there were very few analysts in his country) who had trained in London. It was during this analysis that he started to enact his fetishistic sexual fantasies into actual sexual experiences. Once started, the prowling and sex took over all his spare time. But he was also very adept at work, and within two years was offered a high-ranking job in that country's embassy in London, which he immediately accepted. His analyst had given him the name of the psychiatrist in London who had referred him to me in 1953. He spoke little of his previous analyst, except that she was very kind, but he could sense her intentions to make a heterosexual male of him.

The person who turned up for the 'first analysis' was a robustly built man, dressed like a diplomat. Rather sardonic, as well as laconic of speech. He started off by saying: 'Of course, you want to know about my childhood', and told, affectlessly, rather bizarre 'actual' memories and fantasies from the ages of three, five and eight years (cf Khan, 1970). He paused, expecting a response from me, and I said simply: 'What else have you rehearsed to declaim here?' He was rather taken aback and tried to befuddle as well as placate me by asking: 'Would you like to know about my chief pursuit in life? Seducing young boys. I have made quite an unfailing expertise of it.' I noted his pertinent and lucid use of language. I decided to unsettle him, and said: 'There will be time enough to hear all that. First let us see whether we are the sort of persons who can suffer each other working towards a common goal; a goal which neither you nor I know at present.' He was sitting facing me. He panicked a little, and asked: 'You are not going to refuse me?' I said nothing. He became more and more ill at ease. His blustering stance crumbled. But he wasn't going to give up easily. He enquired: 'Do you always take notes? Dr X never did.' I said: 'No, not always. But it is useful to keep one alert, when nothing is happening clinically.' He paused and asked: 'Will I have to lie down on the couch, and be a good boy?' I said: 'Yes, if I accept to analyse you, you shall have to use the couch. As to the good boy business! You will find it is really not so terrifying undergoing analysis as you dread it to be.' Anyway, we agreed upon his starting analysis, five times a week.

I am quite surprised how extensively I have taken notes of his 'three analyses'. I shall discuss this later on.

In my earlier paper (1965), I had deliberately left out the fact – because the patient wanted me to – that after sixteen months of analysis with me, when he had started a 'stable' relationship with a circumcised youth, he had become so delusionally jealous of the youth that he kept watch over all his activities. Here we explored the enormity of his identifications with his mother. But alas, insight had little meaning or value for him. He resigned his job to devote himself totally to the youth. I could see only too clearly, but helplessly, that he was having a breakdown. Soon he was without money and could not pay any fees, and started taking jobs as a part-time labourer again. I didn't insist on fees or interpret to him his need to be totally dependent on me. I also knew the foreign service job was not *true* to him. Now he was more Bill than he had ever been before, because I was sharing his predicament of being *fated* – without intrusive, precipitate, interpretative 'assault' on him – to show what he was doing to himself and me. This phase lasted some six months. Then he quietened down in his frenzy and the compulsion to render himself destitute and hapless. Fortunately the youth stayed by him, without making excessive demands. He now wanted me to arrange for the youth to have unpaid analysis at the British Institute of Psycho-Analysis, and I did manage that. He 'rewarded' me, because he could not accept any form of being given to, while seeking it frantically all the time, by answering an advertisement for a job with the London County Council as a clerk.

Now something quite unexpected and remarkable happened. Bill came across some very ordinary data relating to animal procreativity, from which he created a hypothesis for research. He started going to polytechnic classes, in the evening, to learn chemistry and biology, since he needed that knowledge for his 'research'. All this went along with his infidelity in his relationship to the youth, and his work at the LCC. Gradually he was able to experiment with guinea-pigs, which he kept in the one room he lived in. I supported him financially whenever he was very needy. During this phase his father died and left him a little money. Within a year he had written three articles on his research, which were published in a prestigious journal relating to his work. On the strength of these he was able to get a research grant, and returned to his country. By now he had been in analysis for nearly five years. I did not try to stop him, though I knew how very precarious his emergent creative functioning was.

Once back home, he kept in touch with me, writing every Christmas for four years. He would also send me, infrequently, a little money towards what he owed me. Then I did not hear from him for two years until one day in 1961 he rang me from London seeking an appointment. The man I met had 'faded' and aged noticeably. The only time he had picked up a youth in his country he had made a mistake; he was arrested and sentenced to two years' imprisonment, of which he served only fifteen months before being released for good conduct (cf Khan, 1970). In prison he had been, from choice, given solitary confinement, and allowed to read books on chemistry and biology. The irony of it all was that during his prison sentence, his researches began to get real international recognition. Nowhere else, either in my clinical experience or reading, have I encountered such a *direct* sublimation of a most absurd sexual fantasy into creative scientific work, as in Bill's discovery of his project for research. After a further year's analysis (Khan, 1970), Bill returned to his country to continue his research. There he now had ample grants and a proper laboratory available to him in a university.

Again he stayed in touch with me, mostly sending offprints of his published research articles. Then one day, fourteen years after his 'second analysis', I received a telegram from him, asking whether he could come for three months of intensive analysis – that being the summer holiday period in his country, whilst it was winter in London. I cabled back: Yes, of course. He arrived within a week and stayed for over three months, attending four to seven sessions weekly – according to my schedule of commitments.

THE FINAL PHASE: THE 'THIRD ANALYSIS'

As I prepared to encounter Bill, myriad thoughts, impressions, apprehensions, etc. scampered through my mind. I was worried, too. Though I knew from his offprints and short accompanying notes that his research had thrived, yet I had no clue as to his private life; which led me to think deeper, and with astonishment, that in spite of having known this patient for twenty-three years, I hardly knew him as a person. For that matter, nor did anyone else. It would be too facile to say that he 'fooled' us all, and *used* us according to his purposes – one cannot talk of his needs or desires even: he was a man more 'lived upon' than 'living'. Furthermore, I had a rather vague and patchy personal recollection of him, though I knew the fatuous and prolix antics of his pathological sexual gamesmanship with the youths in considerable detail. I say 'considerable', and not 'extensive', because I had deliberately curbed any clinical curiosity, even about his tactics and strategies of sexually seducing the youths, and his wilful concern to engender a 'trust' and hopefulness in them, only to abandon them, and be bereft and disillusioned again himself (Khan, 1970). I had very early on in his 'first analysis' taken a hint most seriously as a guide to my clinical approach and relating: he had casually remarked that his first analyst had been too eager to know all about his sexual fantasies, and that her interpretations that he was *resisting*, when he would not talk about his sexual reveries in a session, had somehow led to his enacting his fantasies into real experiences. We had kept a viable distance of relating between us, because I suspected that even what might have seemed to me justifiable as deep clinical interpretative work could, in

fact, be another form of his making me both an accomplice and an
agent to his sexual prowling and practices, and/or be experienced by
him as a sort of *intimacy* between us.

Here I would like to say, in parenthesis, that only now did I become
conscious of what copious notes I had taken both during and after
Bill's analytic sessions. Today, with hindsight, I can say with confidence that note-taking served two main purposes: (i) It put him aside
on paper, as it were; I did not psychically or affectively internalise him.
This helped me to maintain that certain 'distance' that I needed to work
with, and for, him, positively and constructively; (ii) It protected me
from being bored by the compulsive repetitive nature of his sexual
escapades and charades. Here, as in many other respects, I was greatly
helped, during Bill's 'first analysis', by D. W. Winnicott with whom I
myself was then in analysis. This leads me to another aside: the care
and analysis of such patients and persons succeeds only if we do not
imprison them in the *huis clos* of the fifty minutes of analytic time and
space. That leads to an intensification of affectivity, which they have no
way of experiencing except as an ungraspable persecution, or to which
they react by proliferating their mentation and fantasying even more
compulsively (cf Winnicott, 1949, 1971c).

In various ways, theoretically and clinically, Winnicott (1949) has
shown with profound acumen 'how mental activity can be exploited
and become the enemy of the psyche'. I would add: an enemy of true
affectivity, too. I had, at one point in the 'first analysis', pointed out to
Bill that perhaps Dr X's 'nosiness' (as he called it) had done him one
great service towards his *self-cure* (Khan, 1974a): that is, rescued him
from the deadening, encapsulated states of his withdrawn sexual
ruminations, and at least put him 'in life' with *the other*, no matter
how fugitively and pathologically. His enactments with the youths (I
am again eschewing using the concept of acting out) punctured his
phoney sense of self-sufficiency and compelled him to acknowledge his
need of, and dependence on, *the other* for 'personalising', no matter
how precariously, transiently and fretfully. Because, like his mother,
behind his obsessionally smooth facade, Bill was horrifically fretful
and hysterical within himself. All his *expertise* and its successes stayed
external and alien to him.

In the aftermath of these episodes, he experienced only disgust,
dismay and disillusionment. 'Something' had again not actualised

experientially. In Winnicott's (1960a) idiom: '. . . the False Self (like the multiple projections at later stages of development) deceives the analyst if the latter fails to notice that, regarded as a whole functioning person, the False Self, however well set up, lacks something, and that something is the essential central element of creative originality'. This is why I never questioned his escapades. Once he had riled me for being *a*moral, whereas he had sensed Dr X's withheld disapprobation. I also recall another feature of my clinical handling of this patient, namely that, as well as discussing him with Winnicott in my analysis, I discussed him with two very close colleagues, whom I trusted. I rarely do that. And it certainly was not from fear I might make a mistake that could lead to trouble, though that possibility was always present. It was more as if I had to keep him *distributed*: I can think of no other way of saying it.

This leads me to my other major concern while getting ready to re-encounter Bill clinically. I knew he had presented himself as quite different persons to Dr X, to the psychiatrist and in his 'two analyses' with me. There was no deliberate subterfuge or cheating or resistance in this. In his paper on 'Classification' (1959/64), Winnicott states the problem very succinctly:

Now we see the ego of the infant as something dependent at first on ego-support, something which derives structure and strength from a highly complex and subtle system of adaptation to need, this adaptation being supplied by the mother or mother-figure. Also we see the interesting process of the absorption into the individual child of the child-care elements, those which could be called 'supporting ego' elements. The relationship between this absorption of the environment and the introjection processes with which we are already familiar provides great interest.

Along with all this goes a study of the mechanisms by which the infant emerges from a state of being merged in with the mother, a process that demands of the mother a capacity to hate as well as to love. In the theory of the emotional development of the child, the gradual establishment of the individual as a separate person becomes a matter of central importance, and these matters belong to present-day research. Classification must be affected by these theoretical formulations.

As a result of these new developments, narcissism in the clinical condition is seen in a new light. It is as if in looking at narcissistic illness the clinician is liable to be caught up with the absorbed, or internalised, environment, and to mistake this (unless well prepared) for the real individual, who in fact is hidden and is secretly loved and cared for by the self within the self. It is the true individual that is hidden.

In spite of his very abject states of acute dismay, I had no doubt on two scores regarding this patient: one, that he was a very narcissistic borderline psychopath, who would and did manipulate any situation to serve his purposes; and two, that he had a highly developed *innate* sense of preservation and survival. In my earlier article (1970), I had asked why he had not become psychotic, given his relation to his mother or, to be more exact, her endless and ruthlessly callous *impingements* on him (cf Winnicott, 1960b). Also, he had once boasted how, of some seven thousand prisoners of war in his camp, he was the only one who never got abused and hit by the all-too-easily provoked and atrociously punitive Japanese soldiers and officers, of whom we shall hear more later. At this point, I want to say emphatically how my long clinical experience, and 'extended holding', of this patient during his absences abroad had taught me, firstly, never to be in a hurry to 'cure' symptoms and, secondly, to respect the self-protective and self-curative value of a patient's psychosexual pathology, no matter how exhausting, threatening (to both patient and analyst) and boring for the listener. Marion Milner (1969) has given us perhaps the most moving example of this in her insightful account of her decades of clinical care, holding and analysis of her patient, Susan.

It is time we encounter Bill in person. He arrived punctually – as always – to start his 'third analysis'. He had never, even once, missed a session, been late or been physically ill in all the years I had known him. It was nearly a decade since I had seen Bill last. He was sixty-two years old now. He looked physically healthy, alert and relaxed. He did not have that 'faded' tone to his corporeal presence which I had noticed with concern and remarked upon at the end of my 1970 paper. I felt reassured that his private life could not be too vacant and dismal if he had this sentient presence. He surprised me by his opening remarks: (i) He said he had felt sad when he had read that Dr Winnicott had died, and he added: 'You must feel more than a loss. It is a *lack*.' He said it with feeling, and I responded with equal candour, and told him that, even though I had known of Winnicott's failing health for some time, his death was no less painful and a shock. I also said I knew I would not meet another Winnicott. (ii) He said that the porter bringing him up in the lift had told him I was leaving my flat later that year. He added: 'Where will you find a flat as spacious and private as this, and on one floor?' I told him I had been very lucky and had found one. It was being prepared for me. He said he would very much like to see it before he returned to his country, because he would like to have some idea of how I was living, and where. I said I would take him there. We had ample time in the three months ahead. Suddenly I remembered how, for him, time did not exist: it was *now* or never; and contrariwise, it could also be some time, *not now*.

I decided to start this 'analysis' with a playing spirit and style. So I bantered: 'What brings Hamlet to Elsinore?' He laughed, and said he had to make a decision and needed to consult me. Briefly, during the past decade his research project had grown in various dimensions and he was now the director of his particular research unit. He had four colleagues working with him. Two years ago he had taken on a 31-year-old research Fellow, who wanted to do his doctorate on Bill's research project. Hence they had been working very closely. He had got to know him very well, and also his family, who were of humble but respectable status. The young man, Kris, had a fiancée and was getting married in a few months' time. Since Bill had heard about this, an absolutely new and different fantasy had started in him. He had the wish to 'adopt' Kris (as I shall name him) and invite Kris and his wife to share a home with him. He had not yet proposed this to Kris. This was one of the reasons why he needed to see me. 'I have done with my "apprenticeship in monastic cells", as you once called it,' he said, and hastened   add that Kris was circumcised, and not a homosexual. In fact, Bill had never cultivated any sort of experience with a true practising homosexual youth. All his youths indulged in his sort of 'homosexual episodes' furtively, to get some money, while they were looking for a proper job. None of them ever came from a rich or even middle-class family. Not that during his service as a diplomat he didn't have plenty of such youths available and willing.

At this point I could sense that Bill was suddenly in that state of ungraspable panic which he had no resources or ego-equipment to cope with. He asked me: 'How often will you be able to see me? I can come any time, any day and every day, while I am here.' I said it all depended on my work-schedule and previous commitments, but I would try to see him as often as he wished. This didn't help him find his ease. He asked: 'Shall I lie down and start?' I thought carefully, and then said: 'Look, Bill, I know that you *know* all the expertise of being a patient in analysis, and using the couch. I am also fully aware that, at this point, you want to *dissociate* from inter-personal conversation, to talking from the couch, and hearing me, as it were, mock-oracularly. Why not try talking to me face to face, person to person? It would be terrifying for you, but we have both grown up through living, and can take risks.' He was solemn and silent for a while, and then said: 'But can I "retire"' (his exact phrase) 'to the couch when I need it? You do realise that I really mean to have analysis this time. I said to myself on the plane: "No! I shall not play games with Khan. I need him and I shall tell him as much."' He paused again, and remarked: 'Do you know it is the first time we have mentioned each other's name, and called each other by it?' I corrected him: 'No, in correspondence we have addressed each other by name, but it is the first time I have used your Christian name.'

At this point he launched straight into what he had come to ask my 'advice' about. This was also a new departure for Bill. Seeking and taking advice presupposes the capacity to accept dependence, and this capacity, in my experience, is the prerequisite for *in*dependence. Winnicott (1958) discusses it from a different angle, and most insightfully, as the capacity to be alone, and what that entails. Bill continued to talk, disregarding the fact that we had reached the end of the fifty-minute session; another new departure for him in the analytic relating. If he always arrived punctually, with a matching obsessional exactitude he would switch off a minute or two before the end of the session. I had deliberately and purposefully given him the time of 7.00 p.m. – the last clinical hour of the professional day – so that, should he relax, he could continue as long as he needed.

With his typically lucid and pertinent usage of language he stated that he had come, basically, to explore three issues with me and get some insight into how to think positively and creatively about them. It was the first time, again, that Bill had used the concept of 'insight', or even hinted that perhaps 'insight' into oneself towards self-knowledge was the aim of analytic treatment. I make a distinction between self-knowledge and self-consciousness, which is insatiably fed by intro-spection (privately) and often by free associations in analysis. I would go even further and say that it is only when a patient can begin to use insight to *know* himself that he can start to have a new outlook on his life. I think this is what Balint (1968) calls 'a new beginning'. I said: 'Yes, Bill, continue detailing your "agenda".' He could sense I was pulling his leg. I was determined not to let him 'stiffen' the analytic process into a solemn monologic adumbration of data of one sort or another, and ascribe to me the task of editing it with 'interpretative footnotes'. Bill was not to be shifted from his *willed* discourse easily.

The three issues were: (i) Could a man with his sexual past and tactics of non-relating, masquerading as techniques of care and concern (with his youths), take on a real ongoing relationship, at his late age? And if so, how? (ii) He had reread my three accounts of his treatment (Bill could read French: at that time, the second part of 'Le fétichisme comme negation du soi' had not been published in English). He felt I was 'nearer to him' (his phrase) and what he was asking from the youths and offering them, through the sexualised games, in my first account – 'The homosexual nursing of self and object' – and that the 1965 paper was more true to *my* analytic work and insights than to his personal experiences.

What he wanted to go into more deeply now was his childhood, as it had been and not as he had 'wrapped it up' (his phrase) in neat items of fantasies and memories. Because unless he could get some more self-knowledge from that period of his life, he would not be able to cope with living with Kris while he reared a family. He asked me whether I remembered how insanely jealous he had been when the circumcised youth had had a girlfriend, 'provided' by Bill himself in order to keep him. (iii) He wanted to discuss in more detail his experiences as a labourer in the coal-mines, as a prisoner of war (especially in Japan), and during his recent prison sentence. He felt, in a strange and macabre (his word) way, that these were his truest periods of personal living with himself, alongside others (his phrase). And only the understanding of this would enable him to live privately, but companioned, with Kris and his family.

He paused. I was quite amazed by the amount of 'homework' he had done *on* himself during the past fourteen years. I was scribbling, and he remarked ironically: 'So you still take notes', and I parried it by saying: 'We all have our techniques of self-care! This is mine.' Then I decided to end that session by saying: 'Well, Bill, you have certainly set out a very promising project for research here. Let us start work on it tomorrow and not pre-empt what can emerge by categorising it. Let us start at random in the areas you have charted out.' We parted affably on that note. He gave me his address and phone number, and once again I noted a difference: he was no longer in a one-room cell in some shabby boarding house, but in a good hotel with a respectable address.

He arrived for the next session looking haggard. He had slept little, had been restless; but qualified it by saying it was different from the sort of gnawing restlessness that used to make him prowl at night and pick up the youths. He had had a nightmare as soon as he had fallen asleep, and had been awakened by it. He asked if he could 'use the couch' (his pet phrase). I made a point of saying: 'It is not a game we are indulging in. So there are no rules.' He could 'use' the setting as he pleased or needed. He lay down. The nightmare was very brief:

In Japan, P.O.W. sort of terrain. Am sitting too close to another P.O.W., who is rather elderly, and we are talking. At this point woke up in terror.

He tried to make a joke of it: 'Shows you not to ask me to sit up and converse.' I disregarded that, and interpreted: 'You have brought me the dream-text, but unfortunately you have lost the dreaming-experience' (Khan, 1976a). He was irate: 'That is too clever. Tell me in simple terms what you want to say.' I said: 'Perhaps what I want to say to you is something so absurd that I am hesitant.' 'Try it,' he said. I retorted: '*You have no unconscious*, that is the problem.' And I decided to explain what I meant, in a purely didactic manner, without any pretence of it being a long interpretation aimed to foster insight. We analysts 'infantalise' even our most gifted patients through the 'analytic method' (Freud, 1904). We do not give them the credit, at times, of perhaps being both more endowed and *achieved* in life than us. This man had been *sick*, in almost all senses of that word: in mind, body and soul; but he had battled his way from fatedness to destiny, having *existed* en route through a 'false self' organisation that operated effectively in his domain of sexual exploits, and thus had kept himself minimally nourished as a person.

What I stated to him was as follows: 'You know I was trained by Winnicott, and it is his theories that have guided my clinical "holding" and *management* of you. As you once taunted me: "You give interpretations to make this into an analysis. They have little use for me. I do hear them, though." Now, according to Winnicott (1960b), from plus O (birth) to one year of age, roughly speaking, the infant has little existence, except when *in-care* with a good enough environment, usually called mothering or mother. If all goes averagely well, then the infant can begin to internalise the care-techniques of his "holding" environment and the experiences that transpire in the temporal and transitional *space* between him and the caretaking environment (generally the mother). This process continues silently but sentiently, leading to the fruition and actualisation of those innate and autonomous ego-functions and capacities, à la Hartmann (1939), which constitute both the core and the functional apparatuses of all inner reality, psychic life and instinctual (sexual and aggressive) development, in what one day we call a child, and later a person with a self that is both private and *other*-relating . . .

'Now in your case, I am saying there has been an excessive intimacy *from* the mother (excuse the use of "from" and not "with", because you were more *done to* than *doing*), which usurped this temporal space, hence you internalised little and have no "unconscious". You have said yourself that you have, all your life, "existed and observed", which is quite different from living and sharing life with *the other*. *The other* at the beginning is the mother or her surrogate; and only gradually, through maturation and development, takes on that multiplicity of the *others*, which we call family, and social life. You do realise that when I say to you: "You have no unconscious", I find myself talking paradoxically, that is, literally and metaphorically (cf. Winnicott, 1965, 1971b)?'

I have stated schematically what, in fact, had taken me three sessions to say, because I had to allow for Bill to keep me in touch with his daily life and plans, outside the clinical fifty minutes. He had sat up to hear me out. I must also admit that I was taking time getting used to Bill: he was such a different human being from the patient-person I had known. After the fourth session there was a break of two days, because I had no time to see Bill on Friday or Saturday. He knew about it from the first session.

During these two days Bill went to visit a laboratory in a university some five hundred miles away. He was making full use of his time professionally too. When I saw him next, on a Sunday, he started by saying that I had not paid attention to his dream, because in fact it held many clues as to how he had survived the P.O.W. years, without a single injury or punishment, and how this had fated him to exist a secluded and non-participant life after the war, except for his night-prowling. I listened to him. He talked about the way 'accidents' – and sometimes they would lead to mortality – happened in P.O.W. camps, especially in Japan. He had observed very early on, in Singapore, how the Japanese soldiers relished the cruelties they inflicted: the more fatuous and unwarranted these were, the more pleasure they got from them, always laughing maniacally when they beat up a P.O.W. To betray any sign of pain or suffering was to ask for more. Another thing he had registered from the beginning was that the Japanese soldiers and officers could not tolerate any sort of friendship, or 'pairing as buddies' (his phrase) amongst P.O.W.s. Maximal casualties were always the friends of those P.O.W.s who had been picked upon and punished because, if the friends reacted in any emotional way, they were punished three times worse. I hinted that he had seen in childhood, in his mother, the antics of the Japanese style of causing unwarranted pain. Thus he could *observe*, with a totally passive and blank inertia, dozens of 'friends' beaten up so badly that they died of the injuries, since there was no medical care provided. Fortunately he spared me detailed accounts of the atrocities.

He emphasised that after all these years he realised only now that the reason he had survived was that he was 'absent' all the time. He did what he was told. He 'paired' with no one, and stayed a spectator to the horrific and callous 'theatre of cruelty' of the Japanese P.O.W. camps. Furthermore, since their camp was near a harbour and they had to unload food, the most frequent and the most rigorously, as well as severely, punished offence was stealing food. Now every P.O.W. stole food, because their rations were so meagre. He did too, but always alone, and *for himself exclusively*. He neither shared with anyone what he stole, nor did he ever accept any food if offered, no matter how hungry he was; also he never 'hoarded' stolen food, which is how everyone was caught. At this point Bill interpreted the dream himself. He said that during the three years of P.O.W. life he never once felt anxious or afraid. All his panic states started when he was free again and returned home. He had been so frightened by 'something' in his dream that he had woken up in terror. He added: 'You, of course, would say this is the terror I had *repressed* during the P.O.W. years. Whilst I would argue that I didn't *repress* anything, because I never let myself into any situation where I would experience a risk. In the dream I am taking a risk: I am sitting close, very close, to an older person, and there is obvious sympathy between us. I do not mean anything

sexual. But had a Japanese soldier witnessed two P.O.W.s in such a
friendly relation, they would be immediately *marked* as victims, and
the soldier would surely find some excuse to vent his rage on one of the
"pair".'

I deliberately did not link it with the transference, and his 'sitting
close' to me, because he had already jibed at it, self-protectively. But I
did ask myself, and noted for future work, *who* was the 'third' person
watching us. To have given a 'primal scene' interpretation would have
foreclosed the emergent theme. Anyway, we had gone into all that,
interpreting his sexual escapades during his 'first analysis'. Even more
important for me was to keep in mind, not *why* we were being watched
but *how*, in Bill's fantasy, *and to what end*. After all, he had come to
seek advice from me. This was again something new in Bill's
experience: to *fantasise*, instead of his ruminative *fantasying*. Winnicott's (1971c) contribution to our understanding of this difference,
from the analysis of a female patient, is clinically of the utmost
importance:

Dream fits into object-relating in the real world, and living in the real world fits
into the dream-world in ways that are quite familiar, especially to psychoanalysts. By contrast, however, fantasying remains an isolated phenom-
enon, absorbing energy but not contributing-in either to dreaming or to
living . . .
     Inaccessibility of fantasying is associated with dissociation rather than with
repression . . .
     It will be observed that a time factor is operative which is different according
to whether she is fantasying or imagining. In the fantasying, what happens
happens immediately, except that it does not happen at all . . .
     She really lived in this fantasying on the basis of a dissociated mental
activity . . .

For further elucidation of this, in a most novel way, I refer the reader
to Pontalis's (1975b) preface to the French edition of *Playing and
Reality* where he discusses this whole theme in Winnicott's work. I
would say here that the concept of the 'dream-text' I learned from
Pontalis (1977), even though my clinical *use* of his concept differs a
little from the way he states his argument (cf Khan, 1976a). There is,
however, one postulation of Pontalis's in this context that has been
helpful to me in understanding the sexual enactments of this patient,
and the paucity of dreaming in his 'first two analyses':

Further: when a conflict is ceaselessly *enacted* on the stage of the world, we are refused entry into the stage of the dream. 'Real' space takes up all the room. Our objects of cathexis catch the ego's interests and the sexual instincts, confusing them, and mobilize all our energy.

I did, however, point out to Bill that though his interpretation of the dream-text was quite enlightening, the fact remained that the dreaming experience took place *outside* the dream-text: he had felt the terror while awakening, not in the dream-space, to use another of Pontalis's concepts. Pontalis writes:

Dream-object, dream-space: there is a close connection between these two dimensions of the dream. In practice, we are always passing from one to the other. I would like to make a schematic distinction between two modes of relation to the dream-object which represent two specific types of defence against the potentialities at stake in the opening of a dream-space: the manipulation of the dream machine and the reduction of the dream to an inner object.

My only reservation *vis-à-vis* Pontalis's hypothesis is that he rather takes for granted that everyone can achieve 'the manipulation of the dream machine and the reduction of the dream to an inner object'. It is my clinical experience, and it was certainly true of Bill, that a person can be so incapacitated by early experiences that he or she can have no inner object: be it a dream or a person. In other words, I am saying that it takes a certain developmental 'maturity' to achieve what Pontalis so lucidly postulates, which Bill had been cheated of by his mother's incessant impingements in early childhood. Just as inner psychic space had not existed for Bill, similarly nor had time. All those decades could have been *a* moment in time.

In the weeks that followed Bill talked, rather objectively, but with feeling, about how pitiable his mother had been. No matter how affluent her circumstances, and in spite of the devotion of both her husbands, she lived in a 'frenzy of dreads' (his phrase), the main themes being: dread of poverty, dread of being abandoned and the dread of dying. In fact she was a very healthy woman, who outlived both her husbands and her eldest son. It was this frantic state in her which led to her rowing with her second husband until she was all spent and exhausted. Bill could see how he had pursued the same style in his insatiable craving for love from, and sexual practices with, the youths.

He had dreaded being abandoned, though it was always he who abandoned them. Now I took up this theme from another angle. I said to him that he had been so precociously involved in a *demand* for concern by his mother, that he could not even cultivate true sympathy for anyone in later life. His charades of concern and care with the youths were a mask for this incapacity in him. That it had saved him as a P.O.W. was just luck. Winnicott (1963a) has approached this 'developmental capacity' for concern in a very ingenious way. But here I am approaching the issue of concern from another angle.

I reminded Bill how in an earlier session he had said I was nearer to stating his 'experience' of his sexual *expertise* in 'The homosexual nursing of self and object' than in terms of fetishism. I said that his type of 'nursing' was a parody of concern and caring. And that this was why he had come to ask me whether he could 'take on a real ongoing relationship'. The question screened a dread; namely, that he would fail to be concerned, in a true and reciprocal way, with Kris and his prospective family. Thus, would he be inflicting yet another stance of *existing* on himself, where he was self-tortured and frantic because he was not contributing enough? Here he could find himself in a reversed role to that witnessed by him in his mother; he could feel unloving and unconcerned, and so be just as pitiably fated as his mother, only in a different way. Bill dropped the subject, and talked of his time in prison.

Here I noted another difference in his relating to me from his previous 'analyses'. Then he had exploited me, bored me and taken for granted that I would sustain my interest in him. Now his shifting from one topic to another, just as we would be reaching a 'saturation point', had a different intent and dread. He wanted to keep my interest 'suspended'. There was a positive, non-manipulative side to it, too. He could now tolerate being 'scattered' and unintegrated, in himself, without fearing extinction through lack of cohesion. His elaborate narratives during the 'first two analyses' negated this need to be unintegrated and let time and space hold one, through *the other's* care and keeping (cf Winnicott, 1945). His obsessionality was a way of 'corseting' his unintegrated states, instead of tolerating that inevitable non-being which is inherent to personalised living in one's skin. Anzieu's (1974) concept of 'le moi-peau' is, I feel, relevant in this context. An infant *experiences* unintegrated living in his 'le moi-peau' before he can build that psychic apparatus we call the ego and its attribute, which is psychic reality, conscious and unconscious. Here Bowlby's (1960) concept of 'attachment' is relevant too, because 'experiences' of attachment precede the dawning awareness (corporeal, psychic, affective and relational) of what Winnicott conceptualises as 'dependence' in early infancy and in-care. In perversions and addictions I have found it more and more necessary to keep this distinction between the concepts of 'attachment' à la Bowlby and 'dependence' à la Winnicott (1963b) – or 'the container' à la Bion (1967) – clearly defined when 'translating the patient's text' (to use Pontalis's phrase), through our interpretative tactics, into the herme- neutics of the language of psychoanalysis. Anzieu's 'le moi-peau' is, I believe, a necessary auxiliary concept to Bowlby's of *attachment* and Winnicott's of *dependence*. Anzieu defines 'le moi-peau' as follows:

By skin ego I mean an image that the child's ego uses during the early stages of development to represent itself on the basis of the child's experience with the surface of the body. That phase corresponds to the period when the psychic ego is becoming differentiated from the body ego on the functional level but remains confounded with it on the figurative level . . . All mental activity rests on some biological function. The skin ego's support lies in three functions of the skin. In its first function, the skin is the sack that holds in the goodness and fullness that accumulates from being suckled, cared for, and bathed with words. In its second function, the skin is the surface that marks the boundary with the outside and keeps it on the outside; it is the barrier that protects against the greed and aggression of others, persons or things. Lastly, in its third function, the skin – along with the mouth and at least as much as it – is a place and principal means of exchange with others.

To return to Bill. During his 'first analysis', he had fervently and frantically sought to be in *the other's* skin. It had never worked. The *punctured* 'le soi-même' does not travel far. Bill had learned this the bitter way, traversing 'the valley of death' with that *deadly economy* which is sexuality (cf Green, 1975). When he was weaning himself from attachment to the prepuce-penis-youth, during this period, Bill had berated me and said: 'Yes! what an amalgam of fates for me. I have spent my adulthood furtively and fugitively *attached* to a youth by cock, in mouth and arse, without ever having been hugged or *enveloped* with desire, love and longing.' (I have underlined from hindsight, and thanks to Anzieu, in my notes taken at the time.) 'And now my fate is *yapping* with that *arid* mouth to an aristocrat, who is handsome, young and caring but *un-embracing*.' Yes, Bill had made his point then. I picked this up, now, in a different context. I told him he had mocked me about writing on the role of prepuce as a fetish in his life. But the 'economy of sexualisation' à la Green had saved him. Now he was seeking from me the same economy for living, by asking advice as to how to rehabilitate himself, *a*sexually, with a thriving couple, and an infant of *the other*! I told Bill that I had no answers or interpretations to offer. But I could tell him for sure that he had not really *suffered* in his life. Being *fated* is not suffering, but a sort of game *life* plays with one: and what we call living depends on how and from where we live, and with whom. Only then do we either thrive from *jouissance*, à la Lacan (1966), shared with *the other*, or suffer from the lack of its spontaneous reciprocity.

When Bill came next, he was rather elated, and not in the right mood to talk about his time in prison. Some weeks passed, talking of this and that. At the end of one week, in which he had come for seven consecutive sessions, he again asked to 'use the couch' to tell of the days in prison. I said 'Do!'

Bill had arrived in this *particular* prison without a single clue as to what was in store for him. I shall tell his tale as he told it to me, because I asked him if I could take notes and he agreed:

'I was driven in a police van with ten other prisoners some three hundred miles. Only one of us, a crafty youth, had somehow managed to get away with three packets of cigarettes. It was his third term of imprisonment; he had escaped each time. So the *bargaining* started. He kept one pack and sold the rest. Only I said I was not allowed to smoke, medically: a total lie. But I had the P.O.W. know-how behind me. I was not going to be one of them. It took three days to reach the prison, and I sensed they had *decided* against me, because I ate alone, en route, and never "stole" food from the cafés we stopped at. They all did. They started to talk "sex". The boy asked for a packet of cigarettes each day for being buggered. All eight of them buggered him in the van. The driver and his escort took no notice. They asked me: "You want a girl, man? You won't find them where you are going." For the first time I was afraid, but I stayed quiet. I was well-dressed. One by one, they started to take things off me. I just let it happen. I had known the *Japanese*, compared with whom they were small fish.

'When we eventually arrived, I had only a vest and my underwear on. We were "marched in". I was the last. The officer who had checked in all the others hesitated a bit. I stood, wondering: What fate next? He sent for my file. He looked through it, and said: "Take him away separately. There has been a mistake." After some two or more hours – you cannot tell the time in those circumstances – I was called. The officer told me: "There has been a mistake in sending you to this prison. But nothing can be done about it now. I have asked the Guv (governor), and he says I should put you in a 'solitary cell', which is kept for the murderers on second trial. But you have to sign a statement saying you asked for it, and it will be granted." I did. Then he said to me: "Watch out, they are going to pick on you at lunch- and dinner-time, when all eat together. If someone takes away your food, let him. Do not start a fight, or you will be dead. I have read your file. You can count on me." I asked him: "What do I have to do for you to earn this?" He told me that the report said I was a scientist (which was untrue). "Perhaps, when you get out, if you do" – he paused – "then maybe you can do something for me. Go to room 109 (solitary confinement). Undress, have a wash, and put on the numbered prison clothes. Do not make trouble. Go!"

'So I found myself in a small cell, with one small window twelve feet up. Hardly any light even during daytime. I had a mattress, without pillows, to sleep on. Nothing else. Khan, that was the most peaceful sleep and night I have ever had: no responsibilities and total care. I slept like a child. In the months following I *observed* the horrors of what happens in prisons. Not because of those who are officially in charge, but because of the "inmates", as they call themselves. They made their own rules, and *executed* them. I say "executed" because if disobeyed, you were dead: a knife in your back.

'I survived the first ten weeks, but barely. They provoked, taunted, humiliated me in every way. For days they would take away my food. Fortunately, the "officer" would send me a little later on in the cell. Then one day the governor sent for me. He asked me my name. I gave it. He knew it anyway. Then he produced a periodical and said: "Is this paper by you?" I said: "I don't know unless I can read it." It was by me. I was *news*! How ironic. I told you I am fated. I burst into tears! At my age! The governor said: "Listen, prisoner, if you behave as we ask you to, then we can get you every book or magazine you want to read." I

said: "Yes, sir!" He went on: "You will *see* men killing each other here.
So far as you know, you saw nothing." I again said: "Yes, sir!" The
governor said to the officer: "*Try him*. I think we can use him."
Suddenly I spurted out: "No, sir! I will do nothing. You can take your
'protective' cell. Let them kill me. But you cannot 'use' me against
them. I do not know what the game is here, but I do not want to be part
of it."

'The governor was rattled and said: "All right. From now on you
stay in your cell and you'll be fed half-rations." He paused. A form was
brought. I signed it, without reading it. On leaving, the governor said:
"You'll get your books and magazines. With the likes of you, one never
knows." Things were going too well and I started to have "little"
panics. The doctor visited every three months for a general check-up,
unless you were injured, and then you were sent to the "death ward",
as they called it. Because if you were not done in during the fight, you
would surely get your end there. When the doctor examined me, I had
been two and a half months in the cell, without any exercise, so had put
on a lot of weight. He ordered – they didn't prescribe – I should take
exercise, and recommended walking for two hours. I was willing, as
always. But the governor had a brilliant idea: I should take the police
watchdogs, accompanied by one armed policeman, for exercise. This
went on for some eight months. It was the most restful and quiet time in
all my life. I knew it would not last long. I don't know why I was so
sure. We reached the first Christmas, so I had to go to church and
attend the festivities after. During the festivities everyone got more and
more drunk and there was violence in the air. I knew it would explode
any moment. I tried to get away but could not. Suddenly I saw a youth
of some twenty-one years taken by three men, drunk. They tore his
clothes apart and amidst all the gathering started to bugger him. The
police, only a few, let it happen. If they had tried to stop them, the
police would have had it. I found myself *observing* with the same
inertia as in the P.O.W. camp. Someone elbowed me and said: "Let us
stop it." I said nothing. He hit me on the head. Next I knew was that I
was in my cell.

'Afterwards I was removed from that prison and was put on
"probation", back in my own city, in a modern prison. I kept aloof and
apart. Then I was released for good conduct and went into analysis,
because as I told you, I was given a job and I panicked.'

It had taken weeks for Bill to narrate all this, with other bits and pieces. At the end of it, he said: 'Dr X thought I was a masochist and an inhibited homosexual. Now you have never said the latter because by the time I came to you I was buggering every prepuced youth I could find. But what about masochism? Am I a masochist? I have read Freud on that subject, and I can't say I am.' I disregarded his question. I had listened to him for some five weeks, with casual chatter here and there, and made no interpretations whatsoever. He asked me again: 'Am I really a masochist?' I said: 'No, Bill, you are an *inside-out sadist*.' He laughed and retorted: 'Another of the Khanic paradoxes. Explain it to me, please.'

So I told him another yarn: how once I had a patient whose lover was always threatening her that he would commit suicide. One day he took an overdose, and was taken to hospital. He survived. When he returned to his flat she had gone, leaving a note saying: 'The surest way to commit suicide is to provoke someone to kill you. Sorry I cannot oblige.'

I said to Bill: 'Now you have been *killing* through others: non-participant, but as an observer. You have *destroyed* thousands of erections in the youths. Ejaculation – detumescence – death (murder). But because it all happens to a localised organ, you disown the killing! But killing and murder it is – with all the ruses of care and belonging. Now we have to ask why you cannot experience your own aggression and murderousness? Instead you feel *victimised*, which Dr X mistook for your masochism. In your "analyses" you have "murdered"' (I did not use the concept of castration) 'my creative efforts across decades. Which brings me to your third issue: feeling most truly yourself as a labourer in the mines, in the P.O.W. camp, and in prison. In the first you had "murdered" your career and the expectations of your family. You were, by your own account, a brilliant student and very cultured. Becoming a labourer was also a way of being "violent", not to persons, but to inorganic material. In P.O.W. camps you sat on the fence: you were the Japanese soldiers, cruelly "murderous", and also the "third party" – the spectator. In your dream when you align yourself with someone, you dread being "murdered". Now I put it to you that the outrageous hysterical self-pitying assaults of your mother on her husbands were "murderous". You learned then how to "murder" at one remove and sexualise it.'

Now Bill told me a fact about his parents that, he said, he felt was so private to them, he should not say it. When he was nine years of age, and his mother had divorced his father, having already told him that he was her new husband's son, she had said: 'You know why I had no children from my first husband? He only buggered me and made me perform fellatio. Otherwise he was totally impotent.' Now he wondered whether his memories of offering to suck his father's penis, biting the rhubarb, etc. (Khan, 1970), were not actually a child's way of trying to understand what a man-woman relation is. He had, he felt, all his life *enacted* his mother's predicament – to use Anzieu's (1974) concept – on his own 'le moi-peau' and those of the youths. Now could he accept that a man has proper sexual relations with his wife and procreates?

I said: 'I cannot answer that. But one thing I can say and ask: Would you try to humiliate yourself, now that you are finding your status of being a person, by putting yourself in the role of a eunuched-observer? Here perhaps we can start to talk of your masochism – that "living-death" which becomes viable from being sexualised.' He said: 'You don't believe in the death instinct?' And I categorically replied: 'No, I do not! I know what dying and death are, but not the death instinct; just as I know what incest is, but not the Oedipus complex.' I hastened to add that all my colleagues knew about the death instinct and the Oedipus complex (Freud, 1905a). 'Since you read so much, I can tell you where to read all that. But it won't help you with your predicament *vis-à-vis* Kris. You have been coming here for three months. You have found a purpose in *living*, and become a person: *Bill*. Now you have to take the risk of going one step further, and accept that *the other* is not just an *object* to manipulate: a *thing-object*, if I may put it that way. I cannot tell you how to do it, or whether to do it. But you have personalised: that was a terrifying risk for you. Why not take the next step?'

He asked me to be more explicit. I said: 'In your *fated* life you have always been *over*-demanding love – without knowing or acknowledging it. Now you are about to experience sharing, and that most difficult task for any human being, a *companioned-alone* (cf Winnicott, 1975) from *the other*. Now you have to encompass *the other*, and its plurality, which is a family and society, in your personalised selfhood. I can see you smiling. I know it is more easily said than done. But you have always been the *master* of your *being*: from fatedness to destiny. Perhaps you should now try that awesome humility which is shared dependence-independence with *the other*.'

On that note we parted.

That was nearly a decade ago. During this period Bill wrote short letters telling me about having set up a 'home life' with Kris, his wife and their child, and his research unit. Then, after a silence of some months, in December 1983, I received a letter from Kris saying Bill had died, and that he had asked Kris to let me know he was dying a happy man, with a family around him, and his research project well organised for *others* to pursue.

I am fully cognisant that if Bill achieved his destiny, he also left me a legacy – to recount our 'journey' in companionship: from being fated, suffering, and surviving, through all the antics of his 'false' self, fetishistic relating, up to his destiny as a person who has creatively contributed to human knowledge. There is more to be told about Bill, but that another time. In a sense this article is as much my working through a mourning as a case history, written with affection and gratitude for one who will never read it. But the dead live on through those who remember them, as I remember Bill.

[1984]

2

When Spring Comes

'The voyage of the soul – not life alone'
WALT WHITMAN
'Gliding O'er All' *Leaves of Grass*

There was nothing unusual about my visit to D. W. Winnicott this Sunday morning, around 10.00 a.m., in November 1969. After riding I had gone straight to D.W.W. each Sunday morning, for two hours or more, as he wished and needed, for the past two years. I never stayed for lunch. D.W.W.'s health and strength had enfeebled critically during these years. He wanted me to help him get his book *Playing and Reality* written and edited for publication. It was a pleasure for me to help D.W.W. He would present me with some typed scripts or clinical materials and we would work these into a manageable form and shape for publication. It was from such encounters I learned most from D.W.W. He would talk freely and variously, hardly staying with the typed text for long. Quite often he would drift into a somnolent quiet, almost snoozing. These patches of time would give me the chance to read the typed script, or think back over what he had said. He would reassemble himself soon, and start talking afresh. What was most amusing was that sometimes, on emerging into his articulate consciousness, D.W.W. would rebuke me gently: 'You know, Khan' (he always called me by my surname) 'I nearly dreamt. But I couldn't because you being here got in the way of my dreaming.' I would listen to D.W.W. with indulgent mirth, tease him, and get on with the work.

D.W.W. worked on his texts like an ebullient, restive child of nine. He often said: 'Everything had happened to me by the time I was nine. I have never grown older in spirit or style since then,' he would add, rather ruefully. It was just as well. What each of us who worked closely with D.W.W. in these final years of his life, cherished most about him, was his irrepressible ebullience of creative thought and clinical effort. He was still seeing, though for consultations only, children and adult patients. (Most of the latter were analysts from all over the world, of established reputations, who sought *help* from D.W.W., having read his writings. They had all had long personal analyses on one excuse or another, for training or from distress.) D.W.W. discussed only those cases that I could help him write, either into a clinical narrative or for him to organise into some thoughts. D.W.W. never, to my knowledge, wrote what one might say was a purely theoretical paper. He would always start with some recent clinical work and go on to 'theorise' from that. The reason for the paucity and absence of clinical material in his papers, e.g., 'The use of an object' (1969), is that D.W.W. was very particular about guarding the privacy of his patients, even young children of five or so, and would not cite the clinical material that had led him to a particular theoretical *notion*.

This morning I found D.W.W. in an excited state. I had hardly taken off my riding cape and sat down to a cup of tea, which he brewed himself, in the secretary's small room where we always worked together and could be private with each other, before I sensed that D.W.W. was about to make some curious demand. Set me a new task! So little was ever stated explicitly between us. We had known each other for two decades now, working very closely, yet keeping our distance. I was never any part of his social and family life, nor he of mine.

D.W.W. sat down, turned and 'churned' his face in his hands, as was his style, and started with: 'You see, Khan, I saw this young girl, Veronique, yesterday in consultation. She is thirteen years old. Is refusing to eat food or go to her school, because she says she has become "ridiculously thin" (it is her phrase, Khan). I have told her physician, and parents whom I saw last week, that I could not *treat* their daughter but am willing to see her in consultation, and help her find *the right sort of help*.' I had noted D.W.W.'s use of the phrase 'the right sort of help' instead of 'treatment'. I always scribbled 'notes' when listening to such conversations; D.W.W. didn't mean me to take them too seriously, it was his way of easing his *thought-load*, as I called it. These 'sharings' of clinical experiences were rather rhetorical on D.W.W.'s part.

He continued: 'Veronique is a *very*' (he had emphasised that) 'intellectual girl. She speaks English, and also French fluently.' I bantered: 'With that name, D.W.W., she must be French somehow.' 'Yes, her mother is French, but it is not important.' I smiled and let him get on. 'Well, I didn't know, because I had not been told, she was coming to me from a private clinic. She has been there two months now for "food and school refusal".' I noted again that D.W.W. was eschewing the use of any psychiatric or medical jargon. D.W.W. went on: 'She is rather beautiful. Rides. That should make you two friends, Khan.' I knew now that D.W.W. had *decided* I was to take this girl into care. I listened on.

'You see, she is not *really* ill. She is not *really* refusing anything: food or school or sex. I could have easily found out what she was refusing and why, from the consultation, but I decided not to, and to let you find out for yourself, with her help. Yes, you will like her, Khan. She is an aristocrat. An only child. Her father adores her. Her mother is very proud of her achievements as a student and a promising rider. Your childhood almost, Khan. Yes, Khan, Veronique's only ambition is to train to ride for Great Britain in the Olympics.' (So like you, D.W.W.; in 1914 you were to run for Great Britain but the First World War thwarted you.) 'So I thought of you immediately,' he continued. 'Otherwise there are a few other young analysts, medically qualified, who would perhaps be more suitable to *handle* her situation. But she speaks, when she relaxes, in English and French in turn, as is her custom at home; talks about horses and horse-jumping with a *voracious* zest' (I noted D.W.W.'s use of the adjective "voracious") 'and damn it, is an intellectual. By the way, who is this woman Simone de Beauvoir in Paris? She has written a lot about women and sex. Since you read everything, you must have read her too.'

I let D.W.W. have the treat of jibing. I knew he was nervous on two counts: the girl was an awkward proposition, and he was not sure I would take her into care. The private nursing home was some twenty miles from London, and I would have to visit it. D.W.W. continued, after a short 'disappearance' into himself: 'Oh yes, Khan. I promised I would ring them today at the nursing home and tell them what you decide. Could I say I have discussed the matter with you and you are driving over and will be seeing her around lunch-time? Yes, you can, in your car, easily drive there under an hour, especially on a Sunday. The important factor clinically is to see Veronique *when* she refuses food.' 'You mean, D.W.W., *how* she does it.' 'Yes! Yes!! But for God's sake, Khan, do not be too clever with Veronique, otherwise you will never find out what *sickens* her out of eating and going to school.' 'As you say, D.W.W.'

With this much assent from me, D.W.W. was on the phone, and it was arranged that I would visit Veronique that very day, around lunch-time. It was just past 11.00 a.m. D.W.W. walked me to the car. As a parting gesture he said, with his usual irony: 'Oh, Khan, go dressed as you are. Your riding boots and cravat would give Veronique more confidence in you than anything you could say at first. Good luck, Khan.' So I drove away to encounter Veronique.

I had driven to the nursing home in good time for lunch. The whole set-up had an agreeable, gentle air about it. The building was of sturdy Victorian style, with neatly groomed lawns and flower shrubs spread all around it. Down the narrow lane I had noticed a placard stating: *Please drive slowly – Horses and Riders*. The mother, or the physician, had certainly chosen a pleasant place for Veronique; I knew it had not been chosen by Winnicott. I was received by the owner/director, a grey-haired, affable Scotsman. He asked a plump lady in her early forties to take me to Veronique. She was rather garrulous. 'She is such a nice girl, sir. Gets on with everyone. If only the old dear would eat.' I could not help smirking at the incongruity of calling Veronique 'the old dear'. Since she hadn't asked how to introduce me I hadn't told her my name. She went straight to Veronique, who was sitting reading in what looked like a spacious lounge. Veronique got up. She was a very lean, tall red-head, with soft green eyes and a pale, pale face. I introduced myself: 'I am Masud Khan.' 'I know, sir,' she replied in a gentle voice. 'Dr Winnicott has told me about you.' She started to walk towards the door. Turned towards me and said with a suppressed smile: 'I chose a room on the second floor. My food is served in my room. I don't eat with the other visitors.' Trying to establish my presence I said, casually: 'Oh, so you *don't eat* with yourself alone.' She looked at me rather quizzically. We had walked past a few other 'visitors' of varying ages. I felt rather quaint in my boots, breeches and an off-white Irish polo-neck sweater.

Climbing the stairs had winded Veronique. As we entered her room, my eyes caught sight of a lady's riding stick. It had a silver knob on it. The room was furnished in quiet mellow fabrics of pastel colours. Not cluttered at all. 'I like it up here,' Veronique remarked. 'At home I occupy the attic. I like looking at the lawns.' A young woman came in and asked Veronique whether she would like to have her lunch served right away. 'Yes, please!' she replied most genially. I began to wonder whether she had already refound her capacity to eat. With the food came a young female doctor. The maid laid out the food on a table. Veronique sat down to eat. The young lady doctor addressed me: 'You are Dr Khan?' 'Not doctor, please. Just Khan. I am not medical.' She uttered a faint exclamation of some sort, moved nearer to Veronique and uncovered the plate. Paused. 'Are you going to eat your lunch?' 'No, please!' answered Veronique politely but firmly. The lady doctor recovered the plate and floated away, to return with a middle-aged male doctor. As she was entering we could hear her saying: 'No, she had only half a cup of tea for breakfast.' The doctor walked to Veronique, saying 'Hello' to me as he passed. He uncovered the same plate. 'Eat a little, Veronique. What would you like to eat?' he asked, pointing to various bits on the plate. 'Nothing! Thank you very much.' 'You know your mother will be very upset when she comes this afternoon and is told you have not eaten again.' 'I may eat a little with Daddy at tea-time. Daddy is coming, isn't he?' 'Yes, he is,' answered the doctor, rather stiffly.

A little more coaxing and refusal, and both the doctors departed. The maid came to collect the tray. Veronique said to her: 'Wait a bit, please.' Looking at me, she asked: 'Would you like some lunch, sir?' 'No, thank you, Veronique. I ate on the way. A cup of tea I would appreciate. Here or in the garden? It is quite windy outside, so let *us* have it here.' I had deliberately said 'us'. Veronique told the maid: 'A pot of tea, milk and sugar and two cups, please.' I seated myself in the only comfortable chair in the room and asked: 'You mind if I smoke a pipe, Veronique?' 'Not at all, sir. I prefer guests smoking pipes rather than cigarettes. Daddy smokes a pipe all the time and Mummy chain-smokes French cigarettes.' I was unobtrusively watching Veronique. The maid returned with the tea-tray and placed it on the table. 'That will be all for the moment. We will ring for you. Thank you.' She had called the maid by her name, but it escapes me. Veronique took my cup from the tray, put it on the table, poured milk, then asked me: 'Weak or strong tea?' 'Strong, please, with four cubes of sugar.' Veronique smiled mirthfully, poured my tea and passed it to me. I noted she had pulled her chair away from the table and sat down. So she wasn't going to take any tea. I was not going to ask her about it.

An awkward silence followed. Then Veronique asked: 'Are you going to ask me a lot of questions?' 'No, not at all, Veronique. I have driven here so that we can get acquainted with each other. I shall be leaving shortly as I have friends coming to tea at four.' 'And, of course, your wife must be expecting you. Sorry you had to come here around lunch-time.' 'No! it was no bother at all, Veronique. My wife is in Paris, and returns tonight.' Another vacant silence. The riding stick caught my eye again. 'You couldn't be riding in your present condition!' 'No, I am not allowed to. Dr X says I am too weak,' she paused nervously. 'When do you think you will be eating again?' 'When spring comes! That is quite some time away yet. I always have more appetite in spring,' she added. 'I have never been a good eater in winter. Only it got worse this time.' I let Veronique pursue the conversation as it pleased her.

She told me how she had nearly got drowned in her overturned speedboat in Sardinia during the holidays. It was only a few months ago, in early September. 'Daddy nearly fainted when they brought me home. Mummy was furious when she found me so comfortably wrapped up and chatting with the staff who had pulled me out.' Veronique spoke cryptically. She dropped the subject and walked over to the window. Turned round: 'You are sure, sir, you don't want to ask any questions?' 'Yes, quite sure, Veronique.' 'More tea?' 'No, thank you.' I had noticed a watercolour sketch of a male head on the wall, slightly tilted. I got up and straightened it. 'Oh, I did that one of Daddy last summer in Sardinia. I told you I almost got drowned there in September. Daddy still has not got over it. He will be sorry you are not staying for tea. Daddy has met you. Mummy has met Madame Beriozova. I have seen Madame Beriozova dance Giselle. We went backstage. I saw you there.' It was true I had met her father. He was an important figure in political circles. I thought to myself: surely D.W.W. must have known the *whole* family had met me somewhere or other. He had held back that 'information', perhaps fearing I might refuse to see Veronique. In fact, I discovered on returning to my flat that D.W.W. had not been told any of this, and much else.

Veronique talked pleasantly, impishly, around various things. Her school. She missed her lessons in Greek. And her riding classes. 'Here I can only paint. Dr X (the owner/director) doesn't approve of too much reading during the day. He likes us to walk around in the garden. Play croquet. He is very good at it himself. I haven't played here. I feel faint after even a little exercise. I am very feeble at present.' I asked guilelessly: 'Surely you haven't fainted here so far? You are too determined a young lady to let that happen.' 'No, I haven't fainted so far. Nearly, many a time. Even very brave men faint. Daddy nearly fainted seeing me being brought in on a stretcher. And he was awarded the DSO as a commando officer in the last war.'

'Yes, your Daddy is quite some person. Does he still go steeple-chasing?' 'No, not now. He had a mild heart attack last summer. In June, to be exact. That is why I had gone swimming alone with two schoolfriends, when our boat overturned on us. I am a very poor swimmer. Daddy had always gone with me.' 'Isn't that a rather excessive thing to do, Veronique, for just one lapse of companionship?' Veronique looked at me sharply. Got up to pick up something. I got up too. 'Are you leaving?' 'Yes, Veronique.' 'Will you be coming again?' 'I can't tell. Depends on Dr Winnicott. I shall be talking to him later tonight. Shall ring you tomorrow.'

Veronique had quietly accompanied me to my car. I had thanked Dr X as I ran into him coming out. As I was getting into the car, Veronique asked: 'How long do you think they are going to keep me here?' 'Till spring comes, I reckon, Veronique.' And I drove off. I could see her frail, tall figure, loosely draped in a light green dress, wafted by the wind, standing there. As I turned into the lane, Veronique vanished from the view in the rear mirror. The whole encounter had a strange, gentle, sad air about it. All around the countryside was firmly in the ochre-grip of winter.

I decided not to think further about Veronique till I had talked with D.W.W. later in the evening.

It had been a pleasantly eventful day that had not presented any special problems. Veronique had been most accommodating to me, and I had been matchingly unintrusive on her. I had underlined certain obser-vations for myself and arrived at only two 'conclusions'. I began to feel nervous as the time approached to visit D.W.W. and report on my visit to the nursing home, and my encounter with Veronique. Though he had never said it to me, face to face, I knew from others how much D.W.W. expected of me. He was in many respects a most undemand-ing person and this rendered his unspoken and unstated demands outrageously taxing. It was futile preparing one's *texts* for D.W.W. — he had an uncanny way of unsettling one with some guileless, near idiotic, question — so I decided to arrive *chez* D.W.W. blandly unrehearsed.

The time was 7.00 p.m. The door was opened by his sister. Nothing alarming about that. Mrs Winnicott never opened the door to me. I was told: 'Please go up. Donald is waiting for you.' D.W.W. met me 'upstairs' (as we called it) only when he was 'indisposed': our euphemism for his having had an attack of angina, which would incapacitate him for days. The door to his bedroom was open. D.W.W. was tucked up cosily in bed, the gas-fire was warmly hissing. He grinned gently and said: 'So you are safely back, Khan.' Now I knew for sure that he was still in considerable pain. I disregarded what he had said. Sat down. 'Help yourself to some whisky.' 'Only if you have pure malt!' 'Yes, there is some left in the bottle at the back.' I helped myself generously. I was even more nervous now. Any signs of failing strength in D.W.W. made me very anxious. He always tried to hide them from me, and I made out he had succeeded. It was a silly British game, which he played better than me. He was born and bred to it. I wasn't.

I started with the silliest observation from my encounter. Veronique, I told D.W.W., serves tea like an experienced Irish butler. 'Why Irish, Khan?' 'She has a wry sense of fun.' 'I had noted that, Khan. I am glad you have too.' I had not intended to start the telling like that. I decided, rather peeved, to startle D.W.W. I announced a little pompously: 'You were quite right, D.W.W. Veronique is refusing nothing. She is not ill in any way. So what ails her? Well, D.W.W., I think she is harbouring a secret grudge against her mother. Her mellow soulful lambent gaze masks a determined vengeful hating. Its first victim is Veronique herself. So there was nothing I could offer her.'

D.W.W. sat up against his pillow. 'Yes, I didn't think you could or would. Thank you for not detecting on her. Did you talk a lot to her?' 'No, D.W.W.!' 'And she?' 'A bit, but most affably.' D.W.W. paused, and said a little archly: 'Veronique's father rang a while ago. He was very sorry you hadn't stayed to tea. You know each other, Khan?' 'Yes, D.W.W., we do.' 'Pour yourself another, Khan.' I did. D.W.W. continued: 'What do you suggest her parents should do?' 'I don't know about the parents, D.W.W., but I can tell you what her father should do.' 'Yes?' asked D.W.W. 'Her father should take her to Sardinia, alone, with him. Her ladyship has plenty to occupy her in London and Paris, so would hardly notice Veronique's absence.' 'What about the father's political work?' 'I don't think he has a heavy programme ahead this winter. It will be cold summer in Sardinia. Veronique will be able to ride and study Greek with her father. She won't need to drown herself to draw attention to herself.' 'Oh! she told you about it? Her mother says she hates talking about it.' 'I think, D.W.W., it is her mother who is feeling guilty and uncomfortable about it.' 'I am sorry, Khan, I am very tired now. Could you see Veronique tomorrow? Her father will be there for lunch. Mother is opening some fête in their village. So you three can peacefully and positively decide what course to take.' D.W.W. called out to his sister by name. She arrived. 'Khan is leaving now. Please ring the nursing home and tell them he will be joining Veronique and her father for lunch.' The old fox had premeditated everything.

As I was walking out, D.W.W. said: 'Khan, don't leave out – what did you call Veronique's mother? Yes, her ladyship, or she will come back with a vengeance.' 'As you say, D.W.W. By the way, the phone to me will be left open tonight in case you need to ring me.' 'For what, Khan?' 'Oh, out of concern and care, D.W.W.,' I said with calculated asperity. Such bantering was common between us.

The lunch with Veronique and her father went very smoothly. She had rung in the morning to ask what I would like to eat for lunch and my secretary had told her that I usually ate a very light lunch: fish and a glass or two of chilled white wine, dry if possible. I arrived punctually. Her father had come an hour or so earlier than me. There was no need for introductions as we knew each other. Veronique had asked for lunch to be served on a larger table in her room; the room was spacious enough for it. Again, it was quite noticeable that Veronique was not only used to entertaining in high style, but enjoyed it too. At first I was a bit surprised that a nursing home in England should be able to serve smoked salmon and champagne; from Fortnum and Mason, of course, I had chimed in to tease her. 'Yes, sir!' and she had jumped up gleefully to give a pecking kiss on her father's forehead, exclaiming: 'Dear, dear Daddy. He has been so worried.'

I felt reassured that I had done the right thing in excluding her ladyship. Four persons could not lunch comfortably in Veronique's room. I noticed further:

1. Daddy had poured Veronique a glass of champagne;
2. it couldn't have been the first time these two rogues were entertaining a guest without her ladyship;
3. Daddy had made no comment about Veronique not even taking a bite from the very thin slice of smoked salmon on her plate: he had only given her one and nothing else. But Veronique had genteely sipped her only glass of champagne and eaten a bit of Camembert cheese on half a biscuit;
4. Veronique and Daddy were also quite used to making decisions on their own, that is between the two of them, without consulting her ladyship.

As soon as we had settled down to eating I casually, but not tentatively in any way, told Daddy what my recommendation had been to Dr Winnicott: namely that Daddy should take Veronique to their estate in Sardinia for the winter months. It did not appear to ruffle Daddy in any way, though he slightly lifted his eyebrows. He calmly corrected me by saying: 'The estate in Sardinia is not mine. I bought it for my second son. The past four summers we have gone there because Veronique enjoys it more there and feels more free than in Cap Ferrat, where we have a lovely house and I have given it to Veronique. Of course, after me, the mansion and farm land here will go to my eldest son. I have two sons by my first wife, from whom I have been divorced these fifteen years or so.' He laughed a little and went on: 'It was so long ago that I can't remember it now.' Veronique playfully barged in: 'Hold on, Daddy, I am not that old. Yet!' He patted her head affectionately and said: 'She is my only child from my second marriage and the only one who keeps me company riding every weekend.' He paused and added: 'The children get on very well with each other. Both my sons are married. Only my second son doesn't get on with Veronique's mother.' Here Veronique cut in sharply: 'And does Mummy give him any chance!' She turned to me and told me in a determined way, 'Three times Mummy found some excuse at the last moment to cancel going to Sardinia. The real reason was she knows many people around Cap Ferrat and almost no one around our estate. She came grudgingly last summer and it was a mess.'

Daddy looked most uncomfortable so I came to his rescue by saying: 'Now, now, Veronique, you are embarrassing Daddy. I am sure you don't want to.' 'No, sir,' she said, cooling down. 'The reason I want to tell this is that if Daddy agrees for me to go to my brother in Sardinia till after next summer, it won't be necessary for Daddy to stay with me all those months. He has very many important things to do in London. I get on splendidly with my brother. We speak and joke in Italian. I prefer Italian to French.' I noted that preference. 'Dr Winnicott told me on the phone what you had suggested to him and I have reassured Daddy I won't be needing him. I shall not be swimming or speed-boating in the winter months anyway. But I would like Daddy to fly me to Sardinia because then Mummy won't think I am defying her. I have rung our headmistress at school and she has kindly agreed to my being absent for two more terms. Only she is asking for a psychiatric certificate.' 'Dr Winnicott will do that most gladly for you,' I said. Inside I was fuming at D.W.W. for having again taken one step ahead without telling me.

All this while, when Veronique had been speaking rather fast, Daddy had looked on and listened in an indulgent loving way. So it was all arranged: that Veronique would stay two more weeks at the nursing home, spend Christmas with the family in England and depart with Daddy for Sardinia in the New Year. As I was leaving Veronique and Daddy, Veronique remarked: 'Dr Winnicott is seeing Mummy on Friday.' I said rather sharply: 'Good for them both. Saves me a lot of explaining.'

I didn't think there was any urgency for me to meet D.W.W. to discuss Veronique, so I rang him after my evening's patients were finished. He sounded tired on the phone. I told him briefly that it had all gone the way everyone pleased. He said, rather laconically: 'Yes, Khan! Thank you for almost never letting me down. Goodnight.' That was high praise from D.W.W. Suddenly I realised how tired I was, too. Veronique had been a more demanding person than I had bargained for. Anyway, I settled into the routine of the professional week. When I paid my weekly visit to D.W.W. the following Sunday morning, I found him curiously exhausted and pent-up. He made me a cup of tea. I noted he was in no hurry to discuss Veronique. He shuffled a few papers around. Couldn't make up his mind what to settle for. I waited. He dropped a few pages to the floor: there was a 'squiggle' by some child on one. 'Don't worry about that. It didn't work out. I haven't been quite myself this week, Khan. Am getting really old!' He is seventy years of age, I thought to myself. Has had three severe heart attacks in the past twenty years. In fact, it was incredible the way D.W.W. functioned still. I waited. I sensed he was angry on some count.

'Well, Khan, she has beaten you to it. Her ladyship rang me an hour ago to tell me her sister was taken very seriously ill in Paris during the week. Well, she is collecting Veronique from the nursing home around midday and then flying to her sister. The father could not go with them. That louses it up, no doubt of that. Anyway, Khan, I hope the experience was worth the strain.' D.W.W. paused and changed the subject sharply. 'In what way do you reckon her ladyship is going to louse up Veronique, Khan?' I let D.W.W. go on chasing his own thoughts. 'That drowning accident. The mother has only mentioned it once herself. Her daughter talked only of that. I hope she doesn't drown her daughter.' 'You needn't worry, D.W.W., Veronique is neither so frail nor so vulnerable.' 'But she could hurt her husband and that would be very damaging for Veronique. Tell me more. After all, you spent quite a few hours with Veronique last Sunday and Monday.'

I told D.W.W. that I had very deliberately not only abstained from collecting family gossip, but hadn't let Veronique spill it either. So far as I could tell there were three groups. The first group was Veronique, Daddy and her step-brothers (with their wives). The second was Veronique and Daddy only. And the third was Daddy and Mummy. It was the third group that was fraying at the edges. I paused. 'Do go on, Khan. It helps to fantasise with someone. It is only arid when one indulges in it on one's own.' I continued: 'Her ladyship is some twenty years younger than Daddy. She is an ambitious Parisian lady. Highly educated, wanted to be in the theatre like her older, very successful sister. Failed. Her only success has been in marrying Daddy. And she is not going to let go of him. She has *countrified* herself for his sake. She has been a real helper and aide to him in his political career. She runs a very *à la mode* country house. But Veronique has crept up quite unnoticed by her ladyship. D.W.W., I was quite surprised how much Veronique knew about her father's week-to-week daily life. She even acts as his secretary on some occasions. Unlike her ladyship, she speaks Italian fluently, also she rides with Daddy every Sunday. It is then they talk everything over. It is this "intimacy" between father and daughter that is beginning to harass her ladyship. At least that is how I read it, D.W.W.'

'Go on, Khan. I am listening.' 'To aggravate the situation further, Veronique has decided she is going to study languages. Her ladyship had hoped she would follow her aunt's career. In other words, do and achieve what her ladyship has failed to do. Instead she is going the way Daddy had gone: classics, then modern languages, and history. All routes are open to Veronique.' D.W.W. was peeping at me through the chinks of his hands covering his face. He got up. Stretched. 'Interesting! Makes sense. Good work, Khan. Still, pity her ladyship has spoilt it for you.'

'Not for me, D.W.W., for you. If Veronique seeks or needs therapy, I am not going to take her on. I am worth more to her as a caring acquaintance than as a therapist. Anyway, you know full well, D.W.W., that from your one consultation you have engendered an expectancy and trust in Veronique that no one can take over as her therapist. Let us hope she won't be needing therapy. And how are you going to refuse her when she asks you? I have already told both Veronique and Daddy that I am seeing her only because at present you are not well enough to take on a new patient. But that you will arrange everything when she returns from Sardinia in the autumn of 1970. I do not think that plan has collapsed, D.W.W. Veronique will go to Sardinia and she will get Daddy and you to do all the negotiating and bargaining with her ladyship. Because that is what it boils down to. By the way, her sister is not so ill as her ladyship has reported. She was taken ill the week before last and is already up and around.' 'How do you know, Khan?' 'It was in Saturday's *Le Monde*. Her ladyship's sister is quite a renowned avant-garde theatre director in Paris and Nice. My wife knows her. So you see, D.W.W., I am best kept out of your therapeutic strategies for Veronique.'

We were still talking when the phone rang. It was Veronique, ringing from Paris. D.W.W. had got it wrong. Her ladyship had rung him from Heathrow Airport, having already collected Veronique from the nursing home. D.W.W. was furious. He asked Veronique when she was returning to England. She said she was proceeding straight to Sardinia in two or three days' time. As soon as Daddy could come to Paris and take her to Sardinia.

I left D.W.W. alone in the room to talk to Veronique. Afterwards I asked him why he was so furious. 'Everything has worked out as everyone wanted, except for her ladyship,' D.W.W. snapped at me.

'Each one of them is more omnipotent than the other. Reckless meddlers. Veronique won't return to England. Do you know that, Khan?' 'Yes, D.W.W., she will go to Rome. Her Sardinian brother's father-in-law is professor of classical languages at Rome University. The problem now is, what is Dr Winnicott going to arrange for her ladyship? She is going to be at your door hotfoot and howling, D.W.W.' I paused, picked up some proofs from his table and started reading them. We didn't talk any more about Veronique that Sunday morning.

Four days later, on Thursday, D.W.W. rang me around 9.00 p.m. and asked me to come over. He wanted to discuss something urgently. He added: 'Khan, it is pouring with rain outside. If your car is garaged I can easily drive over and fetch you.' I said I had my car standing below, right outside, and would be with him in some five minutes. D.W.W. lived just round the corner. On arrival he took me to the 'den', as we called it between us: his secretary's room in the semi-basement. As always in the evenings the kettle was on the gas-ring, digestive biscuits on a plate with pieces of cheddar cheese, a mug for me and a cup for him, sugar bowl, a bottle of malt whisky, a jug of water and two glasses. It always settled me in the evening visits if I *noted* the objects. I didn't much like going to D.W.W. in the evenings. It ruptured his private living, or so I always felt.

D.W.W. was in a mixed, undecided state. He was excited and worried, at once. He was sipping a glass of very diluted malt whisky. I always regarded that as a barbaric outrage against good vintage malt whisky. He argued that if diluted with water, whisky takes effect more quickly. D.W.W. would sip whisky, to my knowledge, only when pains of angina were starting or when he was recovering from an angina attack. Trying to make the visit short, for him particularly, I asked: 'Has it to do with the Veroniques?' We had started to call the trio – Veronique, Daddy and her ladyship – by that collective plural noun. 'Yes and no.' I realised D.W.W. would get to it in his own time, by his own route. He asked me: 'Have you had time to look at the revised typed draft of Chapter X? Even Mrs Coles is getting fed up with retyping it so many times. I don't seem to get it right about the difference between fantasy and fantasying, so they tell me.' I was a bit short with D.W.W.: 'Why do you ask for their opinion? You never take them seriously.' 'That is not fair, Khan. I do take notice of what they say. But you are right, I should not show it to so many of them. But then they gossip against you; that you are stopping me from relating to them.' 'Does it matter to you, D.W.W., what they say? It doesn't matter to me.' 'Yes, it does, Khan. I am afraid they will harm you when I am gone.' 'We have gone over that a hundred times before, D.W.W. *Laisser allez!* If they pester me over-much I can always go to Paris. Anyway, Miss Freud is still very firmly and healthily around. So please don't worry.'

I knew we were just chattering to ease up, until D.W.W. was ready to tell me what he wanted to, how he wanted to. He made himself a cup of tea, another of his barbaric habits, mixing tea with malt whisky. He sat back, perched up in Mrs Coles's revolving chair. He would keep restively turning round and back. I was always fearful that he would go a full circle and fall off. D.W.W. still behaved as if he was the young, agile athlete he was in 1914, training for the long race. He quietened to stillness. 'I saw her ladyship earlier this evening. They returned from Paris this afternoon.' 'How many constitute "they" today, D.W.W.?' 'The same: Veronique, Daddy and her ladyship. Her ladyship came alone. Said Veronique had enjoyed her visit to Paris. I forgot: they have brought Veronique's ailing aunt with them. Now it is really bizarre. Khan, wait till you hear this. Her ladyship is *expecting*. That is exactly how she said it: "I am expecting, Dr Winnicott!" She hadn't even taken off her fur coat. Sometimes she is brash like the Americans. Distasteful business.'

D.W.W. changed the subject. 'Do you think the revised version is an improvement, Khan?' 'Certainly not! Who has talked you into shoving in a snippet of clinical material? One, it doesn't fit the argument. Two, it is too meagre and casually stated.' 'Well, you rewrite it now. I have done with it, Khan. Let us talk about her ladyship. I hadn't realised she was only thirty-five years old. I have never seen her alone before. She is more vivacious and French when alone. In the company of her husband and/or her daughter she impersonates being a county British lady. Why do these foreigners ape us?' 'These foreigners, D.W.W.? I am one too, and I don't ape. The trouble is, you English, D.W.W., don't like foreigners conforming to your ways.' 'No! No! that is not democratic.' 'But you do encourage them to ape you.' 'Her ladyship is very excited about having a son. She is sure it will be a son.' I didn't comment. 'I think it will do her a lot of good being pregnant and rearing an infant of her own. She was both too young when she conceived Veronique and too busy learning to be a rich country squire's wife. Amazing how much a woman can profit from rearing her own infant.'

I was getting a bit fed up with D.W.W.'s euphoric acclamation of her ladyship's new adventure. 'Did you say her ladyship *will profit* from it?' 'Yes, profit, Khan, profit from it. You are not convinced?' 'No, D.W.W. I know *profit* is a very respectable middle-class English concept, hallowed by usage over centuries, but her ladyship is not English. She is French; temperamental, highly intellectual and a bagful of tricks. She won't hold it to childbirth, D.W.W.' 'What makes you think she will lose her pregnancy?' 'I don't know. I have a feeling she won't hold it. Just getting pregnant must have achieved what she wanted.' 'And why is that, Khan?' 'To make Veronique feel she's *lacking* as a child. A son will complete the equation for her ladyship. Two, she is *news* in her circles today. She won't be in four weeks' time. The novelty of being an expectant mother will give way to the boredom of a *laden* female.' 'You certainly can bitch someone when you don't like them, Khan!' 'It is not that I dislike her ladyship. It is that I don't trust her. You do. You are welcome to her.' 'But you will stay with Veronique?' 'Yes, D.W.W.! You and her ladyship have left me no choice now. I will provide Veronique *coverage* if you will kindly see her in consultation from time to time. And no sending her to nursing homes or for therapy. Not yet! All right?'

I departed. Driving back to my flat I realised that D.W.W. had accepted my terms too readily because they were, in fact, his terms. The old fox really did care for each and every one of those whom he saw in consultation. If he asked a lot from others, including the patients themselves, he gave more of himself to the *situation* than any of the rest of us ever did or could. When I reached my flat, my wife informed me that Veronique had rung to tell me 'Mother is expecting'. My wife said it in a mock-happy voice. I asked her whether she felt Veronique was putting it on. She said: 'Certainly! Please ring her tomorrow.' Spring has already come, I thought, rather paradoxically; not quite knowing what to make of the *total situation*.

What was to happen in the weeks that followed could not have been anticipated by any one of *us*. By *us*, I mean her Ladyship (with a capital

L henceforth! *tout jours!!*), D.W.W., Veronique, Daddy and Khan. Things took a course or were dictated a course. Even a decade and more later I cannot make out whether her Ladyship was the author of the happenings or their victim, or merely a quite unwitting, though a very knowing perpetrator, at least of the first happening. I am taking the notion of *happening* from the 'Theatre of Happening'.

I had rung Veronique just as my wife had promised I would. My wife had said nothing more than what I have reported above. If she did take a phone call from a patient or a colleague, which was rare, she would say the very minimum to him/her or me. Veronique was jubilant. Positively manic. '*Mother is expecting.*' Smothered bubbling giggles in her voice. 'That will keep all of us occupied for the next year. No Sardinia for me. No visits' (the long, long weekends) 'for Daddy in Barcelona.'

After a pause I unobtrusively asked: 'And what of your mother, Veronique?' 'Mother will be busy setting tasks for each and every one of us. Anyone around, or within reach. Yes, sir, Dr Winnicott is the fourth on the list. No, fourth. First is dear Daddy, then our Irish butler, Mac (for MacCoy, sir), then me, Veronique, and then Dr Winnicott. Mother has been on the phone to Dr Winnicott twice already.' 'Does Dr Winnicott enjoy being rung and talking on the phone?' 'He must, sir! They must have talked for half an hour already. It is only 9.15 a.m., too.' 'No, not really, Veronique,' I tried to correct her, to settle her down a little. Veronique was audibly too high. 'Dr Winnicott does not enjoy it. Only he suffers it gladly. Rather invitingly so! There you are right. Now listen to me, Veronique. I am at the outer edge of this "happening". Let us christen it: *Mother is expecting.*'

Veronique had the giggles on the phone. 'Yes, sir!' She still didn't know how to address me. 'Listen! I am, as I said, at the edge, the very mostest outer edge of it, and I am going to stay there. No further away, but no nearer either. So that you can easily reach out to me. Well, I am going away the next two weekends: from Thursday evening to Monday morning.' 'I know about the coming weekend, sir. Daddy has told me. He is going too. To Barcelona, I mean. Only he will be watching and you will be playing. Good luck, sir! You will be playing against the British team. Pity that! We have no strikers from the left. Specially in the deep forward field. You will win comfortably, sir.' 'First it is not *my* team, Veronique! I am only one of four. If the team wins it will be because of the other three: the German, the Spanish and the Argentinian. They are all more seasoned players than me and more fit from daily practice. Anyway it is a fun-match for charity! Not a competitive one.' 'Let us pray your horses don't get lamed by the hard ground in Barcelona. Daddy says it is the last match of the season. He was against it but gave in. Daddy always gives in to the majority opinion. He told me the ground there doesn't suit the horses reared in England. Two of yours are Argentinian ponies. Do I remember right?' 'Yes, Veronique! Well, the weekend after I will be in Geneva. I don't think you will be needing me but if you should, do ring here and you will be told where to reach me. I do not know as yet with whom I am staying in Barcelona and Geneva. Anyway, Dr Winnicott is always there and unfailingly available.' 'Just like Daddy, sir! Anyway, as you say, can you please ask your secretary to ring the headmistress of my school and tell her from you that I am not to be checked on, every hour, as to what I have eaten? Or rather what I have not eaten . . . today . . . so far.' Veronique had said 'rather', 'not eaten', 'today', and 'so far' in a mocking, very English county voice. I could sense she was enjoying herself. At the moment, as Veronique would say.

I received a letter from Veronique in the third week. It was neatly written and stated flatly:

Glad your team only drew in Barcelona; always the best result for me. I am well. Thank you for your letter to the headmistress. Our news. Now Mother wants to kaput the expectancy. Daddy and I want to see you as soon as you can. Everyone has been ringing Dr Winnicott. Even dear Daddy.

I gave them a date and saw them both together in my sitting room. I had decided to make it a social encounter. I noticed Veronique had a little touch, or rather intimation, of blood in her cheeks. Daddy looked harassed and tired. They came at 11.00 a.m. I offered Daddy sherry. Veronique chimed in: 'Daddy likes champagne better, at this hour.' Daddy quietly tried to hush Veronique: 'Will you stop it, I am not a snob.' I rang for my secretary and asked her to bring in a bottle of chilled champagne and three glasses.

Veronique was gloating and said: 'It is all settled. Mother will have the operation this weekend. Good riddance . . .' Daddy stopped her with: 'Shut up. It is not funny.' He turned to me and asked: 'Have Dr Winnicott and you been in touch with each other?' I said: 'No! not for the last fortnight or so. I am calling on him tonight around 8.30 p.m. It is rather dismal her Ladyship has decided to kaput it.' 'So Veronique has told you. It is not funny. They both think it is. It will be *news*. In the papers. What reasons shall I give?' 'Say to them, dear Daddy: the butler thought it would be so much extra work. So her Ladyship decided to kaput it.' I snubbed Veronique: 'You must not forget Daddy has to account for it to more than his family and friends.' I asked Daddy: 'Is there any way I can be of help?' 'Yes, please help me to write a short statement for the press.' We discussed various wordings. I advised against the addition of 'psychiatric' after 'medical'. Daddy thought that was a good idea. So it read:

On medical advice, and for reasons of frail physical health, it has been decided by the parties concerned to terminate the pregnancy.

I called my secretary and asked her to get Dr Winnicott on the phone when she had typed the statement. She did. D.W.W. knew already that Veronique and Daddy were seeing me that morning. He asked me: 'What do you make of it, Khan?' I said, for the moment all I could offer him was the short statement Daddy and I had prepared for the press. I read it to him. D.W.W. was silent; then said: 'Very cunning. Very Khan. Good luck. Pity he has been dragged into it. See you tonight.'

There was little we could do but wait on the events as they happened. Both Daddy and D.W.W. were deeply distressed. They thought it was a ghastly mistake. I thought it was merely scandalous; no worse. In the long run everyone would be glad and relieved *it* lasted only a few weeks and was kaput! I said as much to D.W.W. when I saw him in the late evening. I also pointed out how, since her Ladyship had yanked Veronique out of the nursing home and flown with her to Paris, no one had mentioned the issue of Veronique's food and school refusal. Except for Veronique, once on the phone, when she had requested that the headmistress should be written to.

D.W.W. had borne most of the burden of consultations and advising with the Veroniques. We, D.W.W. and I, had agreed that it should be so till after Christmas. D.W.W. was a medical practitioner of high repute and authority, and with vast connections in the medical world. My role was restricted to talking with Veronique and Daddy. During the past three weeks, two of which her Ladyship had spent in a private nursing home near their mansion, she had seen D.W.W. four times and rung him more times than I care to remember. Veronique and Daddy had rung me only twice in this period, and that to seek practical advice. I had considerable influence with the press and it had come in very handy for Daddy, who was news. I kept in sharp focus, all the time, that the Veroniques had swept under the carpet (and D.W.W. seemed to have joined them in this):

1. Veronique's 'hospitalisation' for food and school refusal. Just as she had not crystallised the 'sickness' in her into proper shape (whatever that means), similarly her 'hospitalisation' was not *proper* either. The nursing home was a genteel county set-up: for respite, ideal! Not therapy.
2. The 'I nearly got drowned in Sardinia' had not been mentioned, except once by Veronique at our first meeting. I felt both D.W.W. and Daddy were curiously silent on that count. I didn't ask. I was sure in myself that there was more, much more to it, than being a droll 'accident'. D.W.W. was already being overworked by the Veroniques. I didn't want to strain him further with my curiosity and conjectures. I was equally certain that D.W.W. would talk about it *one day*, perhaps when *spring comes*.

All the absurd happenings of the month that had followed her Ladyship's declaration to D.W.W.: 'I am expecting', neither interested nor amused me. My only meagre concern was to help Veronique and Daddy have a pleasant family Christmas. It meant a lot to both of them and the two sons. I knew that the Sardinian son and his wife were flying over for Christmas because of her Ladyship's 'indisposition' – that was the family's word for it. But much more important than anything concerning the Veroniques was my adamant resolve that D.W.W. should have a peaceful Christmas with his sisters. D.W.W. was a difficult person to help. He could not stand any sort of dependence on anybody; his sisters excepted!

It did not surprise me that her Ladyship had sailed through her 'hospitalisation' most nobly and resolutely: I have to allow her some praise on this count. But this did not shake me in my conviction that she would eventually 'collapse'. What *did* surprise me was the way D.W.W. joined in with the mood of the Veroniques. The old fox had a strategy up his sleeve. I kept quietly watching all the charades and departed with my wife for Christmas in Paris with friends. Christmas is an awesomely boring social non-event in London, for me! I cannot be an accomplice to the concocted seasonal jollities of English families who never so much as ring up and say hello to each other during the rest of the year. Every culture has its hypocrisies but those of the British are admirably arranged.

A short note from D.W.W. awaited me on my return from Paris, asking me to ring him in the country where he was spending Christmas. I did. He told me Veronique's mother seemed to be having a mild depression. It was to be expected, he hurriedly added. 'Of course, D.W.W., it all happens and always as you arrange it to!' 'Now Khan, I promised Veronique's father you would ring him as soon as you returned. I shall be back for the New Year. Best of luck for the New Year.' 'For you too, D.W.W.'

I rang Daddy and saw him the same evening. He came alone, with Veronique's full assent. He had decided what course to take for her Ladyship to recover to full health. It was as simple as sending her off for the winter months with Veronique, his Sardinian son and daughter-in-law, to return for Easter. I squeezed in: 'For spring!' He didn't get it! I let it pass, and wholeheartedly endorsed his intentions and plan. According to him, everyone was very *happy* with the plan. The English have a most peculiar way of using the word *happy*; it becomes neutral in their mouths. There was one problem, Daddy added nervously: how to 'explain' it to the press. His wife held many positions in charity organisations. I came to his rescue by suggesting the wording as follows:

Lady ———— has been deeply dismayed by the loss of her pregnancy and is going abroad to rest. Her daughter, son and daughter-in-law will go with her.

I further suggested that Daddy should not 'sign' the statement but that it should be sent by her Ladyship's physician. Daddy was hugely relieved. Didn't want to change a single word of it. I read it to D.W.W. on the phone whilst Daddy was still with me. D.W.W. listened pensively and asked me to reread it to him. Stayed silent for a while and said: 'Well done, Khan! Kaput the Veroniques. Thank you for saving me. Happy New Year, everybody.' He rang off.

The Veroniques left for Sardinia a few days after the New Year. That ends my narrative of them.

The real purpose of writing this chapter is to share with the reader my joyous experiences, so very strict too, of 'working with' D.W.W. on living cases. Once the Veroniques were out of our hair, and gone abroad, I kept meeting Daddy at various socio-political functions, as I had done before. D.W.W. stayed wilfully evasive about them for some three weeks. Then, one Sunday visit, he quietly stated: 'That dream of Veronique's is quite interesting, considering all that has happened now.' He restively shifted and shuffled, scrambling odd pages and papers on his desk. 'I did make a note of it somewhere. I remember the dream anyway. She dreamt she was standing chattering quite happily with some guests when she saw her mother seated in a chair, rather bulkier than she is in life, crying. She felt very concerned and started to go towards her mother when she woke up.'

'When did Veronique dream it, and where, D.W.W.?' 'In Sardinia, of course, and before her accident.' 'And she has not trusted anyone to tell it to except your good self, D.W.W.?' 'No, I don't think so.' 'When did she tell it to you?' 'Very hurriedly in the very first consultation, when her mother had gone out to phone some organisation.' I was sarcastic: 'It is quite generous of you to share it with me today, when the Veroniques are safely out of the way, D.W.W. Be that as you wish it to be, we are going to work on the final typescripts of your book *Playing and Reality*. I like the title you have given it, only it is not clear from this that the book is about *your* playing, D.W.W., with *their* reality.' He laughed.

We got it done and the typescript was ready to go to the publishers the following Tuesday. Mrs Coles had many pages to retype. It was always like that with D.W.W. Massive last-hour revisions. One had to literally snatch it out of his hands and say 'Finished now' for him to stop. I was going to keep D.W.W. waiting to tell me more about the dream. We played these child-like games with each other all the time. It is rare that one meets a personage of D.W.W.'s stature and aged maturity and can find such a joyous, spontaneous mutuality with him. D.W.W. was some quarter of a century older than me. But I have noticed that the English have a true talent for fostering such friendships with the younger generations, with proper ceremony and affection. I was always Khan to him and, privately, he was D.W.W. to me, and in public Dr Winnicott.

'What I don't understand about Veronique's dream, Khan, is why she dreamt it. It is not a dream.' I teased D.W.W.: 'Are you quite sure of that?' 'Yes, quite sure.' He realised I was pulling his leg and became defensive. 'Tell me, well-read Khan, where are the dream-features in it? There is little imagination to the making of this dream.' Since I was taking notes rapidly (note-taking rendered us more safely private in ourselves and with each other), he must have felt I wasn't listening. 'All right, to put it your way, there is little primary process. Hardly any dream-work (meaning distortion). Little is repressed or betrays that some material is tucked into seemingly innocuous details. The dream, Khan, is a statement. Yes, as simple as that. So why does she dream it? She could have said it to herself.' 'Just like that, D.W.W.?' 'Yes, Khan, just like that. People do enjoy dreaming! That is no news to me. I have seen over seven thousand children in consultation. Some of them come in dreaming and run back home still dreaming. The clinical task then is not to disturb their dreaming. Not to give *your* interpretations.' D.W.W. had stressed *your* in an edgèd way. Something had irked him. Strange how many ghosts this wise clinician harboured as his judges within: Melanie Klein, Ernest Jones (who had lectured on dreams at the British Society when D.W.W. was a candidate, some thirty-six years ago), and even Miss Anna Freud. They would knock him off his stride in the most ridiculous manner. I had witnessed it during the Scientific Meetings at the Society. Not Jones, of course; I do not remember him coming to hear a paper by D.W.W.

I wanted D.W.W. to go on with his 'thoughts' about Veronique dreaming the dream, so I said: 'Back to Veronique's dream.' But D.W.W. wouldn't let go now. 'You see, Khan, I have had this trouble with them from the days I was training under James Strachey. I never had analysis with Mrs Klein. I can't say I had analysis with Joan Riviere; it is true, however, that she did analyse me for some ten years. And she kept on analysing me during discussions at the Scientific Meetings.' I kept quiet, and let him unburden and be rid of whatever memories had unsettled him. I often used to tease him by saying: 'You know, D.W.W., you do have one thing in common with Freud, and he had *it* in common with Prince Hamlet . . .' 'What thing?' he always asked impatiently. 'You, Freud and Hamlet could live happily in an egg-shell, but that each of you have bad dreams.'

'So let us get back to the dream Veronique could have *thought for herself*, waking.' I noted D.W.W.'s arch phrasing. It was in such throwaway lines that he showed his true genius. But D.W.W. had to settle scores first. 'You see, Khan, I too can identify your Freudian themes in the dream. One, Veronique is showing off her supremacy over her ageing, bulky mother – she is chattering with guests – she has taken over. Two, Mother is "bulky": she is now not a woman who can compete with a young girl for the favours of men. Sexual oedipal rivalry themes. Three, guilt expressed as concern. But she wakes up. Incapacity to hate. Failure of Mrs Klein's depressive position in Veronique. Do you agree with all that, Khan?' 'Yes, D.W.W.: only I hadn't thought of Veronique's dream in those terms.' 'Why not? There is nothing wrong with classical technique.' 'The answer to your "Why not?", D.W.W., is that Veronique didn't tell me the dream. I have thought more on the lines that Veronique hid away something belonging, or relating, to her mother, with you, and you have kept it safely hidden from me till she is out of the way and abroad. You really protect your cases.' 'It is not that, Khan. All that I have said about the dream being oedipal, etc., may be true, but is irrelevant to the meaning and purpose of the dream.'

'So how do you see its purpose, D.W.W.?' 'Simply that the dream is about the mother's repressed (unconscious) hate of her daughter, and not on the sexual level, and neither she nor the daughter could own up to it. Do you understand me? You see, the mother is not crying from rivalry or anguish. But from incapacity. Or maybe for her incapacity.'

'So what is the latent dream-wish, D.W.W.?' 'Simply this: Veronique's wish to rescue her mother from her incapacity to hate her daughter! She had dreamt a dream her mother should have dreamt when pregnant with Veronique. She didn't. At least I don't think she had dreamt. Hence, both she and Veronique are potentially ill, and will wait some time yet to fall ill. You see, Khan, the proof of a patient or person having dreamt a dream is not that he or she remembers it later. I have seen persons fall ill at sixty and more years of age because of a dream they had dreamt in childhood and/or puberty and couldn't recall. Didn't even feel the need to recall! The one positive feature in the dream is that Veronique wakes up before reaching her mother. She refuses to be her mother's repressed hate's keeper. Children do that all the time. When an external not-me factor enters their dream, they wake up. They will have nothing to do with it.'

Now I want to share with my readers my response to the heard-dream, second-hand, via D.W.W. Once he had had his say, we moved on to other issues, particularly relating to his writings and their publication. D.W.W. had a sense of urgency this year, 1970, about getting as much as possible of his 'drafts', scribbled notes, etc., edited, together with me. I had done this once before, some thirty-seven years ago: for, and with, my father, Khan Bahadur Raja Fazaldad Khan, during the last year of his life. I had helped him tidily arrange his vast estates and distribute them amongst his eight sons and two wives, as he wished. He had known and quietly, joyfully, accepted the fact that his end had come. He had had a good innings for some ninety-three years. D.W.W. was only seventy but he had been badly damaged by heart attacks since 1950. Yes! he was a complete and achieved person as he walked and jauntily skipped his route to his end. It pained each and all of us who loved him. I was not the only one. I was one of a very large company. It had been the same at my father's happy end.

No two persons could be more different in most ways than my father and D.W.W., but they had these things in common: an inexhaustible energy for living; an indefatigable capacity for work; a total commitment to the care and well-being of others. Each of them was brutally demanding, without realising it, of the few others they respected and/ or had affection for. So I had come to my relationship with D.W.W. well prepared from some nineteen years of gruelling and loving apprenticeship with my father. I was aware of the *correspondence*. So was D.W.W. Yet we never said a word of it to each other. The onlookers in the profession had their own interpretative versions of it to gossip and spread around.

Let me get to what I 'thought' about Veronique's dream. I have kept notes of my *thinkings*. Somehow I knew that both D.W.W. and I were hard pressed for time, so my turn to tell him wouldn't come. The important thing was to have heard D.W.W. My first response to the dream was: Having dreamt this dream, where was the need in Veronique to engineer the happening: 'I was almost drowned in Sardinia'?

I thought, like D.W.W., that short-circuiting the dreaming experience was self-preservative, but for reasons quite different from D.W.W.'s argument. For me, it signified having another dream, this time not of Veronique's *creation*; only possibly of her making. Her two statements, 'I was nearly drowned in Sardinia' and 'Daddy nearly fainted', I took to be parts of the same 'dreaming experience' (Khan, 1976a), but scattered and spread across time. For me, the accident-dreaming annulled the obligations and concerns of 'mother . . . bulkier than usual'. It asserted her right to live as life offered itself to her. And the largest part of that new life, for Veronique, was *Daddy*. She needed him to underpin it. Here every *actual*, reality-anchored gesture, every act, every word is both *symbolique* and *imaginaire*, in the idiom of modern linguistics. Lacan (1966) has given us its grammar unto utter mystification. What had happened since the dream of 'mother' and 'I nearly drowned' bears out my inferences, at least for me. I leave the reader to elaborate his own responses. In the two further meetings I had with Veronique, after her return to England, I *forgot* with a wilful ease all about these issues, and never even hinted at them.

[1986]

3
Empty Chairs, Vast Spaces

LUCIA

Je ne suis pas toujours maître de moi-même,
que puis-je y faire?
Et je souffre pour mes actions,
que puis-je y faire?
À vrai dire, je crois à Ton pardon généreux
Tant j'ai honte de penser
que Tu as vu mes actes,
Mais puis-je y faire?

OMAR KHAYYAM *The Rubaiyat*
(my translation)

'I am a vagrant. Since my infancy, to be sure. My parents were never in any space for more than a year. I don't remember very much of my infancy, only from three years of age, or about then. And until I went to, what you would call a boarding school, I remember mostly vacant chairs, hours and days of waiting, and strange places. We had few objects. Both my parents are teachers. Real gypsies, the Americans would call us. "Us" is Pa, Ma, my eldest sister Elizabeth, Christina, and myself. I was named Lucia. Every name is a guaranteed misfit to each of us. To make it really comical we three are all different heights, girths and have different colour hair. I am the tallest, thinnest and the blackest. I mean of hair. They say it makes me look exotic-like. A cute sexy kid. I was teased by everyone. I would say I had a very happy, romantic childhood. My parents were on the move all the time. They were, and are, teachers. They are still married, and live together. Isn't that something? They loved their little girls. We are still their "little girls". We have never grown up in their eyes. Oh yes! My parents are fanatical Trotskyites.'

'Can you please spell it for me. A "kiy" in it, or "skyites"? It doesn't bother you I am scribbling notes?'

'No, no. You are welcome. You can stand on your head, if that would help you. My father does, whenever he is angry. But he believes in yoga. You aren't a Hindu?'

'No, young lady, I am a devout Muslim.'

'That is a fine one: "young lady". I have been called many and all sorts of names before, but not "young lady". It sounds so very respectable. Do you understand Spanish? I didn't think you did. Didn't catch sight of any books in Spanish on your shelves. My father had only one book, the *Shorter Oxford English Dictionary*, and my mother always carried a Spanish/Portuguese dictionary. Outside Brazil no one talks Portuguese in our part of the world. She said it had caused her the least trouble to learn Portuguese. Her mother tongue was English. Her parents were Irish. She was born in Shanghai and grew up there. Pa was born in Rio. His father was a real Spaniard and his mother was a half-breed. Indian and Spanish. I was born in Texas, Christina my older sister in Lima, and Elizabeth the eldest in Mexico. She is a doctor. Married with kids. Christina is also married. Couldn't have kids so divorced. Not fair on him, she said. She lives in Rio now. She is a professor. History and languages. I am the black sheep of the family. I just managed a low-grade degree from Mexico. Specialised in teaching disturbed children in San Francisco. My parents were employed there when I was twenty-three. I helped them run the kindergarten, on and off. Please can I have some water? Don't get it wrong; as everyone does, and will continue to. Pa and Ma loved each other. They were god-fearing, simple folks. Went to church every morning, Sundays. In some places the church or the praying place was a mile or so away. In South America and the US there is not always a church in every village or town. I am surprised at how very many churches there are in England. Most of them empty. Church is no longer part of English life, it seems.'

'It is in rural places. That is my experience,' I said. Just to register I was present.

'Maybe so. It doesn't matter anyway. All this is irrelevant to what I have come to seek your help about.'

'You know, lady' (I left out the young, this time) 'as your doctor told you, it is futile coaxing me to agree to an abortion. I just won't do it. First, I cannot. I am not medical. I am what is called here, in England, a "lay analyst". Like the lay priests. The associative link with the lay priests has made the lay analysts respectable. The English have a way of arranging these things. In America most, if not all, of the "lay analysts" are militant charlatans.'

'How can a charlatan be militant? He hasn't the *given* authority to be militant. Would you say Ma and Pa are charlatans and militant as teachers and Trotskyites?' She paused for an answer.

With a calculated intent I answered ambiguously, as well as provocatively: 'I know little about them, but from what you have told me . . .'

'With you analysts, it is always "from what you have told me", in various phrasings, of course. Every one of you makes his patient both a witness and a guilty witness to his/her account. You are objective and never judgemental, you say.' (What an ugly word to use, 'judgemental', I thought.) 'Yet you people are the worst sort of moralists. The morality of Pa and Ma is of the earth, earthy. Nothing phoney about it. Pa has slept with other women. Ma knew it at the time, and all the way. So did we girls; some of it. The middle one most of us three. Ma and Pa both confided in her. You'll say confessed to her. We all five often slept in one room in two beds only.'

'You seem very sure about what I would, or will, say. That is your business. But please, never be sure as to what I will *not* say. I am not responsible to you, or to anyone, for what I will or would think, about what you are telling me. I am, however, responsible only to you, and not to anyone else, for what I say to you from the totality of my thoughts.'

'You know, I have trained as a specialised kindergarten teacher in San Francisco and Rio. Doing a psychology course was compulsory. So I saw many psychiatrists, psychoanalysts and psychologists at work; with us teachers, mothers and children. I had noticed that, from whatever branch, they hardly ever talked to the fathers.'

'That is a shrewd observation, lady. You know your way around, not only living, but thinking also. How come you are in such a mess?'

'Take me on as a patient and find out.'

'For my satisfaction? No, thank you. I have little curiosity about others.'

'We, the girls, grew up sharing Pa and Ma's sadness and their joys. They did have to contend with a lot of hostility in the US when we were growing up. Of course we always thought Pa and Ma were right. Always right. It was always them versus us, where we girls were concerned. Our parents were quite cool about it. They were used to it, for one. And now I can see, since they were the authors of most of the *calamities* – that was our, the girls', word for it – they had to take it on the chin. You have no idea what a strong chin, and a broad one too, you need to survive in the US. It is the most goddamn tight-arsed country you can imagine. Specially in countryside places. They are so generous if you are *proper*. I have seen so many cartoons about the English – or is it the British? – being *proper*. But none can beat the Americans at it. They live by rules and these rules change from place to place. So long as you chew gum and smoke cigarettes, you are in America and are an American. Yes, my Ma and Pa suffered a lot of pain. In the early years especially. They had no money, and when they did, it was soon spent. On us and those whom they thought more needy than themselves. In the US there is one thing that is regarded as Sin. It is poverty. Once poor, you have had it. You earn everyone's contempt. Derision. Hostility. Ostracism. Pa and Ma suffered for their violent and militant political beliefs. The Trotskyites could get away with murder if they had some money. Pa and Ma didn't. So every act, every move, every relationship of theirs was weighed, judged and condemned. They made light of it. We didn't. The girls, I mean. Take this English lady. Ha! ha! I am saying lady too. Truth is we girls called her Lady. I must have been around five when she hitched up with the Pa and Ma commune. We were in Texas then. She had been brought from England to teach some Rancher children. She is still with The Eldest . . .'

'Who are Rancher children?'

'Children of someone whose Pa has a big ranch. Lady spoke proper English. I learned mine from her. She taught me Latin and French too. We loved her. They said Pa loved her too. In a sexy way. It wasn't true. She would have got all confused if he had touched her. She was a happy person. She taught at the school with Ma and Pa. She did very good crochet needlework. My doc. sis. learned that. Not me. Well, Pa and Ma had to leave the little US town because folks started to not send their children to the school, because of the talk about Pa and Lady. Pa thought it was not fair on the guys who owned the school for us to stay there. So we packed and took to the road. Lady always wore long dresses, a little shorter in summer, and was never without her hat. A funny one. French. Said her Pa had given it to her for her eighteenth

birthday. To everyone's surprise she said she would travel with us. She
spoke Spanish. We were going to Argentina. So she came with us. There
was nothing strange about that. We were never just the five of us. In the
"commune" we were always many. When we travelled from one space
to another we were always a *troupe*. Like a theatrical company. Our
baggages were as absurd and bizarre as the way each of us dressed.
Lady's reason for coming with us was that it would be too much of a
burden on Ma to be looking after us girls. She always called us by our
individual names. She had this little dog and her Bible. They never left
her company. Pa and Ma had no Bible. They both knew it by heart,
almost. Pa was a good one for Sunday sermons. He mixed Jesus and
Trotsky in the most convincing manner. Listening to Pa you would think
Trotsky and Jesus were pals and wrote to each other, regularly. We girls
would sit solemn and still in the church or prayer house and tease Pa no
end afterwards. In fact, I became so good at it that when I was seventeen I
would give the "sermons" to local folks if Pa was ill or too busy. The
Eldest, by the time she was fifteen (this is how Pa and Ma called us: The
Eldest, The Older, The Youngest – sounds more chummy in Spanish)
was already not only the family doctor but the kindergarten doctor,
whatever space we moved to. In Lady she found a real ally and teacher.
Only she never came up to Lady's basics for hygiene. It was fun, life and
living. Shared by each and all. Please remember that about Pa and Ma.
Persons and individuals meant everything to them. And one must not tell
lies or cheat. Pa was very strict about the distinction between not telling
the truth, and telling lies. Both were conscious acts and *choices*. Yes, that
was another thing for both Pa and Ma – making a choice. One had to
make a choice, stand by it and take full responsibility for it.' Lucia had
talked herself out of breath. She paused.

'This is really most pleasant, fun as you would say, but it is my task to
remind you that you have to make a choice, and you are here, today,
expecting me to help you make the right, and a practical, choice. Well, I
have some clues as to what would be a positive choice for you, but I need
to hear more on certain issues before I tell you some of my thoughts. Can
you come this Saturday, 4.00 p.m.? That is the day after tomorrow.'

She hadn't needed to be helped with her coat, since she was wearing a
poncho – a most colourful one. As I was seeing her out, shaking hands, I
very smoothly remarked: 'Try not to be so *high* on Saturday. It would
help.' Lucia smiled a knowing smile of recognition. She was no fool.

That was some comfort. She was a 'crazy loony cat', as she had quoted someone saying about her. But I felt she could also be calculating when it fitted her needs.

A word Lucia had employed as she was getting into the lift had caught my attention. Looking at me, rather archly, she had mumbled: 'What a lot of *scrimmages*.' I was sure she had not used the noun *scrummage*, which is a word I had heard from rugby players, so I looked up *scrimmage* in a dictionary. It gave two definitions: (1) a rough or disorderly struggle; (2) *American football*: the period of a game from the time the ball goes into play to the time it is declared dead.

This pleased me. I felt Lucia was a good sport. I could work with her. Reporting on my clinical work with Lucia I am faced with a different problem from the ones I usually have to contend with, namely those of privacy of the patient, and not distorting the facts over-much to mask the patient's identity. As I write this, some thirteen years after my 'clinical scrimmages' with Lucia, and later with her son, I have to guard against what Samuel Beckett (1958) so neatly phrases as perceptions 'distorted into intelligibility'. Since the clinical encounters were infrequently spaced, and were, of necessity, long sessions, I took notes. *Facts* are easy to state. But the *un*-logic of these 'scrimmages' could so easily get hushed by reasonings.

Lucia had a long meeting with her lawyer the next day (Friday) and then had to return to the country, where she had set up a 'commune' with two other girls, to collect clothes to wear. When I next saw her on the Saturday afternoon, she was smartly and properly dressed – by which I mean not casually and exotically. She was never badly dressed. She was wearing a two-piece suit of a navy-blue colour. She had seen her gynaecologist at noon and had lunched with her solicitor. She sat down, and said with a smile: 'Thank you for letting me go on about the Trosts.' She could see I was puzzled by the word 'Trosts'. She enlightened me: 'Trosts is a shortened plural for Trotskyites.' I nodded comprehension. She continued: 'Both my gynaecologist and my lawyer insist I must make a choice, with your help, this weekend. It is growing late by the day. Please can you see me tomorrow? That is rather irregular, I know, but all members of the *gyps* family are notorious for their irregular arrangements, in every situation. Pa and Ma never signed a contract, in spite of the fact that they were taken advantage of, again and again.'

'Please lady, can we stay within the bounded space of the football ground?'

She laughed and said: 'Ask me questions.'

'If you could give me some facts, it would help. We do come from very different cultures and countries.'

'Facts like what?'

'Put it this way. "Factions" that are tagged together by dates. And dates that are important to you regarding the problem facing us.'

'I am thirty-four years old. Not married. First abortion when I was nineteen years of age. In Texas. Didn't know the guy. He was much older. Pa and Ma said: It is your choice. Second abortion when I was twenty-six. A professor. I had been his student in Argentina. Married man, with children. I wanted his child. Pa and Ma and The Eldest thought it was not fair on him. So chose to throw it out. Complications followed because it was done by a local female nurse. We have a special name for them. Unlike the Meds., they do all the irregular things. Was very frightened because the Med. Pa and Ma took me to, after the abortion, said it could be I'll never conceive again. I stayed quiet till I was thirty. Too busy training to be a specialised kindergarten teacher. Then whoom! Pregnant again. I think I wanted to test whether I could get pregnant. Couldn't possibly have an illegit. baby. Was on a scholarship from a goddamn religious foundation. And now this situation. You don't believe any of it, do you?'

'No, I believe all of it, and more.'

'What is the more, please?'

'What neither you, lady, nor I, will ever find out.'

'I told you I came here last year on a grant to study further methods of advanced and more liberal kindergarten education. I set up a "commune" with two other girls, some thirty miles from London. One is British and the other West Indian. We are all "advanced students".'

'Advanced in what sense?' I sneaked in, as comment.

Lucia laughed. 'No, not advanced as everything goes, but in *pursuit* of most noble and honourable methods of educating little tiny tots. The joke of it is the British girl is chaste and the oldest of us three. Not dry stick-like British chaste, but because she is truly committed to her work. Loves the kids. "Slatey" we fondly call the West Indian girl, because she is neither black nor dark brown. She is slate-coloured, dark grey. Not a quite right description. She is the youngest. Knows her way

with men, i.e., youths, and is a great asset to the "commune". Gets us
two often invited out with her "friends" to the movies. We cannot
afford theatres. I am the slack one in every respect. Lazy, spendthrift,
and clever rather than thoughtful. We had run into some money
shortages. One day I was travelling back home to my country-pad, on a
Friday, when I felt very tired. The Third was crowded. I got up and
went to a First. Only one man was seated in it. I barged in and then in
my most American accent asked: "Please Mister, what class is this?"
He looked up from his paper and said: "I think it is First." "Oh sorry!"
And I started to back out. He said, "Sit down. If the guard comes, just
say you are with me. Only don't please make conversation with me. If
you are American, I can tell you I am fifty-one years old. Have a wife
and two children. Travel on company's expense. Have a lovely house
and garden. Am a business executive." And he sank his eyes into his
paper. I noticed he was doing a crossword puzzle. We got out together.
Like in cheap Hollywood films, it was pouring cats and dogs. He asked
me whether I had transport. I said, "Yes, sir, my feet." That amused
him. He said: "I will drop you home. Tell your address to the
chauffeur. Are you a student?" "Yes sir, an advanced student." He
laughed: "Like advancing from Third to First class?" I laughed too.
Net result, next weekend all three of us girls were lunching with his
wife and kids. Four weeks later, after two lunches and one theatre-
dinner in London, I was flying with him to Lisbon. He needed a
translator, *we* needed the money. Yes sir, it was all undertaken and
done with charitable commune intent. The English-Eldest said: "Be
careful." Slatey said: "Don't miss out on fun." This was repeated three
weeks later to Madrid. Net profit: two happy weekends, theatres for
the girls three, some cash (legitimate) and a baby thrown in for free.'

I really couldn't help laughing. She had a cute turn of phrase. She
asked ponderously: 'Well sir, what is the professional advice choice-
wise? Right now. The *lover* wants to have the kid. So do I. So do Ma
and Pa. The Eldest says: "No! not if he doesn't give you a roof over
your head." The Older says: "What the hell. If you want it, keep it." I
am not decided. From the commune The Eldest says yes, but
conditionally. Slatey says you can always go to Barbados and stay with
my parents, have the kid and teach for fun. Gynae. says it is risky to
have it done. The lawyer says that since I have an American passport
and he is British, with two daughters only, and considerable wealth,

the snag is if the baby is a boy he will claim it, that is, can claim it. That is the galaxy of my problems, sir. What do you recommend?'

I asked if we could break for a cup of tea. Tea was brought to the consultation room. Casual chatter but significantly oriented, by both, and each, of us. After tea I said I read the situation thus. I reminded Lucia how what she remembers from the age of three to eighteen are *empty chairs* and *vast spaces*. Well, she has replaced 'chairs' with phantom prams; the space-stretches are the same. Another feature to take into account is that she is ageing, with a near-damaged uterus. Since the relationship with 'the lover' is positive, and the wish for a child both mutual and commune-al, I would certainly recommend keeping the baby. But before I endorsed my recommendation, I would like to talk it over with her gynaecologist, to whom I was professionally answerable since he had sent Lucia to me. But the three of us should meet together.

Lucia got up lithely from her chair and asked permission to use the phone and make an appointment for Sunday. I said she could go to the secretary's room for more privacy. She replied: 'One, there is no call for privacy, and two, I will be speaking in Spanish.' After the phone call, during which an appointment with her gynaecologist had been made for 4.00 p.m. the following day, I did not let Lucia tarry and chit-chat. We met on Sunday afternoon at Mr X's rooms in Harley Street. He was a genial, friendly person who knew of me, although I didn't know of him. We were meeting for the first time. He was a friend of the *gyps*, and had met Pa in Mexico City during some international multidisci-plinary conference. He was willing to take Lucia into his ward for labour and childbirth. She would have to pay the hospital fees, but none to him. Mr X suggested he should write to me, recommending keeping the baby because of fear of damage to the uterus, and that I should endorse it. This was to get an extra grant for Lucia. She would have to stay in hospital some two weeks.

During our threefold and threesome exchanges I discovered a great deal about Lucia's way of going about living. What I learned endeared her to me. I offered to charge mere token fees because travelling to sessions at weekends would be expensive. Neither I nor Lucia had time during the week. The issue that concerned me most was who would look after the baby. Lucia said she had rung her older sister the night before, and if she were to decide to keep the baby, then The Older would fly over to stay the length of time it would take Lucia to finish her advanced course. The Older was now the richest of 'the girls' and said she needed a sabbatical.

The Older had also said she would pay all expenses, so Lucia would have no financial burden from the baby. At this point Mr X raised the issue the lawyer had thought about; namely, 'the lover's' possessive interest, if the baby was a boy. Both Mr X and the lawyer had met with 'the lover', and agreed that he was a decent, caring and honourable person who wanted and needed a son. As we were talking, the phone rang in Mr X's room and it was the lawyer, who talked with Lucia and Mr X in Spanish. I said I would not see the lawyer at this stage and 'the lover' never, if I could help it. It was not from hostility, but that I would be able to help Lucia better if I didn't tangle with 'the lover' now. In fact, I knew 'the lover' socially, but I didn't say so. There was no point in revealing this at present.

It was mutually agreed amongst Lucia, Mr X and myself:

1. I would take Lucia into psychotherapeutic care from now on. This did not constitute a promise to analyse her in any accepted sense of the term psychoanalysis, as I would explain in writing. I would try to see Lucia every Saturday and Sunday. I did warn them that I would be in America lecturing for four weeks, departing on Good Friday which was in four days' time. Also that I would not be able to see Lucia some weekends in June and July, and I would be away for the summer vacation for six weeks from mid-July.

2. All three of us would keep each other informed of our actions regarding Lucia in the given context. Mr X would send me copies of all letters, abstracts of telephone conversations and consultations with Lucia, 'the lover', the lawyer, the family *gyps* and anyone else who became involved in any way. For my part, I would write in fuller detail to Mr X before I left for America, and on my return would keep him informed of all significant developments, clinical and extramural. I would not correspond directly with 'the lover' or the lawyer but, should they wish to write to me, I should be accessible and available, and also to all members of the family *gyps*, including the English lady who was still trekking and living with them.

3. I would not communicate with the English-Eldest and Slatey of the mini-commune, but I would be open to any communications they might wish or need to make about Lucia. However, in general I would like them to talk with Mr X first, on every count.

With this agreed amongst us, I gave Lucia a third appointment for the following Wednesday. When I returned home, I was positively elated and happy. The going was good and the running had been fast. I had found Mr X not only most co-operative, but also very positive towards our working together. I couldn't help smiling at the fact that Lucia had opened another 'commune of three': herself, Mr X and myself. It would be fun to explore the possibilities of such an *open* situation. It was my first chosen venture for such an unprogrammed and non-bounded relating with a patient, clinically, to help her find her own true limits and boundaries.

By starting on a new style, and scope, of clinical work with a patient/person and his/her total environment, as was appropriate to the patient's needs, I was freeing myself of the rigid Yiddish shackles of the so-called psychoanalysis. I say 'Yiddish' because psychoanalysis, for better and worse, is not only Judaic in its inherited traditions, but also Yiddish and Jewish. The three are quite distinct in my experience. Even though only two Jewesses played an important role in my education (Melanie Klein for a short while, and Anna Freud mutatively and for much longer), the impact of the Judaic-Yiddish-Jewish bias of psychoanalysis was neither small nor slight on me. If it undoubtedly nurtured me, it has also cramped my personal and ethnic styles. It was an ego-alien ferment, as well as an increment, in my totality of experiences. In the year 1974 (when this clinical work took place) I was to be fifty years of age. Time to be my own person.

The third 'scrimmage' with Lucia was quiet, sobering, and not easy to balance for either of us. I learned a lot more and all I said to Lucia was that she would have to sustain herself for long breaks, with the help of Mr X, as well as the English-Eldest and Slatey. I promised to let her have a copy of the letter I would be writing to Mr X before my departure. She affectionately asked: 'Can you please ask your secretary to send me your itinerary in the US? I would like to know where you are and be able to write to you. Every one of the *gyps* writes amusing and not plaintive letters.' I said yes, of course. We parted on that happy note.

From my letter to Mr X:

As promised I shall briefly, even if awkwardly, state some of the thoughts I have about Miss L. Trosts. The first is about what I am offering her by way of 'therapeutic care'. You raised your eyebrows when I said to both you and her, during our 'commune-consultation' last Sunday, that I am willing to provide psychotherapeutic care. That this would not constitute a promise to *analyse* her in any accepted sense of the concept of psychoanalysis, I repeated to Miss L. Trosts when I saw her yesterday. I further added that, should I consider she needs analytic treatment during this period (between now and giving birth) or after, I shall find her a suitable colleague for analysis, with your agreement, of course, and continue to provide psychotherapeutic care myself.

To spell out more elaborately what I mean, may I tell you that I have been trained in the strictly classical traditions of psychoanalysis at the British Institute of Psycho-Analysis. As you know from attending the late Dr Michael Balint's seminars for physicians, or so you hinted, there are three traditions of classical psychoanalysis at the British Institute. The longest-established is The Middle Group (now rechristened The Independents, to give it more, and better-defined, 'gender identity', not that it has made much difference). Then The Kleinians (a most militant lot, who are gathering power by the week and are almost there); they are wagging the British Society now that the stalwarts like Winnicott, Balint, Fairbairn and such personages as Glover (Ed), Marjorie Brierley, and the Stracheys are all dead. The third group is the misnamed (or perhaps the intention to make it 'second class' was not that larval) 'B' Group, led by Miss Freud. Members of the last two groups are largely Jewish and refugees (with two exceptional immigrants, invited and much honoured, Mrs Melanie Klein and Miss Anna Freud).

Now I was trained in all three traditions, having been supervised by Miss Freud and Mrs Klein (for adult cases) and Dr Winnicott, Mrs Milner and Dr Clifford Scott (for child cases). I have never entertained the conceit that I enjoyed this almost unique 'training career' from any large virtue in me as a candidate. I was bright, no doubt, but also too young and naïve at the start. Years have aged me, but I have kept the naïve bit. The reason is that my father, the late Raja Fazaldad Khan, had left me very large estates and immense wealth to pursue my studies. So I could afford not to have to earn a living; could take five non-paying patients and pay supervision fees to four supervising analysts. Only Miss Anna Freud did not charge me supervision fees. Mrs Klein charged me outrageous fees, thinking it would make me balk. I paid readily, even though I was learning the least from her. She was a status symbol, and I was young, clinically inexperienced, of noble birth, a Muslim from the Punjab (then Northern India of the British Imperial Raj, now Pakistan). I knew I needed 'status symbols', so I collected them. It was a fatuous pursuit. Miss Anna Freud, Dr Winnicott and Dr Clifford Scott were the analysts I learned most from. With me, Miss Anna Freud was most liberal and facilitating, in spite of the Kleinians gossiping about her rigidity. I found Mrs Klein's spate of supervisory interpretations about a patient she had never *met*, not only over-self-determined, but rather boring as well. Both Dr Winnicott and Scott had seen a boy of seven and an adolescent of sixteen, in consultation with their parents, before deciding that I was suitable for these patients.

I am writing at such length to clarify what I mean by distinguishing between 'psychotherapeutic care' and analysis proper, so called. The former I learned first from my father from the age of nine to nineteen. The 'care' was of our peasants, and it was total care. This was augmented by Dr Winnicott's teachings in particular, and by Dr Clifford Scott's open-minded and helpful comments about one of my cases (the sixteen-year-old boy). From Miss Anna Freud I learned, without dogma or strictures, Freud's psycho-analytic method (1904). As I have gained in experience, and learned *with* my patients, I now clearly state to them whether I am taking them into analysis (which is never less than three times a week with me) or into psychotherapeutic care. Even so, there are periods in analysis when I find I have to cut down on, and curtail, interpretative work and augment caring as such. Therapeutic caring entails explicit and mutually agreed *management* (another basic Winnicottian concept, or rather notion), and this inevitably involves the family and friends of the patient.

When I had agreed to give a consultation to Miss L. Trosts, on demand from you, I had little doubt, from the letter you sent me, that she would need psychotherapeutic care more urgently than insights, as such. And this is what I am offering her now, on a long-term basis. I have told Miss L. Trosts that during the periods I am away (like now, for four weeks) she will have to find the humility and honesty in herself to seek help from you, the lawyer, 'the lover', her mini-commune and, of course, her Pa and Ma, even at this long range.

About Miss L. Trosts, I can tell you this much only. I find her intelligent, imaginative, playful and a joyous prattler. It does not bother me in the least that in her narrative most facts, offered as facts, are *factions*, both fictive and true, and paradoxically so at the same time. In fact, Miss L. Trosts tells *more* through her factions than those miserable creatures, the neurotics, addicted to being analysed.

I also feel quite confident that I can help Miss L. Trosts, and for the one reason that I feel I can learn a lot from her. She is an awkward person, but an authentic one.

I enclose my itinerary in the USA. Please write to me or ring me as you wish and as Miss L. Trosts' demands dictate.

With this letter written, typed and dispatched, I took off for my lecture tour in the USA. During the twenty-eight days I was there, I received some ten letters from Lucia. She never failed to reach me. She was right:

the Trosts were talented and dedicated *épistolaires*. Her letters were convivial, sharing, and a pleasure to receive. I answered each, briefly: brief not from costive policy but because I was always short of time. Somehow flying, landing, delivering the goods, taking off for the next appointed space gave me a sentient feeling of what Lucia must have meant by 'I am a vagrant'.

When I returned and saw Lucia, she was hugely, nearly seven months, pregnant. She had been shown straight to the consultation room. When I entered she got up and walked, a duck-like, Chaplinish, pregnant-lady walk, towards me. It amused me very much. I noticed my houseboy had served her coffee; most unusual for him to have done that without my explicit instructions. So, I thought, one more person had been enlisted to the mini-commune. I am not going to detail here all that she told me. Only this much: Lucia had moved her mini-commune from a flat to a house with a small garden. Pa and Ma, The Eldest and The Older had sent 'donations' – unsolicited contributions – and the two girls of the mini-commune were willing and voluntary helpers. She said: 'Yes, sir, it is all free, happy service around me.'

She got up, turned a full circle and exclaimed: 'Isn't it goddamn good!' I looked at her with indulgent affection and said: 'Now, now, Lucia, what are you fattening me up for? Let us have it.' 'Oh, for Pete's sake, don't spoil it for *us*.' I noted the use of 'us'. I said: 'I am sorry, Lucia, these have been four long weeks for you. Thank you for keeping me alive in memory, and with you, yourself, all these weeks. But please, I have to deliver a bit of "homework" now and then. So come on, tell it.'

She shuffled nervously, and said in a quiet voice: 'I have cheated a little. Couldn't help it. Lover-man has been so kind and attentive. He loves me as dearly as his circumstances allow. After all, damn it, I am not much, especially filled up and out like this . . .' 'Ha! ha! Lucia. You see, language speaks better and more wisely than we can ever make it speak for us. You said in the first consultation: "All I remember are empty chairs, vast spaces." Then, in the second consultation, you said you had got pregnant to prove that you could get pregnant and then had thrown *it* out. Today you are talking of being "filled up and out". Isn't that great, Lucia? Emptiness has been haunting you, somehow, and in many ways, since you started to have "the red wets".'

She leaned forward and asked: 'Have you been talking to Mr X?'
'No, Lucia. I arrived home only four hours ago. How is he?' 'He has
been writing to you. He loved your letter. You meant it to be loved.
There are two small errors in it. Anyway, the lover-man asked me a
favour. I agreed. It was that I give the baby his surname. He says his
name is quite a common Welsh name and so there is no risk of leakage
to the press. He is quite famous, you know.' 'No, not famous,
important! Get it right, Lucia.' 'Of course you know him and you held
out on me and Mr X. Not fair!' 'What would you have gained if I had
told you?' 'Nothing, I guess. Anyway, do you think I did right?' 'Yes,
more than right, Lucia, you have behaved with generosity and with
honour. Your Ma and Pa have certainly reared their *girls* well.' 'So can
I write to them? I mean now.' 'Yes Lucia, but why not ask Mr X first?
He really cares about you.' 'Oh Lord yes! Without him I could have got
into panics many times these five weeks. Did I write to you it was he, or
one of his nurses, who got us the house, and very cheap? You will visit
us, won't you? I will say it for you – *one day*.' 'Yes, Lucia.'

I gathered more information. I had established the *significance* (both
fearful and curious) of 'empty chairs' for Lucia. Now I would look for
what 'vast spaces' signified to her.

We reached the summer break. Fortunately the English-Eldest's aunt
invited all three of them to spend two weeks in her country house. The
lover-man had lent them a car for two weeks. Thus we parted. Since I
would not be easy to reach on the phone, moving from place to place in
the south of France, I told her I would ring her. I had rung her three
times. Once a week. When I had rung her the third time, she had asked:
'How long are you staying there?' 'Till I fly back to London in six days'
time.' She asked me to ring her in two days. The Older was arriving
from South America; it would be a pleasant surprise-gift for her. I fitted
in with Lucia's whim.

As I have said, Lucia was by now truly full and overladen. She made
light of it, as she did of everything. 'Manic defence' is a jolly good thing,
I often thought in relation to Lucia, but only if you can make it work
for you. I kept pace with Lucia, as she wished and needed me to. She
never once took advantage of it. She was nearing what she called 'The
Trosts' D-day'. I had noticed that *naming* events, dates, places (in her
own way) was Lucia's way of underlining for remembrance. In fact,

what I had called 'factions' to Mr X were never, or rarely, distortions of facts. They were merely playful, child-like elaborations, and always funny. I was to discover soon that each of the Trosts had their own brand of humour or wit.

Important to report here is the fact that by the time Lucia went into hospital for her confinement the mini-commune was almost over-populated. Out of the blue Pa and Ma had come to spend six months in England to study. They had brought with them a Mexican professor of humanities whom Lucia had not met before. He was writing a book on an English poet and would be staying in Oxford. The problem now, for Mr X, me and the lover-man, was how to clear some space around Lucia. I teased her by saying: 'Goddammit, Lucia, forget the vast spaces, you are cluttered. All chairs are full and more.' She had laughed.

The labour was quick and healthy. She gave birth to a son. Everyone was overjoyed, especially Ma and Pa. They had a grandson. Four weeks after Lucia had returned to her house I gave a lunch party on a Sunday. She had hinted that this is the gift she wanted for her son, who had been most typically named: Juan (father's Christian name) Trosts (to include all the family) Hamley (the lover-man's surname; I have changed it here, for obvious reasons).

The guests were: Lucia and Juan (aged four-and-a-half months), Pa and Ma, The Older, Mr X, the lawyer, the English-Eldest, Slatey, the lover-man (Lucia had asked for him to be invited, and since he had met everyone else, and I knew him, it would have been churlish to exclude him), and 'the Mexicano Don', as Lucia had named the professor: a grey-haired, handsome, swarthy man, tall and lean, about sixty years old.

It was my first encounter with everyone, except for Lucia, Mr X and the lover-man. I had a casual buffet-lunch, served with casual ceremony. Lucia was driven home afterwards by her *aides*, as she now called them. The lawyer had come with the lover-man and returned with him. Mr X had gone on to his Harley Street rooms; he attended to his mail on Sundays. Pa and Ma went to the Tate Gallery. The whole lunch-affair had been a most joyous venture for everyone. No one had felt strained.

Lucia could not come for the next two weeks because she had to put in extra work on her dissertation. She was determined to get it finished and return to Mexico with her baby, Pa and Ma and The Older. I knew, by now, what a resolute character she was, and had little doubt that she would get it done. Things were happening fast and rapidly. Mr X had to go abroad on a lecture tour, so most of the responsibility for guiding Lucia now fell on me. Pa and Ma were, most strangely, just sympathetic onlookers, although always willing to help, and available whenever Lucia needed them. I could see clearly how they had reared their daughters. They were most unintrusive parents, participant with the two girls and equally calling upon them for help. Lucia went to the British Museum to help Pa find the data he was looking for. Ma had joined a nearby school run by a potter, where she worked some three hours daily. The Trosts were such motivated persons, each one of them. Most enviable.

When Lucia came next, she sat meditatively, then she burst out laughing. 'Idiot me! It is not going to get any better holding it back. Well, sir, I am in love. With whom, you must be wondering. The Mexicano Don. I don't think I have ever been in love before. We are not intimate. I have told him I am not going to be, till after marriage. He should not go by my past. I am an unmarried mother now, and must think of Juan before I indulge my passions.' I kept listening. 'What do you make of it?'

'Well, Lucia, I know from Pa and Ma that the Mexicano Don is a widower. His wife died tragically of cancer some six years ago. He has two daughters, one of fourteen, the other ten. He is sixty. Five years younger than Pa. So far all is smooth sailing, Lucia. The only issue to be resolved honourably is, how are you going to bury the lover-man?'

'Oh, him! I have had no intimate relations with him since my pregnancy was diagnosed. Everyone knows it. So he has to muff it.'

'What does that mean?' I asked sharply. 'Don't push me to take his side or you will have no baby returning with you to Mexico City.'

'You got me wrong. "Muff it" means take something quietly. I have told him about the Mexicano Don. He understands the situation. You can talk with him. He trusts you more than Pa and Ma. But then you have had almost the same education. You know I have never created any uglinesses for others, only vast messes for myself and around myself.'

'So now it is vast spaces spread out with vast messes?'

'Why are you being so touchy today? Is it because the lover-man is English or British, or whatever they call themselves? We call them gringos! In our part of the world they are the wanderers. Homeless, friendless, and most of them just strays.'

'Come, come! Who is being hostile now?'

'Yes, I am afraid of you, and so is the Mexicano Don. He has found out a lot about how much influence you have all over the place. He came last night after dinner and asked me, rather pathetically: "If Khan doesn't approve, would it mean it is all over?" I told him you will listen first. He loves me and needs me. His daughters have known Ma and Pa since they were toddlers. His wife helped with the summer school. I had heard of them. Strange I had never met them. Anyway, please tell me bluntly what you think. Of course, I won't do anything you don't go along with. Not until Juan goes to kindergarten. Then I will be independent again.'

'Again? When were you in shackles before? It is no fun talking to you today, Lucia. You are irritated. Better ask Pa or The Older to talk to you.' We agreed it was better to part for that day.

Next time I saw Lucia, it was after a three-week break. First she couldn't come. Then I had to go abroad for a weekend of lectures. Even time seemed to help us out. When we met, each had cooled down. I had seen the lover-man at his request, and with Lucia's agreement. Finally it sorted itself out. The only person who was hurt, and behaved most honourably, was the lover-man. Lucia had left peacefully with Juan, Pa, Ma, The Older and the Mexicano Don in May 1975. She had finished her dissertation. The person most upset by her rather sudden decision to depart was the English girl from the mini-commune. Lucia and the Mexicano Don had decided to marry immediately after their arrival in Mexico City. That decision had been a relief to me. I had thought her marrying here, in London, would be a bit much for the lover-man. It had happened just as everyone had wished.

I heard infrequently from Lucia. She was settled in her chair and her spaces were firmly bounded now. I had told her exactly that. I did stress that being settled was going to be rather *un*settling for her, at first. We had parted with an almost familial affection. It always surprises me how, when a clinical relationship fares well, it doesn't hurt anyone when it ends. Actually, it *never* ends. A person grows out and away from it. It is only when it gets stuck in some manner that partings are experienced as rejections by both parties. That, at least, is my experience. I had retained my fondness and admiration for Lucia and I think she always had happy memories of me.

JUAN

(aged six)

'*Dites, qu'avez-vous vu?*'
BAUDELAIRE 'Le Voyage'

When I went to collect Lucia and Juan from the waiting room, Lucia got up, came forward and kissed me on both cheeks, lightly; a normal manner of greeting for a Spanish South American. On first sight I noticed she had slightly greying hair. A little more filled out in body, but still sleek and tall. Hair was closer-cropped now. With a gesture I asked silently, where was Juan? She smiled and pointed down under the table. So I stepped forward and knocked on the table, saying, 'Knock! Knock! Come out, you young rascal. Greet me and tell what have you seen. What have you been doing?'

A sprightly lad jumped out and up, grinning, and gave me a hug, saying: 'Good morning.' He had his grandfather's reddish mop of hair; his mother's eyes and mouth. A tall child. Gleeful and restive. All three of us walked to the consultation room. Juan was chattering away as if he had known me all his young life, calling me Uncle. He was carrying a Pan-Am travelling bag. The spaces of my flat were new to Lucia also. In 1974 I had seen her in my previous flat.

Lucia sat down. Juan took out all his things and, when he had arranged them half neatly, asked something of Ma in Spanish. She said: 'Uncle will tell you where.' So he asked: 'Uncle, can I have a Coke?' He spoke English fluently. I gave him directions as to where to find my houseboy or secretary or chauffeur. Any one of the three would give him a Coke. He departed. Hop skip and jumping his way.

This gave me a chance to ask Lucia whether she had seen the lover-man. We still called him that. She said: 'No, there has not been any time. We arrived only last night.' 'How many make "we" today?' She smiled. 'Only Juan and me. Mexicano will join us in Madrid, where he has to attend a conference. I am here only for one day. Am seeing my lawyer this afternoon. Then meeting the lover-man, and you will please tell me, after you have talked with Juan, whether you want him to see his father or not. He knows Mexicano is not his father. He calls him Uncle Hosay.'

Juan had returned holding a tonic-water bottle in his hand. Evidently we had no Coke. Lucia got up and said something to Juan, then asked me: 'Where is the drawing room here?' Juan said: 'I can show you.' And off he scampered with Ma. In her letter Lucia had cautioned me that Juan was a very ebullient, sportive boy. Could be a nuisance at home. He returned, took out the rest of the things from his bag, arranged them and asked: 'Some paper please, Uncle.' 'For what, Juan?' I teased him, handing him tissue paper for fun. Juan kept his cool and asked again: 'And now some drawing-paper, please, Uncle?' 'You mean any paper to draw on, or real drawing-paper?' He said firmly: 'Real drawing-paper, please.'

I got up and took some dozen sheets of blank white paper I had ready to hand, and gave them to Juan. In a very professional way he took one sheet, held it up against the light, felt it and said: 'It is OK. Thank you, sir.' I laughed. Juan continued: 'Gran doesn't like thin paper. It doesn't take, I mean, absorb the water well.' 'But there is no water in here, I am afraid, Juan.' 'I saw that,' Juan said, 'but I have pentels. They will do. What shall I draw? Please tell me. I cannot draw make-believe.'

I thought, and said: 'Why not tell me a little about yourself and why you are in London?' 'Uncle, you know. It is to meet that "Guy", my father. Have you met him, Uncle?' I said yes, and asked: 'Why do you call him "Guy"?' He scratched his head and said: 'Well, it is like this. He doesn't like me to call him "Daddy". And not Uncle. He said, "Call me Guy; it is funny." So I call him "Guy".' 'How often have you met him?' 'Twice, I think, but I remember the last year only. Guy took me and Cachita to Disneyland for two weeks.' 'Who is Cachita?' 'She's four years older than me.' 'Who is she?' 'Auntie's younger daughter. She spends all her holidays with us. She lives in Rio now. We are good pals.' 'Are you looking forward to seeing "Guy"?' 'Yes I am, but Ma is not. I will get nice things. He is very kind.' 'Why is Ma worried?' (I had put in the word 'worried' deliberately.) 'Will tell you after I have gone and done the drawing.' I told him where to find someone. 'I know. It is James I go to. Yes, he drives your car. He gave me the I-don't-know-what-it-is-called. There was no Coke. Must rush or I'll bust.' He ran off.

I had a sort of *déjà vu* feeling. It had all happened before, between his Ma and me. He was an infectiously likeable child. Chattered like an adult. Carefree. A bit muddled, I thought. Don't know why I thought that. I knew I was losing ground with Juan all the way. I would never get anywhere close to a 'consultation' this way. I decided to start afresh. Pretend we were beginning. Juan, thank God, was taking his time returning.

I decided to play it for real. I could hear Juan scampering back. The consultation-room door was open. He stopped and knocked, shouting: 'Knock! Knock!! Coming in!' The little devil, I thought, is going to give me no footage here. He squatted down, with the blank white paper in front of him, his pentels arranged neatly on the left. He had put the other stuff back in the bag. Juan asked: 'What shall I draw?' I kept scribbling on the pad in my lap and said nothing. 'What are you writing? Please tell me!' I read out: 'Juan asked: What shall I draw?'

He rolled back in a somersault. He was agile. 'That is a real funny one. Must tell Ma,' and off he ran to Ma. I didn't stop him. It was going to be another 'scrimmage' for sure, I thought. And I had only this one consultation to get somewhere with him. What constituted that 'somewhere', and how we would voyage there, I didn't know, and as his Ma would have added: And goddammit, I don't care!

Juan returned. I decided to let him set the sights, and as he pleased. He said, pensively, looking at the paper: 'I will *quickly* draw *a* funny me.' He shut his eyes and scribbled wildly on the paper. I knew Juan had seen a reputable child psychiatrist/psychoanalyst a few months earlier. I noted the words 'quickly' and 'a' and underlined them. He paused and said: 'Let me draw Ma.' He bent low over the paper and went berserk on the page. Looked at it (drawing no. 1). 'Well, it is a try. Not much like Ma though.' For the sake of saying something, to stay in the game, I asked: 'When did Ma have her hair cut?' 'In New York. It was a birthday gift from Grandpa.' 'What did Juan give?' 'Uncle Hosay and me gave one together. Uncle Hosay paid the cash, I chose the thing.' 'That was nice for Ma.' Juan changed the subject. Almost soliloquising: 'I wish Ma wouldn't worry so much.' I decided to try a pointed remark: 'Has Ma always worried?' 'Nope.' He took another blank sheet of paper and laid it out lengthwise. Another hurried scrimmage with pentel. Looked at it (drawing no. 2). 'That is a good

Fig. 1

one. You like it, Uncle?' 'Yes! I do. Please don't read it for me. Spoils the fun. Who reads your drawings for you, Juan?' 'No one. Must show it to Ma.' He jumped to his feet. 'Ask Ma who reads your drawings for you and tell me.'

Juan was gone in a jiffy. A moment later he was back. Grabbed his pentels and the paper and asked: 'Please, Uncle, let us go to Ma in the other room. I like it better there. It is bigger.' I said, 'OK, Boss,' and

Fig. 2

went along. Lucia got up and asked mirthfully: 'How are you doing, sir?' I mumbled fondly: 'Like son, like mother!' She laughed. 'Uncle, ask Ma who reads my drawings.' 'Well, you have asked her now yourself.' 'Well, come on, Ma, don't keep us waiting.' 'Who says that, Juan?' 'Uncle Hosay. Ma is always late. We came here early because I won't wait.' He went to the other corner of the drawing room, where there was a flowerpot and some indoor shrubs.

I was sure that drawing the last picture had made him very anxious. I knew what Ma was worried about. Now Juan had told me. He knew it too. I said nothing. Lucia asked: 'Can I get you a cup of tea, or shall I pour you a sherry?' 'I am not English, Lucia. Pour me a long, mild whisky. But no ice, please.' Lucia poured me a drink. She made herself a Bloody Mary. Yes, she was pent-up about the day. When she sat down, I remarked, fully aware that Juan could hear me if he tried: 'It is tough, isn't it?' 'No, no, it is not that. It is not now it is tough. I have no worries today. Amongst you, Mr X and my lawyer, you will sort it out with the lover-man.' 'Who is he, Ma?' came a voice. 'You call him "Guy".' 'And what do you call him?' 'I forget.' Juan hadn't persisted. Lucia told me she had nearly had a breakdown last winter. She was very down and irritable all the time. 'You weren't fun, Ma,' Juan interrupted. 'Only Grandma could talk to you. Poor Uncle Hosay. How he was upset. Then I got upset.' 'About what?' I asked. 'I dunno,' he said.

The phone started to ring. My secretary had forgotten to switch it off in the drawing room. I took advantage of it and said: 'Please take the call, Juan.' He jumped to it. So activity was his standby too. Like Ma! 'Whom do you want, please?' asked Juan. Put his little hand on the mouthpiece and said: 'Ma, it is the Doc. Says when should he come and collect us.' I said, 'Please pass it to me.' He brought the phone over. The secretary had arrived. I took the phone. Had a few words and said: 'I can't be sure when. Why don't you come over, please. It is no bother. I don't have to buy it or cook it or serve it. Come when? As soon as you comfortably can. See you.' And put the phone down. Asked the secretary to send my houseboy. He came fast.

I asked Juan: 'What would you like to eat?' He asked Ma: 'Are we eating with Uncle? I would like to.' Ma said, 'Yes! Doc is coming too.' 'Yes! Then I have to choose.' 'Not choose but decide,' I teased him. 'I want a double-decker.' The houseboy asked: 'With meat or cheese, sir?' 'I don't know which is better here. You know, Juan, the shop is only some two hundred yards away. You can choose your double-decker there.' 'Yes, sir. Double-quick, sir. I'll get my coat.' 'And your scarf and your gloves, please. This is London.' 'It is not colder than New York last year, Ma.' 'Oh, last year. There will never be an end to it.' Lucia was noticeably irritable. Not her style.

Juan didn't fuss. Dressed himself and returned. Meantime I had told the houseboy what to get for lunch. 'Uncle, I haven't picked up my things in the other two rooms. Can I go now and do it when I come back?' 'Of course, Juan. And remember everyone walks on the right-hand side here. Have you been here before?' I asked mischievously. 'Yes, Uncle, for six months, I think. I was tiny and don't remember it.' 'You rogue. You are not lost for words, are you?' He rushed off blushing. Juan was an adorable, buoyant child, coping precociously with the problems of others.

I had taken advantage of the phone call from Mr X to find some private space and time for Lucia and me. Juan and the houseboy had hardly banged shut the front door when Lucia collapsed, crying loudly, on to my lap. I let her cry. She gathered herself together. Sat up. Asked if she could have another Bloody Mary. I said, 'No! Have some wine.' She asked: 'Which wine?' 'I think we shall have a rosé wine. Please go and get my secretary to open a bottle.' Lucia went and soon returned. Even the walk to the kitchen and back had balanced her. I had hoped it would. We were both short of time, and one achieves little in my sort and style of work if things get too pent-up and intense.

Lucia and I had some twenty minutes to ourselves. Things always seem to work out for Lucia. She was in acute and chronic distress today. I shall abstract only those details from this conversation – it was *not* a scrimmage – which could help the reader to assess for himself why I changed course again. The conversation with Lucia was a necessary 'interlopation' (my invented word for 'interloping') in the totality of the scrimmage with Juan. This is what Lucia told me:

Three years ago she had started trying to have another child. Juan was now going to kindergarten. Lucia's new life had achieved a steady balance. She was living in *one* place and had a home-life quite different from that of the Trosts. She had given up teaching and had moved up to take a university post as director/instructor of kindergarten teachers. It was less taxing and she could write more. Everything was going fine.

Then, in 1977, she was told by her gynaecologist in Mexico that only surgical 'grafting' could perhaps help her to conceive again. Mr X had flown over. She didn't know why she had hidden it from me and not written to me. Then she had met someone from London and heard about my cancer operations. She had felt that God was turning against her. She had been thinking of coming to London for a few months and having treatment, as she got dangerously incapacitated by depression. She could see that Juan was drawn into it. But the worst of it was that both her Pa and Mexicano Don went down with minor heart attacks in 1978. There was no *space* left for Lucia to be ill in. She had pulled herself up to nurse them. Happily they had both made good recoveries and returned to their professional lives.

Now that the only two males in Juan's life had collapsed, he had no grown-ups to play with. He started to refuse school, steal, and stay away from home at the slightest excuse. This worried Lucia more than not being able to have another child. Here I chose to say something. 'Do you realise how much of your predicament Juan has known all the time?' She insisted he didn't. Not very much. I went and brought the two drawings that Juan had made and asked her how she 'read' them. She insisted she had managed to stay cheerful whenever Juan was with her, which was not so much now because he went to kindergarten in the mornings and chose to spend the afternoons with his friends.

I asked: 'Did you stop working at the university, or curtail it?' 'Both, but only for short patches.' 'But the fact is, Lucia, that from the age of three or just over, somehow Juan did become aware of the "empty chairs", to use your metaphor.' She became very anxious, and asked: 'Do you think Juan is very disturbed now? The child psychiatrist in New York thought he was. She saw him five times in two weeks. Juan *hated* her. She talks nonsense about Grandpa and you and sex, he protested. He is so grown-up in his acquisition of languages: Spanish, English and Portuguese. It was Grandpa who stopped his going to that woman analyst. Actually Pa had rung you in London in August 1978, but you were in Pakistan. Then The Older at last decided to get divorced and was very depressed about it. She came to stay for three months. She also insisted I should take Juan to see you. Then Mexicano said, out of the blue, that he wants Juan to have his surname. I told him, and I have told the lover-man, I am not going to choose this time. They have to decide between themselves, and tell me, and then I will decide after consulting you. But now Juan says he wants Uncle Hosay's surname and not "Guy's". I really do not know what Juan wants. I will accept what Juan wants. Please find out from him. If you need more meetings I can cancel going to Spain and stay here two weeks.'

I could hear the lift coming up so I hurriedly said to her: 'I have still half an hour, and more, with Juan. Let us see what happens. Let us decide after that.'

Juan thundered in shouting happily: 'Look, Ma! I bought something for Uncle Hosay and Grandpa. It was a nice shop. Please give money to Uncle for those.' Ma asked: 'How much?' 'I dunno how to count English money.' I chose to act now, and said: 'Mr Dunno, you are coming with me to the other room and we are going to do some hard work together.' 'Please, Uncle, can I get a Coke and take it with me? We bought Coke in the shop.' 'Yes, of course.' He scampered off. I met him in the hall and we went together to the consultation room. Juan settled down to drawing spontaneously and easily. We had been together some half an hour when I heard the front door being opened. 'It must be Mr X,' I said to Juan. 'Run and open the door for him, if you would like to.' 'Yes! I would.' And he ran out.

I detailed the essentials of my *scrimmages* with Juan in a letter to Mr X, because he wanted me to. I shall quote from the letter further on. Suffice to say here that Juan and I covered a lot of ground in the half-hour and I felt confident that I could give the right advice now, both to Lucia and the lover-man. I told Juan, when we had finished 'reading' his drawings, that I thought it was best for him to shed 'Guy's' surname and take on Uncle Hosay's; that I would be telling this to Ma and Doc now. He said: 'Oh, thank you very much. Please send telegrams to Uncle Hosay and Grandpa too. They will be worrying.' I was quite amazed how stress and strain had 'precociously matured' Juan. I said: 'I certainly will.' He asked further: 'And please, a copy for me and a copy for Ma, too.' 'Yes, sir! What more do you want, sir!' He was putting his things in the bag. He paused and looked at me shyly: 'And can I have photocopies of the drawings?' I said: 'Well, run to my secretary and ask her to make three photocopies. You take one . . .' 'No, two for me, please.' 'Two for you, and I keep the originals and one copy.' He rather quietly walked out of the room with his Pan-Am bag and holding the five pages.

The lunch went smoothly. When Juan had returned with the photo-copies, I told Ma and Mr X that I agreed with him that he should take Uncle Hosay's surname; that I had given Juan my reasons for agreeing and would explain them in my letter to Mr X, to be written later that day. After lunch we parted happily. I note how many times I have used the words 'happy' and 'happily' in this clinico-familial narrative. It is true to my experience.

From my letter to Mr X:

I agree with you. The past two years have been very hard on Mrs L. Hosay. She is such a proud and authentic person. That is why we have all worked to help her. It has been worthwhile for us too. You have been exemplary in your devotion to her. Thank you for saving me from any involvement with the lawyer or Mr H [the lover-man was mentioned by name]. I had to take a tough line with Mr H, who was a friend of mine before Miss L. Trosts arrived on the scene. He has behaved most honourably. But then he is a real Scot. A very lost and unhappy man now. He rang me yesterday and I shall be seeing him. Please drop me a note if you agree to take medical responsibility for him. It doesn't matter that your speciality is gynaecology. You are a physician and you have seen him. Mrs L. Hosay also rang from Barcelona. She had started to say: 'Juan is much better', when he piped up on the other extension, 'And Ma is less worried. Hi! Hi!'

I had a few words with Don Mexicano. He thinks you don't really like him. Not as much as you do Mr H. So I laughed and said: What did you expect? You are a Scotsman like Mr H and not an outsider like me. That reassured him. Thank God they all have a good sense of humour and are likeable, each in her/his own right. Juan is just adorable. You said you are most curious to know how I tamed Juan. You are right, the little rogue is quite irrepressible. But I fooled along with him till he had picked and played all his cards and I had still one to pick. I had cheated a little but he found me out immediately and said, patronisingly and pompously: 'A little cheating is in order, here and there,' in a heavy voice, like his Uncle Hosay. Anyway, let me share with you my scrimmages with Juan. You have heard their versions. Here is mine.

Juan had emerged, jumping up from under the dining table where he had hidden to surprise me. 'How are you, Uncle?' 'We are well, you little rogue. Where have you been these six years?' He turned to Mrs L. Hosay and said: 'Have I met Uncle before?' She replied: 'Yes, sonny, when you were tiny.' 'That doesn't count, I cannot remember that far back!' He turned to me: 'Do I bring my own drawing stuff or will I be given some, please?' I said: 'You can borrow a few pentels.' Thus we walked to the consultation room, Juan and I. He was commenting on everything he saw. His way of coping with strangeness of persons, places and things, I thought. Juan is a strange amalgam of tidy habits and almost eruptive, messy excitednesses. He has a lot of confidence, though some of it is bluff. He cannot bear anxiety – stress. Takes to action at once. Just like his mother. He sat down. I handed him a few blank white sheets of paper and half a dozen pentels of various colours. I remarked: 'Sorry, Juan, I have no toys for you. We will talk instead.' He said: 'I prefer that, sir! Only girls play with toys. The lady in New York kept pushing toys on me and making silly remarks. I draw now, sir.' I said: 'I like it better when you call me Uncle. You know, Juan, I was as nervous about meeting you, as you were of meeting me. I feel easy now.' He looked up, smiling. 'Me too! Only Ma is still worried.' 'Well, we will see what we can do for Ma later.'

Juan turned the paper around once or twice, as if he were going to wrestle with it. Said: 'A quick one of Ma.' And went berserk on the page. Stopped. Looked at it. Pouted. 'Not very like Ma, is it?' I looked at it (drawing no. 1) and asked: 'When did Ma have her hair cut? She has long hair in this drawing.' Juan was thoughtful. 'Better not talk about it, Uncle. Poor Ma. She has been so worried these two years. We went to New York for Ma to see a doctor and me to see this lady. Neither was much good. Ma had her hair cut then. I don't like Ma with short hair. Nor does Uncle Hosay.' I noted that in many ways he was identifying with his Uncle Hosay. This I found reassuring, because I wondered whether the wish and need to change his surname to Hosay was Juan's or had been implanted on him by Ma, Grandpa and Don Mexicano himself. I was getting more convinced by each utterance of Juan's that it was his own. He had run off to show Ma the drawing. So the little rogue was more worried about Ma worrying than worrying on his own account. He returned and said authoritatively: 'One more drawing I make. Then a break, Uncle.' I said: 'Yes! as you order, sir!' 'No, Uncle, I am only asking.' I rumpled his red moppy hair. He beamed. The next drawing he made rather carefully. He was pleased with it. Got up. Showed it to me. Wanted to show it to Ma, and I went along. He didn't want me to say anything about it, I sensed, and I didn't. He was fidgety now. The drawing had *spilt* out of him (no. 2). It had embarrassed or frightened him. I knew what it meant. So did he. Ma didn't. Or rather chose not to. *So the denials were hers.*

I didn't let Juan settle down with Ma, but hustled him away to the consultation room. This was a bit of cheating on my part. I said: 'Juan, we are going to settle down to half an hour of hard work together.' He asked me, quite sincerely, 'Why can't we do hard work with Ma around? I do it with Grandpa and Uncle Hosay.' I owned up instantly and said: 'There has been a bit of cheating on my part, Juan. I wanted us to be alone. I want us to have some privacy together, so that we can "read" your drawings.' 'Oh! I see,' Juan said, in a grown-up way. I quoted his words back at him: 'A little cheating is in order, now and then.'

Juan made one rule about how we were to read the drawings. 'Each party can stop, after starting, if they want to, and no "read" of the stoppage,' he said. Exact words of his. I was simply astounded by his self-protective, as well as *other*-caring, capacities, but I didn't want Juan to have it all his own way, for his sake. So I offered generously: 'OK, when either reaches the point of no-more-read, as you say, you will blow the whistle to stop.' Juan sat down behind the paper and pentels. He remarked: 'How would I know when you want to stop the "read", Uncle?' I blithely said: 'You would know, Juan. You are very sensitive and clever.' He thought a little and said: 'All right, Mister, I did say a little cheating is in order.' 'Who says that, Juan?' 'Uncle Hosay. He is always making and breaking rules, and now you are doing the same.' I liked it that Juan had put me in company with Don Hosay. It is a big responsibility, I thought.

I sat down in my chair, planning the next move. There is no overall strategy possible in one-consultation encounters; one stumbles from tactic to tactic, changing course, or pursuing the same one, depending on how I and we fare. I wasn't doing too well with Juan. I had neither bargained for, nor anticipated, his precocity of mind and intellect. Lucia had not mentioned it either. For me it constituted the biggest problem, and the most urgent one, in handling and managing Juan and interpreting his drawings. I wasn't going to interpret his behaviour, movements or conduct with me, anyway. I have had four or five rather sad experiences with precocious children, and such precocity is not always of the mind, mental. It can be of any one ego-capacity or a cluster of ego-capacities. When I had erred, it was on one of four counts: under-estimating precocity and its role in that child's functioning and living, or over-estimating it; then either interpreting too late or too early. With these other children I was able to rebalance the clinical stance in the next consultation. With Juan there was to be only this one consultation, and too much was being expected from it, by Ma, and Juan also. I let the situation develop as it would.

Juan asked: 'Shall we read the first two drawings first, and draw after?' 'Yes, Master Don Juan, as you please.' 'You are a teaser like Grandpa. Let us start. You read first. Drawing number one coming forward.' As I took it from Juan I said: 'On the double trot and halt!' 'Trot' was a deliberate pun on *Trots*. I meant Juan to *dig* it, and he did. I looked at drawing no. 1 and said: 'Ma seems to be having a good laugh at someone.' 'Yes, Uncle. At the lady in New York. Ma also thought she was silly and crazy. Uncle Hosay said she had sex on her mind.' 'Do you always tell everything to Ma and Uncle Hosay, or do you keep some things private to yourself?' 'No, I have no secrets from Ma and Uncle Hosay,' retorted Juan. 'I didn't make myself clear, Juan. Secrets are not the same thing as keeping things private to oneself.' 'I understand now,' said Juan. 'Like I keep my toothbrush private to myself. I don't share it with Ma or Uncle Hosay or anybody.' 'Yes, like that, private.' Under my breath I muttered: Damn your instant-quick precocity. Still, this 'read' had given us one clue and served one function. By introducing his toothbrush, as something private to himself, Juan had linked the drawing, Ma and mouth, just as he had linked me with Uncle Hosay and Grandpa earlier. I recalled he had feeding problems. I didn't say any more.

Juan said: 'Drawing number two coming up. My turn to read. A long mare with a baby horse. Each looking different ways. Your turn, Uncle.' I said: 'I cannot make out whether long mare and baby horse are separate or is the baby horse inside the long mare?' 'Stupid me. Shall I change it?' 'No, please, Juan. Let me read more. I cannot tell from this drawing whether baby horse is inside or outside long mare,' I repeated. 'Shall we agree it can be both, inside and outside?' 'Why not, Uncle? It is only a drawing and I am giving you a penalty-warning now. You are cheating again, Uncle, taking a long time. I have to wait.' Juan bent over the paper, took a black pentel. Drew one shape. Turned the paper round a bit and did another shape (a cone). He paused, turned the paper all round and drew a third shape (cone with lines). The first shape was drawn with sepia pentel; the second with the same pentel; in the third, the cone was drawn in orange with the lines coming out in green.

Juan said: 'Your turn, Uncle,' and passed me drawing no. 3. 'Let me see. Three shapes. No. Three things. Each has to do with food and eating. First could be a mug with a handle.' Juan jumped up with glee: 'Bravo, Uncle. Very good. It is my mug at home for morning coffee, and for chocolate at night. I

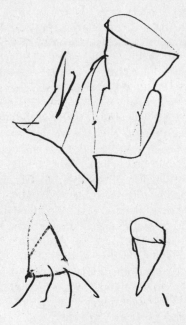

Fig. 3

never refuse anything I can eat or drink from my mug. Grandpa cheated once
and nearly spoilt my mug for me. He put strawberries in my mug so I would
have to eat them. I don't like eating sloshy squidgy things. Stop writing, Uncle,
and read me the other two.' 'It is rather upsetting, Juan, not to be allowed to
finish all of one's "read".' 'What more did you want to say, Uncle?' 'No more
about this one, but about the one before. Number two.' 'All right, Uncle, you
can look at it again.' I looked at it. 'I knew there was something different about
it.' 'What? What, Uncle?' 'It is drawn with a blue pentel.' 'Oh yes. Ma always
wears blue when she is happy and not worrying. Like today, Ma is wearing
blue. So Ma is a happy happy person! Yes, everyone loves Ma: the kids, their
dads and mums, everyone. They are careful with Uncle Hosay. One better be
careful with Uncle Hosay. You never can tell what will upset Uncle Hosay.
Uncle Hosay, unlike Grandpa, is very correct. That is the word! Grandpa
always teases him that way. Says all Spanish men are very proud and correct.
And Uncle Hosay, Grandpa told me once, has Indian blood in him too. And
Grandpa said these Indians were even more proud than the Spanish. Grandpa
gave me books about them, with pictures. I like the way they draw. Long mare
is a bit that way. I mean their style . . .'

I barged in with: 'So there is a bit of Uncle Hosay in the drawing too.
Anyway, you naughty prattler, you have not read drawing number three.
Your turn to read.' He sulked a bit. 'This reading job is a bore. Anyway, there
are three things or objects. No! One is mine (the mug). The second is Ma's. It is
an ice-cream cone. Ma loves ice-cream. I can always make Ma happy when she
starts to worry by getting her an ice-cream cone. And third is a bulb to plant.
You know what I mean?' 'Yes, what one plants in a garden!' 'Yes, Uncle, or in
a pot, if it is for a room. Uncle Hosay is always planting, in whatever mood.
When Ma wants to be alone and get rid of us she always says: Go with Juan,
Don (Ma calls Uncle Don, not me as you did) and plant or pot some bulbs. It is
always fun to work with Uncle Hosay. He doesn't talk much. Everyone else
does.' 'Perhaps he doesn't get a chance, like me today,' I added. 'All right,
Uncle, I'll draw another one. A new one.' He drew no. 4, signed his name
under it and said, laughing: 'Ma will like that.'

'Your turn to read, Juan, please!' 'It reads: I haven't a worry at all . . . That
is a good one.' He rushed out to show it to Ma and was back, leaving it with
her. He realised what he had done. 'You haven't read it. Shall I go and get it?'
'Don't worry, you happy rascal. I am glad it is with Ma. Keeps her company till
Mr X comes.' 'No. Ma is busy reading your books. You have plenty of books,
Uncle. Every one of the Trots, and even Uncle Hosay, reads books all the time.
I get bored. I like it outdoors. Doing things. This is why I spend more time with
Grandma than anyone else. She paints a lot. And she makes pots too. Very nice
ones. She is teaching Ma how to pot now.' 'I thought Ma had *done her share of
potting*,' I said pointedly. But Juan didn't get it. Said: 'I make one last drawing
and then we finish and join Ma in the big big room.'

Fig. 4

He took some time drawing no. 5. Could not quite decide what more to add or not. I took it to mean he was not sure how much to tell me and how much to keep private. When he had decided to add nothing more, he said: 'Well, Uncle, here it is. Quick please. I am timing the "reads" now.' 'You bully critter,' I protested. 'What is a critter, Uncle?' 'A creature like you: naughty, playful and bullying, and a friend and a good-boy-sonny, all in one.' Juan laughed: 'That is a good one. Critter. Will remember that. Can I call Grandpa critter, Uncle?' 'Nope. You can call persons critter only of your own age and younger, but not those that are older.' 'Goddammit, you can be a spoilsport, Uncle. Grandpa wouldn't have known it. Nor me neither, if you hadn't told it to me. Now it will be rude to call Grandpa that.' You are infernally precocious, Juan, I thought to myself. But, like Ma, you tell the truth. You create and guard your privacies by not telling, not eating . . . 'Well Uncle, I am waiting!'

I now introduced the theme of naming, on the quiet. 'Top left: outdoor plant, on the verandah, not in the garden, I think.' Juan had come over to my side to look. 'One tree in the garden (top right). Three flowers and three flowers again, two separate bunches in the same pot. A worried-looking small horse, looking my way now.' 'Very good, Uncle, that is my mare. Please go on.' 'A flying eight-branched tree.' 'You are funny, Uncle. More, please.' 'Three houses, one rather at a distance, two close to each other.' I deliberately stopped. Juan urged me: 'More, Uncle, please.' 'I am stuck, Juan. Help me out a little, please, Juan.' He took the paper. 'You see, Uncle, there are three chairs, bottom right, as you would say.' Juan stopped. 'But they are empty, Juan.' 'Everyone knows which is whose. On the left is Ma's. Then Uncle Hosay, and then me, Juan,' he said, beaming. 'You got it, Uncle?' 'Yes, Don Juan, I got it,

Fig. 5

and more too.' 'What more, please?' 'Let me give it a title,' I said. 'Yes, please, but don't write on it. I want to show it to Ma, Grandma, Grandpa, Uncle Hosay and Auntie, just as it is. Our chairs back home are red. So red chairs in the drawing. What is the title for it, Uncle?' 'You see, Juan, all these various things must occupy a lot of space, outside and inside. So I am going to name it: "Empty chairs, vast spaces".' Juan laughed. 'Funny man you are, Uncle. I will miss you.'

   Then we joined you and Lucia Hosay. The rest you know. One last remark. Naming things, or calling persons by new names, in consultations, serves a very particular function for me. For example, by calling Juan Don Juan twice, I had, as it were, given Juan my blessing to change his name to Don Hosay. I never said anything more explicit about it. He got the message. I never interpreted anything explicitly to Juan. Once it was in the open between us, and significantly named, like mug, pots, potting, long mare, food, spaces, chairs, I left it to Juan to go on making connections now and later. I am sure he will remember this consultation a long time. Of course I have fears and apprehensions about his precocity. I know it will be a long wait for him before he can be all there, in himself, as one whole person-self: Juan Hosay. Now he has only smash-and-grab raids and thrusts at it and from it. He has no choice. Farewell voyager, Don Juan!! I had said to him.

From my letter to Mrs Lucia Hosay, written after the phone call from her, Juan and Don Hosay:

It was a pleasure to hear your buoyant voices from Spain. Yes, English damp cold weather was no fun for poor Juan. I hope the conference is fun for you all. I enclose a copy of my letter to Mr X.

You asked me to write to you about whether you and Don Hosay should push Juan to return to school for the remaining part of the summer term, or not. Also about his feeding *reluctances* (they are not *problems*, as yet!). About the latter, I would say that Juan is playing at *being too adult*, to be one with you grown-ups. He is happily, but devilishly, precocious. And this must neither be exploited nor ignored. Let him *refuse* what it pleases him to refuse. Please do not make an issue of it with him. Refusals constitute a large part of a child finding and becoming his own true self and person. Like you do over reading books. Children at his age learn better from studying thematically illustrated books. Juan is interested in Mexican-Indian pictograms. I saw a sumptuous illustrated book of Mexican art and legends at a Spanish friend's house recently. It is published by Abrams of New York. You are passing through New York. Pick one up for Juan, and post me a copy too, please. Thank you.

This school business is rather more complex. I understand from Juan that he goes to two schools. One for book-studying (as he called it), and another for riding lessons. He wants to return to the riding school, but the book-studying school presents a problem for him. He is cleverer than the other children; thinks they are 'dull and stupid', his words. If he goes next term to a class of one-year-older children, he will be OK. I am sure of that. So please do not push him to return to this school, this term. Juan would like to spend more *day-time* potting and pottering about in the garden with the gardener and his son. Says Uncle Hosay goes to the garden only in the evenings, when it gets suddenly cold. I think he should spend more time with the gardener and son, in the garden. This way he will have experience of another kind of adult who does different things. You are all 'with books' (Juan had said) most of the time. He likes outdoor life; let him have plenty of it.

Next, Juan doesn't want to learn to play baseball. Says it is a gringo game. In fact, Juan doesn't care for American kids. Too spoilt, and 'not so good manners', he told me. I agreed with him. He is quite happy riding. Please encourage him to take care of his mare himself, and polish the saddle and shoes. I told him he was too young to wear riding boots like Uncle Hosay and Grandpa. The critter piped up with: But I can wear longish moccasin boots over my jeans, Mexican-style. I told him yes, he could. I have promised him a pair of riding boots when he is eighteen. It is nice to be waiting for something pleasant. With an uncanny innocence he said: Will you be around, Uncle? I laughed and said: Even if I am not, my *Estate* will. I shall now write in my will: 'One pair of black riding boots, from Hermes of Paris, for one Juan Hosay of Mexico, to be measured, made and delivered in the year of Our Lord 1992, from Masud Khan, now hopefully resident in Heaven, Block D, Appartemento 18, 3rd Floor. Knock three times and come in.' Juan rolled around with laughter. He thinks I am very funny. So do I. You don't. As Juan would say: Minority vote does not count. Please do not let another six years pass before we meet.

Affectionate regards to you, Juan and Don Mexicano.

[1986]

4

A Dismaying Homosexual

The warm water reminds
me each morning
that I have nothing else
alive near me.

GEORGE SEFERIS

'I was born in a Jewish ghetto in Chicago. It was a mistake. So my parents would tell me. A ghastly mistake. They were Russian émigrés; wretched poor and determined to stay so. Father never did a day's work. He worked hard at night. In the bed. Result: thirteen children in fifteen years. Mother always told us she never liked sex. I love my mother. My father died before I could hate him. That has damaged me a lot in life. He was a livid Trotskyite. We had many of them lying around in our apartment. Poles, Spaniards from South America and Russians. The only thing they had in common was smell. Awful musty smell. It would get worse in summer. They ██████ each other, any time day or night. All of us children looked on with amusement. To us it looked silly and funny. I am the youngest of the thirteen. Hence a mistake. Not of intentions, but of biology. Mother thought she couldn't conceive so she had not used the contraceptive. The contraceptive was stuffing a rag up your fanny. I saw my two sisters prepare themselves like that. Quite often. We were a liberal family. Sex was the only thing everyone had in plenty. They were much older than me. Of thirteen children ten had died before they reached the age of three. From malnutrition or colds or both. No one would tell.

'When I came into it all I was the only male child. My sisters were fourteen and thirteen years older than me. Everyone in the apartment loved me. Some would get carried away by it, and make me ██████ I ██████ my first ██████ when I was nine. I was frightened the first time. I lost my virginity at eleven. I bled. Elder Sis said it hurt only the first time. She put grease on me and said always use that. I never did. Too greasy. I delivered newspapers in the Black ghetto. We were much of the same kind. Only they had longer cocks. The women bulged in their sweaters. It is not a myth about the Blacks in the USA. They do have longer cocks and fuck merrily. Anyone they can lay their cock into. Boy, man, girl or an ageing spinster. One laid it into my Elder Sis. Not the eldest. Sis started to fatten out. Pappy asked: Is he a goy? Mother merely sighed: What can a poor Yiddish girl do for fun? Mother has not learned to speak American yet. She left Odessa when she was ten. Landed in Chicago when she was eleven. Married at thirteen. Is still going strong some fifty-five years later. Sis got the clap and a foetus. She got rid of the foetus all right. Not the clap. Had to have hysterectomy done at seventeen. If you can survive American charity medical care in Chicago you can survive both Archipelago Gulag and Belsen. She has never recovered – lives at home and looks after Mother. Pappy died. Quite anonymously. We realised he was dead two days after he was really dead.

'I paid my way through school. Doing chores of all sorts. I was a beautiful child. Had no inhibitions about sex. Primal scenes have seasoned us all for a life of sex of all varieties. Won scholarship to college. Became editor of the college magazine. My writing-cum-literary-agent career started then. Blacks in Washington arse-financed me. I mean I gave the arse; they gave the money. A goy politician took a fancy to me after I had finished college. Perhaps my only talent is that I never miss an opportunity. He couldn't stand the Blacks taking turns on me, with him. I could never refuse them. They were real passionate and kind. I have learned better since. Freud is right: abstinence whets both the appetite and the lust. The goy shipped me off to Barcelona to a Spaniard/Americano, who took me into his arms. He was a leftist writer. He loved me on first sight. Dave wasn't a homosexual. Not a real one. I have stayed with him ever since. Not chastely (I am incurably promiscuous). For twenty years now. Shall stay till my end.

'Has this Parisian head-shrinker told you what I went to him for? Dave sent me. I made a New Year's resolution that I would end my life this year, on my fiftieth birthday (that is how old I will be in August; five months left for the *reprieve éternelle*). I told Dave. He tried to persuade me to give up the crazy idea. The head-shrinker thought I was blackmailing Dave, the fucker-man, who has kept me. Not true. Dave gives me everything I want. All liberties too. Only I must return home every night, no matter how late, and never leave him alone. Not difficult to do. Since eight years of age Dave has had this fear that he would die suffocating in a dream. I sleep with him. He stays awake till I come. Has had analysis in every capital of the world. None could shift his symptom. He is a successful writer and has private means. We have an apartment in Paris and a house on the beach in Spain. He lives in style. In Fascist countries the few who have money have power, and vice versa, and these goys live in grand style. Saw it in Madrid, Paris, Berlin, Athens, Prague, Budapest, Rome, Cannes, Warsaw, Japan, Moscow. India as well.

'I have travelled a lot with Dave. I have to go everywhere with him. He collects phobias like some folk collect butterflies. We have been very happy together. He never loses his temper. Can be very cruel. I am very calculating but always teetering on the hysterical knife-edge. My dream is one and the same dream, repeated with different stage-sets, depending where I dream it. Someone is walking heavy-footed in the dark. He approaches nearer and nearer. I start to pant. I see a gleaming dagger in his hand. He is going to thrust it in my arse, I think. Wake up screaming. Always find I am holding my wee-wee, and it is erect and I have come. I can never get an erection anywise, waking or sleeping, except in this dream. I am a passive homo. Totally so. Never even wanted anyone to suck me. Touch me, yes! What are you scratching on that paper all the time?

'So this head-shrinker talked with Dave some three weeks ago. Said he could not dissuade me from committing suicide. He couldn't help any more. Dave asked: "Who do you think could?" He told Dave there was this Monsieur in London, he is a prince and well-known as an analyst. He could, but he doesn't accept patients easily from others. The head-shrinker gave Dave some reprints of yours in French, German, English, Italian and Spanish. I was very impressed at first by the number of languages you could write in; I thought at least four. I can speak six: Russian (mother tongue), English, Spanish, French, German and Italian. But I write only in English. Dave disillusioned me. You also write only in English. All others are translations from the English. Even so, you certainly do get around. That has given me faith and confidence in you. Perhaps you could help. I know you are very expensive. We can afford you, Dave and I. Can you, please?'

Now I spoke, after having listened to Mr Luis for some seventy minutes (only some of it stated above). 'Yes, I think I could, but I don't think I want to. You are not ill or sick or neurotic, or my sort of patient. I shall learn little from you. Yourself, you are not a true pervert either. Just a mixed-up Yiddish kid who has started to age suddenly, and is terrified of ageing further. I can well believe you were a beautiful child and a beautiful youth: with your dark gleaming eyes, dark hair, you were, I reckon, smartly sleek of girth and tall-woman height: five foot eight or nine, I guess. You have earned your right to die before you start to putrefy. As you surely will. *And* you know it. Dave does too. You are already faded and wrinkled behind that heavy make-up you are wearing. Rather ridiculous, isn't it, to paint yourself up and around each day, at your age. You dress almost elegantly but the ghetto screams through, here and there, in unmatching loud colours. *And* your tiepin, cuff-studs and your one tooth (capped upper eyetooth, left) are all gold. *And* that is about all you are worth. The rest are have-beens and had-beens now. Mere reminiscences. No, I don't think I want to even try to help you. *Also*, I think for me it would be much harder than for some Yiddish colleague of mine, here in London. Some of the best analytic clinicians you could find, practise in London. You are a good patient, with some nuisance value only. That is about all. You won't kill yourself. Someone may kill you; that is, stab you in the wrong place . . .'

He asked: 'Why won't you treat me yourself? It would help me to know that. I will go to anyone you recommend. But please tell me why you won't, and don't, want to help me. Is it because I am a Jew? Not classy. A mere poof from nowhere. I stink in your nostrils. I can sense that. But you are a professional, so should be able to rise above all that. I need help. I can pay for it and you can provide it. So why do you refuse?'

I quietly and ceremoniously filled my pipe and lit it, then said: 'You have guessed right on many counts. I have little use and less praise for self-made Jews who pretend to be artists, atheists, writers or dancers. Actors seem to manage it better in America for some reason. I have met all types everywhere. Even in Moscow. The yids certainly know how to climb up. My profession is no exception. Yes, I can rise above that. You would not be the first Jew I would be treating. As to class: well, there is no *class* in America, so I cannot hold that as a negative indication in your case. Poofs, especially the gilded ageing ones, do fill me with instant disgust and disdain. I have met lots of you. All are the same in the Homo International Jetset. Isn't that what you call it? I have treated some Jews and non-Jews of that sagging plumage. So it is not that.'

Mr Luis asked: 'Please tell me, what is it?'

I said: 'Why do you want to be humiliated by me, by insisting on an answer . . .? Since, Mr Luis, you won't give up, I'll tell you. It is that you have *very little sense of privacy* in any sense, or in any context. This I could not remedy at once. And without some capacity, or need, for privacy in a person, I cannot relate to him. So better let someone else try it. I am further handicapped by the fact that I am all things you are not, and you are many things I could never be.'

He sat forward, asking: 'Like what, please?'

I said: 'OK, if you also relish paying to be humiliated, here goes. Let us look at each of us. I am tall, handsome, a good polo and squash player. Fit. Only forty-one. Very rich. Noble born. Delightfully married to a very famous artist. Live in a style of my own making. Am a Muslim from Pakistan. My roots are sunk deep and spread wide across three cultures, from the Punjab of Northern India, Rajput Indian and Shia Persian. So where do you, and I, Mr Luis, meet? Can possibly meet? And how? Not *why*. Though "why" is in it, too. I don't desire or need your "I can afford it". You can't seduce me as you have seduced everyone else. Not because I am better or more than them, but because I am *different*. And this *difference* matters most for me. Why waste your time and money, from sheer wilfully hurt pride now, Mr Luis?'

He said: 'Let me take care of that. One more thing I ask before you throw me out. I can see the light flashing on and off in the corridor. Must be your houseboy. A handsome lad. But everything is in superb taste around you here. I am not flattering. Nothing overwhelms me so much as vintage style. And you have it. Briefly, please tell me why you think I shall kill myself on my fiftieth birthday.'

I stared at Mr Luis, hoping he would give up. He didn't. So I said: 'Well, sir, if you want it this way, have it. You have paid for it. As you folks say: the customer is always right. And you are more of a customer, and less of a patient, as yet. I think you want to kill yourself for one reason only. You are *non-procreative*, I mean physically and literally. If you had been a girl, beautiful and lush as you would have been, and lived with a virile loving man for twenty years, you would have at least three, if not thirteen, children to show for it, not mere scattered lewd reminiscences. If *your man* had not been able to give you a baby, for some reason, then one of the dozens of others would certainly have. But no, Mr Luis! After some forty years or so, having been perfervidly at it, you have nothing to show for it. You are a withering sac of a body today. The mouth and arse yield pleasure, but cannot procreate. Nature made the wrong choice for you. There I feel sad for you. And, Mr Luis, you have every right to punish nature.'

I noted that Mr Luis had started to cry quietly. I had finished my say. He got up, picked up his neatly rolled black silk umbrella and beseeched: 'Please give me one more consultation. That is all I ask.' I said: 'How abject of you, Mr Luis, but OK. Arrange it with my secretary, later today, by phone, between three and five p.m. God be with you, Mr Luis.' Even as I was saying it I started to wonder why I was giving this phoney, murky character a chance to waste another two hours salaciously prattling about his non-being.

Mr Luis was rather swarthy of taint. I had jibed with him: 'Mr Luis, how come you are swarthy of taint, I mean tint of skin?' He had been unabashed: 'From lying by the sea, upwards!' The bastard, I had thought then. Which reminds me of another nasty bit from Mr Luis's reminiscences: Mammy (as Mr Luis called his mother) had been faithful to Pappy, not from loyalty, but from laziness. She had once told Sis Liz: 'Don't let them spread you wide. They all do it, different ways. Better stick to one goy. The Blacks do it differently with the same woman. Not the goys. Them goys talk more dirt, but do less. They also fall asleep after. The Blacks want to be up and dance or eat till next time.'

I had stopped Mr Luis's spate of remembrances of what Mammy said, by saying acidly: 'What Mammy once said, you now enact. It doesn't amuse me. So leave it, please. You are wretched enough, don't make it heavy, man. Isn't that what the Blacks say in Chicago?' 'You have sure been around some places, Khan. Good memory you have, too. Strange someone like you should visit those places. But then a man will follow a dame anywhere. They call it loving.'

I warned Mr Luis: 'One more personal remark about me, my wife, my staff or my things, and I will throw you out, you accursed nobody Jew. Find your own people then. Shoals of them drift around, just like you. Yes, I am anti-Semitic. You know why, Mr Luis? Because I am an

Aryan and had thought all of you Jews had perished when Jesus, from sheer dismay – and he was one of you – had flown up to Heaven, leaving you in the scorching care of Hitler, Himmler and the crematoriums. Don't fret, Mr Luis; like the rest of your species, you will survive and continue to harass others, and lament, and bewail yourselves. Remarkable how Yiddish/Jewish you are. Vintage quality, too. Only you have gathered too much moss on your arse. Face you can mask with paints. Do you hear me, Mr Luis? It is not that difficult to splurge obscenities and outrageousness. Now, is it? I can be a deft hand with it at times, when provoked. But what will be the point of that, with you? Playing your dirty games your way. Still, I am giving you one more hearing and shall decide then. Goodbye again, Mr Luis. Don't hang around in the hall, please. Try, or at least pretend, to respect the privacy and rights of others. Goodbye, Mr Luis, till we meet again. If we meet!'

When Mr Luis arrived for the second consultation he had dressed down. Casual expensive clothes: no gold tie-pin or gaudy tie or gold cuff-links. Of course, the golden tooth even he couldn't paint over. Almost no eye-shadow. As I have said, he was swarthy of colour. I had forgotten his parents came from Odessa. He started by saying: 'Everyone and everything around you is beautiful, just beautiful . . . including your houseboy . . . And these Braques and Giacomettis on the wall. Just beautiful . . .' I was determined to keep my cool, and said: 'Please, Mr Luis, no personal comments or we stop right here. I am your last chance. Protect me from yourself. Yes, Mr Luis, *you* protect me. If I have to do it, it would be too sad and bad for you. Please take the chance you have given yourself. You have boasted that is your one talent: making the most of chances. Prove it to me!' Mr Luis started to cry again. Gathered himself, and departed.

Dave had rung me the same night. I accepted the call. If convenient, he would like to see me before he and Mr Luis left for Paris and Barcelona. They had lots of arrangements to make, now that I had agreed to see Mr Luis, at least until the Christmas break.

I saw Dave next day. He was a tall Texan: gaunt and handsome of face. I noted that Dave, like me, was everything Mr Luis was not, and none of what Mr Luis was. I felt concerned and caring about Dave. He told me he was a really mixed-up character: a Roman Catholic by faith, and a Lenin Marxist in life-style. The only thing that didn't fit was his inherited wealth. I sneaked in: 'And also Mr Luis, as you know all too well.'

I had seen Dave for some forty minutes only. That was all the time I could spare that day. I didn't play at being a professional analyst of international repute. I told Dave that, as yet, I owed Mr Luis nothing by way of either privacy or concern: I should do when he started his analysis in a fortnight's time. I also told Dave frankly that I feared Mr Luis was going to hurt him deeply; that I should be available if that happened during Mr Luis's analysis. 'I am, and I feel, responsible to you, Dave,' I said. 'I shall provide you coverage.' When Dave had told me he would be sixty next birthday, that he was exactly ten years older than Mr Luis, I *digged* the malice and venom in Mr Luis's resolution to kill himself on his fiftieth birthday. It was not blackmail, as the psychiatrist in Paris thought. It was an explicit intent to murder Dave. I told Dave as much and asked him to tell Mr Luis what I had said.

When Mr Luis started his analysis he was in a very subdued mood. He and Dave, he told me, had rented a large flat within walking distance of me. He had got a secretary for both of them. After Christmas they had the option of another two-year lease. He boasted: 'Of course, I had to do all of it. Dave cannot do a thing. He only writes.' I couldn't help putting Mr Luis down. Well, he does pay excessively for a Hausfrau. I had deliberately used that word; I had heard it used in Stuttgart about ageing poofs. This had pulled Mr Luis up sharply. He said: 'Well, you *have* got Dave neatly wrapped round your Muslim Mongol feudal little finger. Obedient-wise. Am I correct, Prince Khan?' 'Yes, Mr Luis, very much correct. May I add that Dave is safer in his person wrapped neatly round my Mongol Muslim little finger than he ever has been, these many years, wrapped round, and into as well, your dirty Jewish arse.' We both paused, glowering at each other with matching contempt. Hatred is so addictive, I thought. Now Mr Luis and I are trapped in hating and loathing of each other. A strange therapeutic alliance.

I shall skip across months of tedious, though not boring, clinical work. Mr Luis did not commit, or even attempt, suicide. Dave, coaxed by Mr Luis, gave a belated party in October (two months *after* the date) to celebrate the giving up of a morbid wish. That was Dave's phrase. Mine to Mr Luis was: 'So you didn't carry out your Jewish harikari! It would have made more of a spectacle than your party last night. But then, of course, you would not have been there to enjoy it, not that you enjoy or care to enjoy anything for long. And Dave would have been your executioner. Now he has a long wait for his execution by you, while you wail at the Wall.'

We made it to Christmas anyway. Our relationship had improved. Mr Luis provoked less and I insulted him less. I suggested that Dave, Mr Luis and I should meet and talk candidly about whether Mr Luis should continue his analysis with me, or whether he should go to someone else.

We met. Dave said he and everybody thought Mr Luis was benefiting a lot from his analysis. I said: 'If he is, Dave, I surely am not. It is a chore for me. I am going to cut it down to three sessions from the New Year. You can move back to your headquarters in Barcelona. I am willing to see Mr Luis Fridays, Saturdays and Sundays – but I will double my fees. They are already exorbitant, I know that. He can earn the extra fees easily in Barcelona. Here, Mr Luis has too much time on his hands. And literally, physically, I mean. And that is Mr Luis's primary and only symptom: over-permissiveness, not from desire or for profit, but from hate and incapacity to put limits and walls round his person. He couldn't help it as a child. Now it has become his sole expertise. Rather sickening, Mr Luis, isn't it? And please don't cry again. Spare Dave that humiliation.' I said to Dave: 'Why don't you take Mr Luis to the Wailing Wall in Jerusalem and shake all this phoney crying out of him?' Mr Luis smarted at that and said: 'You two feel so comfortable with each other. Christian and Muslim. All right, I am a Jew and sell myself as one. That is what you so disdain, Prince Khan, isn't it? All right, I'll stop whoring. I will work in Barcelona. I know how to work.' I said quietly: 'And everyone respects you for that, Mr Luis.' Oh Holy Jesus, does this man never descend to earth? In a most theatrical way he knelt down, raised his hands, turned his eyes heavenwards and prayed:

'Oh Mary,
Mother of God,
Send my roots rain . . .'

Flatly I said: 'Please get back into your chair, naughty, naughty boy! There, there, don't wet yourself . . . with tears . . . Yes, Mr Luis, I can place the last line of your prayer. It is from a poem by Gerard Manley Hopkins. Good, poignant good taste, Mr Luis. So what have you decided?'

It was agreed Mr Luis would come on Thursdays, Fridays and Saturdays, for a maximum period of two years. That, I had stated, was all the time I could spare him.

Mr Luis surprised everyone, including me. After another four months of analysis he started an *affaire* with a Spanish orphan-youth of seventeen. The youth was half gypsy and half Spanish; very handsome and tall. Dave, Mr Luis and I met together again. Dave was convinced Mr Luis was in real love. The boy, Mario, was 'honest' and wanted to study. Was willing to do part-time housework as an *au pair* and live with them. I told Dave: 'If you can take it, I accept it.' So that was settled. End of second round. We all dispersed for our summer vacations.

Events took a course in the August break that moved everyone deeply (me included) and were tragic for Mr Luis. For their summer vacation Mr Luis and Mario had gone to Greece. Dave had gone to Hollywood. A novel of his was being scripted and filmed. While he was there, Dave had an acute attack of the blinding, piercing headaches he had been suffering for two years now, with increasing frequency. He was admitted to a private neurological clinic. An inoperable cancer of the brain was diagnosed. Dave had only a few months left to live. They had given him pain-killer tablets, and prescriptions for injections when the pain would get unbearable towards the end. Dave had insisted he must be told all. They told all. He returned to Barcelona and waited for Mr Luis and his boyfriend. What nobility in him! He rang me requesting an immediate consultation as soon as Mr Luis returned.

I saw Dave and Mr Luis together. Dave was a ghostly skeleton of the man I had met eight months earlier. Mr Luis couldn't even utter a word. He was genuinely traumatised by hearing of Dave's ailment. I was lost for words too. Dave begged me to let him keep Mr Luis near him all the time and he would pay all expenses and extra fees for my visits to his seaside house in Spain. There was an airport within miles. I requested Dave not to beg. I said it didn't become him and it both demeaned and hurt me; that of course I would fly over as frequently as I could, even for a day. I realised both he and Mr Luis would need therapeutic coverage. I would charge my normal fee, and travelling expenses. I was doing this as much for Dave, I said, as for Mr Luis. And perhaps for the young boyfriend too. I said: 'Dave, let us' (meaning Mr Luis, Mario and myself) 'make the end sing for you. You deserve it.'

Dave started to cry with choking sobs. He took my hand and kissed it. Mr Luis did *not* cry. Those dry tears were the only tears Mr Luis had ever shed or perhaps would ever shed. We parted.

Dave died on Christmas Day in his seaside house, at 5.00 p.m., just as the sun was setting, Mr Luis told me. That was what Dave had cherished all his life in Spain. Sitting on the balcony of his house, on the second floor, and seeing the sun set slowly into the darkening sea. Mr Luis had given me an eloquent account of it. I had attended Dave's funeral, three days later. Dave had wanted a very private Christmas, so there were only the three of them: Dave, Mr Luis and the boyfriend, Mario. And the old, fat gypsy maid. Dave and Mr Luis believed in symbolic acts and gifts. After lunch Dave had taken the ring – which had been his grandfather's – off his left hand and put it on Mr Luis's finger. Mr Luis had taken off his ring and put it on Mario's finger.

After the funeral, when I was alone with Mr Luis in the lounge of the hotel where I had stayed some nine times when visiting Dave and Mr Luis, between September and Christmas that year, Mr Luis had quietly said: 'Now the cycle is complete. Please, Prince Khan, help me not to hurt this boy. I have done with "killings" and hurtings.'

Mr Luis was being quite genuine and true to himself for the second time. I agreed to see him five times a week. He sold his 'agency' in Barcelona and moved with his boyfriend to a house in the suburbs of London. His reasons for this were that he felt more quiet, less excited and more unsolicited in the suburbs than living in Chelsea, and that he couldn't 'launch' his boyfriend in Barcelona: everyone immediately identified him for what he was. Mario could not take on a new identity in Spain, anywhere. In London he was anonymous and starting with a clean slate, as it were. I was impressed by Mr Luis's concern for, and caring of, his boyfriend.

But all this is incidental to the relationship between Mr Luis and me. During the three and a half months that Mr Luis had nursed Dave, our attitude towards each other had gradually changed. We were no longer all the time on guard with each other. Mr Luis did not provoke me too often, and I learned to desist from putting him down at the slightest hint of intimate insult on his part. I would say, scanning my notes from this period, that Mr Luis and I were beginning to relate to each other, not only from withheld hating, but from almost neutral affectivity.

I kept my distance, firmly and adamantly, with Mr Luis. All his perversities, phoney charades, excessive and exaggerated attitudinising derived from one source and one source alone: all through his childhood Mr Luis had known *no limits*. It was total permissiveness to everyone in the apartment in Chicago. The only limit was, no goys! And that was more a prejudice than a limiting attitude. Nature had endowed him with high brain power, so that as he grew he had brought everything, almost everything, under his ego-omnipotence. What he couldn't manage was to get into himself, to be his own person. He lived scavenging on the desires, the wealth, the intelligence, the good will of others. It was a sordid existence. Dave had offered him both space and scope, but Mr Luis couldn't use it. He didn't know how to. He had no available capacities within, with which to operate. The miracle was that he had survived at all. After all, ten of his parents' children had died. One sister was maimed for life and lived off doing menial work and the money Mr Luis sent her. The other sister had gradually become an alcoholic and perished in some dingy mental-care set-up.

With this history, what could one expect of Mr Luis for himself? The acute illness of Dave had compelled Mr Luis to devote himself entirely to Dave and to one task only: not survival, but chosen caring of another. I had stopped his treatment. The nine times I had visited Dave and Mr Luis in their seaside house, it was to be with Dave. Each visit I would meet Mr Luis in the lounge of my hotel, for an hour. I charged for that hour and never let it spill to more. But what had helped me most in getting to know Mr Luis was watching him manage the house, the nursing staff, the doctors, etc. He was an extraordinarily cool person when called upon to be responsible. I began to respect him. But I knew that one slip on my part and he would pull me down into his mess-makings. I also learned that his verbal 'texts' were a parody of what he was and what he did. He over-amplified everything when he talked. He had to paint it red. When I saw him act, it was a different Mr Luis indeed. No hysterics, most things in measure and everything organised, and not just manipulated. There was a creative core to Mr Luis.

When he started his full analysis with me after Easter, i.e., after a break of six months, I set my sights differently. I knew now one could put positive limits round Mr Luis. So far I had worked by putting up negative hostile barriers. They had served their purpose. Now a new way of relating was needed and necessary: a mutual way of relating, trusting and working together. So far we had worked *with* each other, in the service of a hypothetical Mr Luis; this is the only way I can describe it. Mr Luis had been, and still was to a large extent, a hostile mocking witness to himself. His psychosexual pathologies were as polymorph and viscous as the rest of him. If he was permissive to everyone and let them in, he also leaked them out with equal ease. He had once said: 'I go to bed full in the mouth and arse. I wake up famished, empty and dry.'

These metaphors were true for *all* of Mr Luis. He was a polymorph, unintegrated, could-become-a-person creature. One encouraging sign was that he no longer enjoyed witnessing his self-degradations, or wittily saucing them up with obscenities. His language became more expressive of himself and more reflective of reality. He became a tamed, not timid, person.

In the total and teeming mass of material I gathered in the months that followed, Mr Luis's boyfriend, Mario, featured prominently. Once installed with him in London, Mr Luis started on the boy's education. The first problem was Mario's impulsive stealing – from Mr Luis. Mario never stole from shops. I had decided that I would abstain as much from interpreting Mr Luis's relationship with Mario as I would from interpreting Mario on Mr Luis's insinuations. When he asked me why Mario stole, I replied: 'Mr Luis, I can never tell *why* any of my patients do anything. All I try to sort out is *how* they do it.' However, I did advise him to try three things with Mario. First, ask Mario to keep strict accounts of all outgoings, and to make a list of everything in the house, right down to Mr Luis's toothbrushes. While Mario was doing this, Mr Luis should put a few unneeded articles around the house, and also a little cash, randomly placed. Second, instead of trying to educate Mario day and night, Mr Luis should teach him English for an hour in the mornings only and talk to him in English all the time. (Mario had worked as a waiter in seaside hotels in Spain, so already knew quite a lot of English words.) The third thing, and I said this was the most important, was that Mr Luis should not check up on Mario every ten minutes. At this Mr Luis burst out laughing.

I said: 'You can do us a favour too, you and me, and that is please forget about Mario during the fifty minutes you are here.' It had all worked out well, allowing for lapses here and there.

Slowly and painfully Mr Luis and I had managed to establish some sort of a 'working alliance' in the clinical situation. I had been, strangely, very classical in my mode of relating with Mr Luis. I had no extra-mural contact with him (the walled space being exclusively that of the clinical room). I could not avoid running into him in the foyers of theatres, the Royal Opera House, art galleries, etc. It was explicitly understood between us that Mr Luis would not accost me, or I recognise him, in such gatherings. Each party had honoured their promise. I had gone to the extreme of taking other precautionary measures. For example, I had noted from Mr Luis's first aberrant remarks that his eye had marked my houseboy, a tall handsome Italian youth, so I asked my secretary to open the door to Mr Luis. She was a well-bred young English girl, and so quite safe from Mr Luis's snarings. I also instructed her to take Mr Luis to the consultation room.

As I write on, I am more and more convinced that the reader will learn little from the 'texts' of Mr Luis during this period because I had learned very little, so far, from analysing him. It was he who had named his excessive verbal outpourings in the sessions his 'texts', because in spite of their bizarre, lewd and very personal character, these verbal charades were impersonal to Mr Luis. He knew it, and so did I. The two and a half years he was with me, and he was an addictively regular patient, I collected masses of mere data. Analysing Mr Luis was like peeling an onion. Skin after skin peeled off, leaving a meagre Self behind. Why I had stayed with Mr Luis was from a totally impersonal compassion. I had learned soon enough how primarily resourceless Mr Luis was in himself, and for himself. All his acrobatics of sexual expertise and whorings were unnourishing ventures that left him sapped, empty and desolate. Mr Luis's affectivity could be described as basically that of dismay, not depression. His sexuality was febrile excitedness, with little true desire or appetite to it. His aggression, or rather aggressivity, expressed itself through *wasting* others. There was no actual thrust or venom to it.

The most painful experience that I encountered in Mr Luis was his gradually acquiring the capacity to mourn Dave's death and absence from his life. He realised and felt with excruciating pangs how he had wasted Dave and what Dave had to offer him. Mr Luis's primary resourcelessness was augmented by his dismaying inconsolability. One could claim for Mr Luis that he lived, had lived since childhood, in a state of deep chronic grieving about a Mr Luis that never was, never would be. It was within these parameters that I had to help him find a *modus vivendi* with himself and amongst, if not with, others, that would not be merely wasteful of himself and them.

In some ways, Mr Luis had a reptilian capacity for scanning his environment for 'food'. He had expressed it in a rather vivid image in which he compared himself to a cobra who swallows everything, small or huge, and experiences nothing. He had said: 'The cobra doesn't even chew!' And I had replied: 'I reckon you know best what a cobra does.' No doubt Mr Luis was a venomous creature. But like cobra's venom, Mr Luis's was not registered by himself, only by others. At some point he had offered another image to describe himself: 'I have the over-famished scanning eyes of all reptiles, and I sense things *from* my skin also. I am highly musical like the cobra.' On another occasion Mr Luis had stated: 'When I can stop invigilating what I am doing, especially in sexual charades' (his word) 'I will start to heal.'

I could offer the reader heaps more 'texts' from Mr Luis but they will tell him as little as they told me. For example, self-consciously commenting on his gaudy clothes, Mr Luis had said: 'I wear these bizarre colours because I feel so colourless, I am so colourless. How very colourless I am, Prince Khan. You know it, I have to live with it.'

From my account of Mr Luis's analysis so far, it will be evident that, while I had learned a lot, and was the richer in personal experience, from my encounters with the other patients who feature in this book, the same could not be said of my clinical relationship with Mr Luis. His analysis had been a tiresome exercise in 'earnest professionalism'. I couldn't, hadn't been able to, get any purchase on Mr Luis's modalities of relating from his cohabitation with Dave. So I tried to see if something could be gathered from his new adventure with Mario.

Mario was a beautiful, non-literate gypsy youth of nineteen, not seventeen as Mr Luis had first told me. Mario had done the rounds with the homos, hippies, and females also working as waiters in the seaside resorts of Spain. He was no one's fool, and yet his native *pride* had somehow helped him not to get embittered or lax in habits. During the first months of living with Mario, Mr Luis had stayed *chaste* with him and others. What was most interesting, as well as amusing to witness, was how gently, but firmly, Mario *habit-trained* Mr Luis not to take everyone into himself, anywise. However, when they had been living together for a while, Mr Luis cheated Mario, who punished him cruelly. I shall give a detailed account of this episode because it marked the start of the mutual re-education of Mario by Mr Luis and of Mr Luis by Mario. It was not sordid for a change. There was nothing sordid about Mario; he knew his onions and played his cards carefully and, I must add, compassionately. Mario was neither greedy nor possessive. This left little room and scope for Mr Luis's expertise in corruption. Most things in Mr Luis's way of life were going to take on new colourings henceforth, and were to be progressively less sordid and murky.

This is how the chastisement of Mr Luis came about. After some three months of 'celibate cohabitation' (his phrase) with Mario in the London suburbs, Mr Luis had begun to chafe. An opportunity offered itself and he took it. Mr Luis went off to Paris for three days, leaving Mario behind in the house in the suburbs. It was their first parting since they had set up a ménage in Spain, some ten months ago.

I had unobtrusively hinted to Mr Luis that Mario might panic, finding himself alone in the house and not speaking English adequately. Mr Luis had immediately perpetrated one of his obscene 'texts': 'I hope he will, Khan. If I am lucky, he might even choose someone who will open Mario up for me. I have not been tough enough to achieve that. I am Luis, and not Mary, celibate Mother of Jesus. I need food.' It had outraged me but I kept quiet.

Mr Luis had departed on a Friday evening, leaving Mario with plenty of money and his address in Paris. He had rung Mario from Paris on Friday night, Saturday morning, afternoon and night. All was going luxuriously for Mr Luis so far. Then on Sunday morning the milkman had called to collect the monthly payment. Mario got confused, and rang Mr Luis in Paris. From the apartment, which a friend of Dave's had let Mr Luis have for that weekend, a young French voice had answered. Mario understood just about as much French as he did English. He had got the message all right, and so put the phone aside, not down. (I am giving Mr Luis's version, as I got it the following week.) About ten minutes after the phone call from Mario, Mr Luis had rung him back. No one had answered the phone for some three hours. Mr Luis had got into a confusion of rage and concern. He had taken an earlier plane back to London. On reaching his house he had rung the bell. No one had answered the door. He had gone in. On the entrance-hall table there was a written note for him, with cash. Since Mario could barely write Spanish, the note had been written in English, in a very calligraphic style. It read:

Sunday 12 noon. I have gone away for some time. I think it is best for us. I am being taken by someone. Shall ring you at night and tell you who. He is a friend of yours. I am leaving all the money left after weekend spending. The fridge is stocked. There have been some phone calls for you. I didn't take any names. Told them to ring back on Monday. I am taking only a few clothes to wear with me, the rest are folded and placed on the bed in my room. Please do not ring the police. It will not be fun for anyone.

It was signed by Mario himself, with a different pen and ink.

Mr Luis had gone stark raving mad. He said he had never been so insulted in all his life. 'The wretched bastard' (which Mario factually was) 'has hurt and humiliated me. I will teach him a lesson for life . . .' Mr Luis decided to play it cool. Took the phone off the hook. Put it back soon after. Mario rang near to midnight. He was very cool and asked how Mr Luis had fared in Paris. When Mr Luis asked: 'Where are you, Mario, and with whom?', Mario had quietly given the information: 'In the countryside in some hotel with —' and added the person's name. Mr Luis had exploded with fury, banged the receiver down, and broken the phone.

A very desolate and inconsolable Mr Luis turned up for his next session. In spite of all his hysterics with himself, and calculated histrionics with his friends and acquaintances, I was grateful Mr Luis had not rung me. He had not been able to trace Mario. He was beginning to dismay, feverishly. At the end of the session he asked me, looking very bewildered: 'Do you have any clue as to where Cato' (that was the name of the youth who had *taken* Mario) 'could be? You know how these English behave! How ugly to steal someone's lover!!' It amused me to hear Mr Luis look at his dire straits that way. I asked:

'Does Mario have the keys to your beach house in Spain?' 'Yes, and those he has not left behind. I know what you are thinking. You are right, he has gone there all right. Please, can I miss the next two sessions? I must find Mario . . .' I just shrugged my shoulders. Mr Luis left for Spain.

Mario turned out to be quite some character, in spite of his raw years. When Mr Luis arrived at his house in Spain, he found Mario alone. Mario had not taken Cato with him, nor accepted any money from Cato. He had immediately found employment as a waiter in a nearby hotel. When Mr Luis had tried to play the jilted lover, Mario had pleasantly told him: 'I am still a *virgin*! That hasn't changed. What has changed is I cannot trust you any more. You cannot throw me out of this house. Signor Dave has left half of it to me. You can bring anyone you like to live in your section of the house. I'll take the second floor, the use of the drawing room, the kitchen, etc., etc.'

Mr Luis returned from Spain a most chastened lover, and a defeated person. Now everything started to change in his life-style. For once he became truly dependent on his analysis. Up till now Mr Luis had only played at being dependent on his analysis. This 'dependence' was put on more for the benefit of others than experienced in, and for, himself. Mr Luis also began to withdraw into himself, which was rather anxious-making for me. I feared for his well-being and health. He was suffering terribly, there was no doubt of that. He didn't ring Mario once. Nor did he pick up *lads* to feed his terrified famished state.

Three months passed. Mario had written cards to Mr Luis, in poor Spanish, every three or four days. Mr Luis was utterly lost. So he said, and I believed him. Then, one Friday, Mr Luis asked me: 'Please can you help me refind Mario? One last chance, please . . .' I thought carefully and said: 'All right, Mr Luis, I will try. But I don't think it will succeed.' I wrote the following a short note:

Mario! I have met you eyes to eyes, but we have not spoken with each other. I respect and understand your stand, but I think if you persist with it, you will not gain any more. Both you and Mr Luis need each other. I trust you more than I can bet on Mr Luis. I do not say if you return Mr Luis will stay chaste. One thing I *can* promise you. He will neither cheat nor humiliate you again, while he is in analysis with me. Think carefully about it, Mario. If you do return to London, with or without Mr Luis, and want to see me, please ring and make an appointment. God bless you. Take care.

MASUD KHAN

Mr Luis struggled very hard not to howl, reading what I had written. He simply said: 'Dave was right. Deep down you care about me. You always have. A very strange man you are, Mr Masud' (as he now called me).

My note worked. Mr Luis returned to London with Mario. He had been away only one week.

The analytic work that Mr Luis and I did together in the three months of Mario's absence in Spain was to prove most fruitful, as well as decisive for Mr Luis and his future. It was the first stretch of time that Mr Luis and I had been together, in the clinical situation, without a third party hogging Mr Luis in his social or domestic life. Mr Luis had little private life, or privacy with himself, as yet. I shall now narrate, again in some detail, what had transpired both clinically and socio-domestically with Mr Luis during these months.

The house in the London suburbs was too vast for Mr Luis to live in by himself. As things turned out, he was not alone there for long. Some friends of Mr Luis were going to the Côte d'Azur for four months. They had a newly employed Portuguese housekeeper and had asked Mr Luis if he could accommodate her while they were away. The housekeeper, Maria, would cook and clean for him. Mr Luis rang me to ask if he should. I said: 'Most certainly, yes.'

With this new set-up at his house, we could work without fears or anxieties. Mr Luis cultivated instant-fears and panics. No *impingement*, from within or without, could last long enough for him to react with anxiety. The element of *held-time* is crucial in the transformation of tensions into an anxiety-effect that can be used positively by a person. Without this, there is what Winnicott (1962) awkwardly phrases 'unthinkable anxiety'.

One of the first tasks of the 'ordinary good-enough mother' (Winnicott, 1952), is to enable the maturing infant to hold larval and fleeting anxiety-states. When there is a failure here, then 'that is a "fault"'. The consequences can be dire indeed. The infant cannot 'kill', but learns to do something worse! *Waste*. Mr Luis was a consummate *waster.* His 'Mammy' had been very devoted indeed, in every way, to everyone, but in no sense was her devotedness ordinary, as we were able to reconstruct from Mr Luis's 'texts'.

'I continuously translate my impressions, sensations, memories, fears, into these "texts", in which I am always literally speaking to myself, audibly when alone, silently when with others. This translating into "texts" doesn't let me hear anyone. It was the same at the summer camps, and with that Black couple before.' Mr Luis said that the memories of his mother, that began to emerge now, were of a woman lost, terrified all the time, and all the time busy doing something. 'These Russians have a genius for finding private cures for themselves. Like Mammy had, and like Pappy had. I saw others contrive similar cures. My Sisses couldn't; they had got too Americanised – alas! Only the Russians can do it. Being sick and ailing of soul is an art with us, Mr Masud. I mean *us*, because I am very Russian, as you have found me out to be. I successfully hide that from others. I am the typical yid whizz kid, American-style, where they are concerned. You could say I am a Russki/American Peter Pan. The English stage directors are very wise and perceptive when they always cast a young girl in the role of Peter Pan in their Christmas . . .' 'Pantomimes,' I supplied, and allowed Mr Luis scope to indulge such 'texts'. He was going through a grim time. He grieved for Mammy, Pappy, his Sisses and Dave. They had all suffered so much. He was the one who had got away. 'Hardly,' I said. 'You, Mr Luis, are loaded with *imprintings* from each of them. These are the onion-skin layers we have been peeling off. Do you understand me, Mr Luis?'

'Oh yes, Mr Masud. I am very relieved you did not say "full of identifications" like that head-shrinker in Denver kept mouthing all the time. I did tell you I was given a sort of "house-arrest" by the army in Denver for almost four years and had to see a head-shrinker goy, who tried to cure me of homosexuality. I had done all my training in Denver. I got a lot out of being in the army. They taught me to type and keep records. I did clerical jobs only. Mostly in Denver. But sometimes in other army bases too. I spent little, since I did not drink or smoke. Out of desperation I had become a vegetarian from the age of eleven. Thus, I didn't have to eat Mammy's food. It was always a ghastly greenish-brown stew. We ate it dunking chunks of stale bread in it. Same pot, only different pieces of bread, hands and mouths. I started to be given good food when I was taken over by the Black couple and went to live with them. But I stayed a vegetarian. They weren't rich and had taken me to lighten Mammy's burden . . . Even one mouth not to have to stuff, was a real saving for Mammy.

'I don't think, Mr Masud, you can have any idea what real poverty is. Just as I cannot begin to imagine what it must be like to be born to *luxury*, and plenty, like you, and have it all the way. And not be corrupted by it. It wasn't others, I can see it now, but abject poverty and its insatiable terrors that made me take to stuffing myself with sex — as they say it in French — both orifices-wise. Mammy was always muttering to herself in some Russian dialect. I learned later that it wasn't remotely like Russian, as written and spoken by, say, Chekhov. She had a Pandora's box of apprehensions, and matching superstitions to reason them with. In my mother's world everything was perfectly reasoned. One example: Pappy had tuberculosis! Why?! He shtarted to shwake when he be eight . . . Mammy always made "sh" sounds of "s". So Pappy had not taken enough oxygen into his lungs. Result: had eaten-away lungs. Cure: don't do any work; eat only vegetable soup, white meat and barley rice. Pappy loved his cure-diet, largely because it was cooked separately and did not come from the huge communal pot . . .

'I was telling you about my gains from army service . . .' (this had taken three sessions, I see from my cards. I have left out plenty!). 'I saved money and was able, with the help of the Black couple, to buy Mammy a three-room tenement flat in the Jewish ghetto area. I paid monthly instalments for five years . . . On release from the army, when I had got the admission to college, a grant, plus some cash, I had given most of the cash to Mammy and felt free. Some of the money I had spent lavishly, by my standards, on clothes. I had realised the importance of three things during the two years of summer-camp vagrancy. First: never say no to anyone or anything. This was easy for me. We had not been taught to say no! Second: the importance of knowing languages. I already spoke, and could read and write, Russian and English. Now I learned Spanish. At college I learned French and Italian. Third: the importance of the clothes one wore. One *is* the clothes one wears. Proof: why are the Blacks most and best dressed when naked, both males and females? Because the Blacks have been skin-dressed black by nature. They don't need our clothes for them to have skin. The whites do, goys especially, all the time. A naked goy is a pathetic plucked bird, Mr Masud. Take my word for it, please!' I did. Mr Luis had taught me something: the role of clothes, not as decoration and fineries, as in my culture, but as *skin*.

Mr Luis's Pappy had died when he was fourteen years of age. It was after that event ('crisis' was Mr Luis's word for all events and happenings) that he had moved out of the apartment to live with the Black couple. There Mr Luis started to attend church services and Sunday school, which had a profound influence on him. He read his Bible. Knew it by heart, almost. The Bible was distributed free in the Gideon edition containing English, French, Spanish and Italian versions, all in one volume. It was the first book he owned for a long while. That is, for some three years! Slowly I had begun to realise that Mr Luis's experiences and measures of time were quite radically different from mine, and that of most others (Europeans included). A basic confusion of his was that both parents lived and worked by the Russian Calendar, so their dates were always out of step. Another was the awesome precariousness of life-in-health, habitat- (his word) and job-wise; if anything lasted from Easter to Easter (Russian Calendar dates), it was ritualistically and communally celebrated by each and all. This celebration of dates and *crises* had become quite a custom with Mr Luis.

Mr Luis had added, when he reached this point in his 'text' bespeakings with me, that a minor but most useful thing he had learned from the army was the '*tricks* of discipline, if not the *habits* of it'. The distinction is important, Mr Luis had said, because, with American GIs, discipline is a bag of tricks to carry around. Once out of the army, you throw the bag away. Every American is too much himself to learn anything from anyone. And discipline as a *habit* had to be acquired and learned from others. 'The GI, Mr Masud, is the first and last denatured natural man of the primeval jungle or desert, wherever the species started.'

Gradually a true picture of who Mr Luis was, and how he had become so, began to emerge from the clinical process. Mr Luis, in these months, applied himself to his analysis with a frenzied and understanding zeal. He wanted to know himself and he did get to know himself. Knowing himself entailed shedding a lot of *imprintings* (Bowlby, 1969) from others: individuals and environments. This *imprinting* process had not started in, and ended with, childhood. It had continued right up to and through his college years. It was with this 'load', and the weaponry (his word) of 'never say no' – the ability to talk in many languages and to dress well, plus 'tricks of discipline' – that Mr Luis had sailed for Europe/Barcelona in 1950. A real American innocent in the classical Henry James style, same vintage, Mr Luis had told me. He had given me *What Maisie Knew* to read and I read it with pleasure and profit. In fact, Mr Luis was to introduce me to some very nutrient American writers: Walt Whitman, Poe and Emily Dickinson as well as Henry James.

Mr Luis repeatedly protested against, lamented, and cursed how the Europeans, all brands and breeds, had exploited and abused his innocence. His only profit from these encounters was that he always won. The tactics of winning were simple: 'Stay with no one person for long, and let the next push out and away the one you were found with.' Dave was the only exception. 'But then he was an American aristocrat (by our standards, for sure, Mr Masud), and even you respected that quality in him.' 'I certainly did and I do still,' I said. 'But then there was not much sex or intimacy between Dave and me. He loved me, was devoted to me. Couldn't make any sense of the way I let myself be picked up and would then slide away, snake-wise. So like Mammy, I can see now. You have revealed one thing to me: how all of me is a *collage* of imprintings, particularly from Mammy and Pappy. I couldn't help it then. I can't easily divest myself of them too quickly now. But I have learned from you the necessity of staff to protect one, from oneself even. Maria is a darling. So fat and amiable. Does everything. So at least I am eating well. My house is tidy. Dave was stark but not tidy. You saw the stark bit. The tidy house in Spain that you saw was my work. Dave had neither patience nor time for patience. It was the same with his writings. He couldn't, wouldn't, even complete a long sentence. I was the best secretary he ever had. The only thing I did for poor Dave: typed – completed his sentences. If he had worked a little harder on his texts he would have been a really great writer. As it happened, he was taken up by Hollywood directors and producers to *script* novels and plays for them. He earned the money he never needed, and was kept busy in a way he hated. If I heal, I shall not fall into that trap.' (Mr Luis hasn't.) 'I am already healing, Mr Masud, being fed and protected by Maria – she receives all the phone calls and doesn't understand some three-quarters of them – what a respite that is! – and from your vigilant care. Living with Mikhail is no honeymoon . . .'

Mikhail was Mr Luis's Christian name but he only began to use it in the sessions during this period. How much more absurdly Russo-Français could he have been named? He told me his Pappy spoke good French, poor English; was a scholar of Russian; gave lessons to graduates at home. Refused to take any money . . . said the ones who came to him couldn't afford to pay. Yes! even the imageries of his father started to change: 'For one thing Pappy owned books. Well-bound Russian editions. Some forty books. They were sacred. No one was allowed even to touch or look at them. They were neatly heaped up in a corner of the family's one bedroom. This is why I had to sleep with the Sisses. There was no extra room except for the space taken by the books, and you were not allowed to put more than five books on top of each other. Destroys the bindings, Pappy said. The books are still with Mammy. Feather-dusting them, putting them in the sun, etc., is like dressing Pappy for her. I am sure it is, because Pappy has never died for Mammy. She used to dress him, feed him, even wash him in later years. Pappy never learned to tie a bow-tie. He only wore old-style bow-ties. He polished his shoes daily. I never saw him buy another pair. But then he rarely went out. Once a year, on their wedding anniversary, he would take Mammy to a concert and dine out. That is, if they had money, the weather was good, and there was a concert on. I don't think the three conditions were met more than four times in all the years they were married. The concert programmes are still hanging on Mammy's bedroom wall, wrapped in cellophane. I have offered to have them framed, but no! . . . cellophane and ribbons are sacred.'

I still allowed Mr Luis to indulge in these 'texts', taking all the time he wished to devote to them. If I could listen to them, only then would he start to hear his own 'texts'. That was my strategy with Mr Luis. It worked. Show him how to conduct himself, or even how to experience something, and he would/could learn, and change. Mr Luis was a sensitive, observant and willing learner. When he had rung me to ask if he should employ a housekeeper, and I had said: 'Most certainly yes!', he had said: 'But Mr Masud, I have not employed a servant in my life,

nor even my ancestors.' 'Holy Jesus!' I said, 'please do not employ a
servant. Engage staff instead.' 'Does it mean I will have to eat with
her?' 'No, Mr Luis. She will serve food to you and your invited friends,
etc. Please take her into your service now. My secretary will explain the
rest to you. Only don't start with giving too many concessions.' It
might bore the reader to have to read all these ordinary details, but it is
precisely such everyday things that one is called upon to attend to in the
management, and holding, of the person of a patient. I have almost
never suggested to a patient, even through devious normative interpretations, 'Do this or do that.' At the most I say: 'You could try that,' and
leave it there.

The character of the analytic setting had changed to the extent that
now Mr Luis would be, and could be, *playing* in it. Where before he
had merely spoken, flaunted and exhibited his 'texts', now he would
change what he was saying and telling while he was speaking.
Speeching changed into conversation. Playing has rules but no rigid
fixities or shape. Mr Luis was no longer frightened of giving himself
away. Even his paranoid scanning was an *imprinting* from his
relations with his father. 'Pappy was a militant Trotskyite, as you
know. Many persons gathered every Sunday around lunch-time. One
would think it was a meeting of some revolutionary group in Moscow
or Minsk. They were all so confiding in each other, yet the moment
someone left early or came late he was Fifth Column, an informer.
Their Sunday meetings were a sort of political Black Mass, Mr Masud.
My role was to give and take away endless cups of tea. Yet these were
happy gatherings for Mammy and Pappy. For me too. Everyone
laughed and everyone cried. I wake up some nights remembering those
meetings and crying. The goys are so stupidly clever and their sex is
dirty sex. I never heard a dirty joke in all my childhood. I saw a lot of
sex but then I wasn't meant to be looking or knowing. We lived in an
atmosphere of pervasive innocence. No one had enough money. No
one tried to earn more. Everyone was living borrowing and pawning.
Yes, the visits to the pawnshop were always a treat and a spectacle.
You know, Mr Masud, every Russian is a poet, a novelist and an actor.
And a terrible naïve liar who is totally unashamed if found out.
Amongst themselves they play the game of no one finding anyone out.
It was when I tried to fit all this "inheritance" to the rules and ruses of
goys that I became corrupt.'

Mr Luis claimed, and rightly I believe, that not all the *imprintings* were negative. He said Pappy and Mammy were forever optimists. 'They believed in the power and efficacy of *good works* . . . a very Russki concept, Mr Masud. I have both in large quantities. They believed in converting others to the *Cause*. Theirs was the one and only true cause. I can see I have tried to convert Mario to the Cause . . . only I don't have a cause, with a capital C . . . open doors and orifices don't add up to a cause.' I let the obscenity pass. Mr Luis was on the right track.

This was all narrated in the few days before Mr Luis was to ask me to help him refind Mario. Mr Luis could sense and see Mario's larger knowing in keeping away from him, which was why I had readily agreed to write the note to Mario. I felt that Mr Luis could, and would, respect Mario's rights and feelings now. Also that he wouldn't try to take over totally. Even the education of Mario would be different. Mr Luis could learn one thing above all from Mario: the arrogance of the poor, the unyielding pride in one's person, a very Spanish attribute. Mario was a half-breed. Most gypsies are half- or rather multi-breeds in Spain; an amalgam of Spanish, Arab and French strains. Mr Luis was well-informed about all that.

Once he had returned with Mario, the Portuguese housekeeper, Maria, went back to her employers. Mario insisted on looking for a waitering job – he felt he was good at it and he enjoyed the work – and found one in a hotel near their home for after the summer holidays. So, with all things arranged to come back to, Mario and Mr Luis left for their vacation.

I am nearing the point in this case history when I can bring the curtain down on Mr Luis's 'texts' and my clinical efforts with him. But this is by no means the end of the saga and, so as not to leave the reader with too many untolds and unknowings, I will report this much further. Mr Luis had a pleasant and unexpectedly fruitful vacation in the USA, where he had taken Mario for two reasons. One was that his mother was in very poor health and not expected to last many more months. In fact, she had died in his arms two weeks after their arrival. Mr Luis had buried her with dignity and without fuss. Then he and Mario had gone to Hollywood to explore the possibility of living and working there together.

The vacation had also served the purpose of introducing Mario to the American *civet*, Mr Luis's somewhat nasty, but one has to grant him pertinent, euphemism for the civilisations (in the plural) of the USA. Mr Luis, who was born to displaced Russian immigrants and had never really settled in America before he had been pushed over to Europe, had quite a knack for perceiving realities, that others missed, and phrasing them with an impish, dry, often salacious wit. I had not come across the word *civet* when Mr Luis used it, so I asked him what it meant. He sat up and said joyfully: 'Good. We can learn something together. I know only vaguely what it means. Please can I look it up in both the *OED* and Webster?' I said: 'Please yourself. I can't think of a better way of squandering this session today . . .' As Mr Luis was putting on his coat and arranging himself to go to the waiting room, where the dictionaries are kept, he said: 'Please warn your secretary that I shall be in the waiting room for some ten minutes. This is so that she can keep others out of harm's way . . .' Mr Luis's sarcasm wasn't lost on me. I replied: 'Don't you think, Mr Luis, it has served you well that you weren't tantalised and teased by the handsome looks of my very youthful houseboy? Well, I reckon it has.' Mr Luis sighed resignedly.

Mr Luis always took off his coat before lying down on the couch. He wore very tight French/Italian-style hand-tailored clothes. This he had picked up from Dave who, however, unlike Mr Luis, was determinedly casual, cowboy-wise, in his dress. As Mr Luis was buttoning his coat, he had said: 'Something for you to think about while I chase up *civet* in the other room. The USA has no – or very few – citizens in the English or French sense of the word. It has *cits* instead. Now a *cit* is a clever and expert lowly trader. Always a yid or a goy. Almost never a Black or a Red Indian. The *cit* is a practical trader. In English you would say a pragmatic trader. I wrote an essay about it at college. This is how I know what *cit* means. I looked it up in Webster. My argument was then, as it is today, that the USA is the first nation known to Homo sapiens that has created a scatter of civilisations, spread all over America, without creating any culture of any sort. This is what confuses all Europeans when they go to the USA. They look for culture and, not finding it, they berate us for the lack of it. Well, we never wanted culture so why should we have it? Just as we have very few citizens, like, say, George Washington,

Abraham Lincoln, Roosevelt, and now the Kennedys, and we choose
our Presidents from amongst them. In this we are unique. We are the
first, and I can predict the last, of Homo sapiens who breed a special
category of *cits* – not peasants or gentry or noblemen – known to us
as "citizens" in quotes, from whom we elect our political leaders. It is
somewhat like the Elders of the Athenian city-states, the Consuls of
the Italian oligarchies, and the kings and queens of Europe. After all,
the English also breed their kings and queens most carefully. So do we
our citizens . . .'

I had been writing very fast, but had missed a lot of spicy asides all
the same. Mr Luis had a quaint vocabulary and employed it most
peculiarly, according to his needs and wishes. I had started to
appreciate it only since the Mario-crises, when Mr Luis had become
more private with himself, at his house, and in the clinical situation.
Such usages of the English and French language constituted a large
proportion of our 'playing' in the sessions. Mr Luis returned bubbling
with laughter. 'You can't beat the English for deodorised, aseptic
double-crossing. Listen to this, Mr Masud!'

Mr Luis was holding Volume II of the *Oxford English Dictionary*.
He read out the whole entry for *civet*, nearly one column, but I shall
quote only the relevant part of it. Mr Luis read well; the years of acting
and stage-speaking in summer camps and at college had not been
wasted on him.

a.F. *civette* (15th c. in Littre, both for the beast and the perfume), It.
zibetto, med.L. *zibethum* . . . all originating in the Arab name *zabād*,
zubād.
1. A genus of carnivorous quadrupeds, yielding the secretion called by the
same name. Specifically, the central African species, *Viverra civetta* . . .
2. A yellowish or brownish unctuous substance, having a strong musky smell,
obtained from sacs or glands in the anal pouch of several animals of the *Civet*
genus, especially of the African Civet-cat . . .

Mr Luis then went to return the dictionary to its proper place; from
Pappy he had learned to cherish and tend books. When he came back,
he was beaming. 'This has been a really fruitful session. We have both
learned something from it. Thank you, Mr Masud, for letting it
happen. Any other head-shrinker, and the worst of moralists amongst
you are the Jews, would have clamped down on me at the very start of

the playing, saying it is *resistance*. It wasn't only in Denver I had psychiatrists. Also at college. They had to keep checking on me because I had this grant. I was tagged "a very bright non-believer, with abnormal tendencies". How telling! Like these *OED* descriptions of *civet*. So you see, Mr Masud, what I wrote in my essay was that the *cits* in America cultivate the *civet* of African cats – of course I couldn't say the Blacks, though I meant them – to manufacture their civilisations and sell them all over the globe, for profit only, without soliciting conversions or convictions.'

I had ended the session by saying: 'That is really very neat. Do write it up, Mr Luis, and lest you think it was lost on me, the use of the nouns "conversions" and "convictions" is very astute in its *double entendre* and bite . . .'

I have written of this interchange at some length to give the reader an idea of the changing role, character and usage of the analytic situation, for both Mr Luis and me. Since, at the beginning of this case history, I repeated again and again to myself, and frequently to Mr Luis, that I had little to offer him by way of growth and cure, and he had even less to offer me to learn from, it is important to show how much I had learned, after all, from Mr Luis's treatment. I was to learn more in the concluding four months of his analysis, and after it had finished, too.

When Mr Luis returned to his analysis in the autumn, after visiting the USA, he asked me whether it would be possible for him to complete it by the New Year, when he and Mario were planning to start their new life in America. I told Mr Luis emphatically that though I couldn't tell how complete his analysis would be by then, I saw no reason why he should not end it by the New Year, that is, in some four months' time. It was during this period that I met and talked with Mario, at Mr Luis's request. They had two options open to them. Both entailed little change of roles for Mario, but one option meant Mr Luis starting a new career altogether. He wanted to try it, in spite of the risks. I, too, thought that he should give it a try.

So Mr Luis and Mario returned to the USA early in the New Year and settled into a home of their own, in a new city, with Mr Luis pursuing a new profession. Since his analysis finished some fourteen years ago, Mr Luis has never sought further treatment, with me or with anyone else, and I have met Mr Luis and Mario at yearly intervals. Mr Luis is over sixty-five now, healthy and going strong. Mario is thirty-five and positively life-oriented.

[1987]

5
Outrage, Compliance and Authenticity

Probably every psycho-analyst would agree with the general statement that affects have a peculiarly intimate relation with instincts but
that they are essentially ego-experiences. As Freud (1915) said years
ago: 'It is surely of the essence of an emotion that we should feel it, i.e.,
that it should enter consciousness.' Further, we should probably agree
that affects constitute a specific kind, or mode, of ego-experience; that
they vary both in quality and quantity, and that individuals differ
markedly both in the range and in the intensity of their affectivity. It is
when we try to make these general statements more precise that we
encounter difficulties . . . We must have logical theory, but we do not
work with theory, we work with living impulses and feelings. Hence,
we should do well to check our theory by constant reference to our
working experience of affects.

MARJORIE BRIERLEY
Trends in Psycho-Analysis

In the forty-five years and more since Marjorie Brierley (1937) wrote
her pacemaker article, a great deal has been written about affects of
various sorts. André Green (1973) discusses this literature exhaustively
and critically in his book *Le Discours Vivant*. Yet, to my knowledge,
the affective ego-states of *outrage* and *outrageousness* have never been
discussed, in spite of the fact that as early as 1920 Freud himself singled
out 'the outrageous' as one of the precipitating causes of war neurosis:

We (the psycho-analytic school of psychiatry) had further asserted that
neurotic patients suffered from mental conflicts and that the wishes and
inclinations which were expressed in the symptoms were unknown to the
patients themselves – were, that is to say, unconscious. It was therefore easy to
infer that the immediate cause of all war neuroses was an unconscious
inclination in the soldier to withdraw from the demands, dangerous or
outrageous to his feelings, made upon him by active service.

I am proposing that the affective ego-state of outrage and/or
outrageousness should be clinically considered as a distinct syndrome

in its own right, just like love, hate, grief and rage, etc. First I shall present clinical material and later my theoretical inferences. Outrage and outrageousness can be both ego-syntonic and a social asset. The American cabaret comedian Lenny Bruce, for example, made millions by being outrageous to live audiences.

CASE MATERIAL

A physician rang me to ask whether I would take on a rather elusive and difficult patient, who had been refusing to go to work, off and on, for the past three years and had now totally packed up. The patient had been, he said, in analysis with two analysts (both of whom he named and I knew) and had jettisoned each. He was in his early thirties, married, had children, and was a successful businessman. As a last resort he had been given abreactive therapy, after which he had collapsed and retreated into refusals of all types of psychotherapy. He was, however, willing to have a consultation with me. As diagnosis, the physician gave on the phone: obsessional character, with acute depressive phases and non-relating. I agreed to give him a consultation, but nothing more. I reserved the right to take him into analytic treatment or not, and told the physician to inform his patient accordingly. I have no idea why I made this clause.

The 'patient' arrived rather early for his appointment. I was on the phone, and instructed my secretary to take him to the consultation room. Now this was atypical of my usual tactics for the first consultation. Normally patients are taken, by the secretary, to the waiting room when they come for first consultation, and I deliberately keep them waiting five or ten minutes; then I go personally and escort them to the consultation room, walking behind them. The first visual observations in the waiting room and their style of walking to the consultation room, and puzzlement as to which chair to occupy – since there are always three chairs and a couch in my consultation room – plus their manner of taking off overcoats or raincoats, and placing what they have brought with them, has always yielded me rich data (at the time merely 'registered' and *noted*, but not made interpretative use of).

Now, when I went to encounter Mr Roberts (as I shall call him here), after some five minutes, I found him standing in the middle of the room. It was winter and he was wearing a beige-coloured cashmere overcoat, a neatly tied woollen scarf and a black Russian-type hat, totally incongruous with his very pale, gaunt English face and skin. He was of slight weight and medium height. I said: 'I am Masud Khan.' He faintly, almost inaudibly, replied: 'I am Mr Roberts. Dr X has referred me to you.' I asked him to make himself comfortable by taking off his scarf, overcoat and hat, and pointed to the chair I wanted him to sit in. He most neatly folded his scarf, then his coat, and placed them in one chair. Then he took off his hat. He was balding rather much for his age. When he sat down I noticed he clamped his hands and was very tense. His shoes were impeccably clean and polished, and he wore a well-tailored suit; but he was wearing an outlandish tie that didn't fit the rest of his dress. Years later, when I got to know him better, I asked him about the hat and the tie he had worn at the first consultation, and he told me the hat was a Christmas present from his wife, and the tie from his children. Then I asked: 'What about the clean shoes?' And he said: 'I hate going into houses with dirty shoes, so I carry tissues in my coat to wipe them when getting out of the car, or coming up in a lift.'

We sat. He looked vacant, exhausted and opaque. After a while I initiated conversation by saying: 'Yes!?!' He paused, and said: 'What *outrage* are you going to commit on me?' I was taken aback by his use of the accusative noun 'outrage'. I gathered my wits, and said: 'It depends on how much you are going to provoke me!'

He sat immobile, looking down at the floor, totally and wilfully (I felt) oblivious of the aesthetic ambience of my consultation room. I felt a bit *outraged* myself, because I could sense he was a man of culture, and was *rebutting me*, which is more than refusal. I let it be, and terminated the consultation by saying: 'Well, we have encountered each other, at least, corporeally. Perhaps, if you choose to come again, you will tell me a little about yourself. But please, feel free to ring my secretary and cancel the appointment, giving at least three hours' notice.' This puzzled him, and I myself have no clue why I picked on three hours. I had added: 'No fees will be charged for the cancelled second consultation.'

We had been together for thirty minutes at the most. He got up, carefully dressed himself, wrote the date (a week later) and time of appointment in his diary, and left. I noted he was carrying a 'take-away' plastic food bag on him: another incongruous feature in his total self-presentation. He did not protest at the abrupt brevity of the consultation. I noted that he was *compliant*. So from the very beginning *outrage* and *compliance* became closely associated in my experience of this person, Mr Roberts!

He turned up punctually for his second consultation, I noted not a minute early or late. He sat down. Silence. Clamped hands as before; so tense I feared he would crack some bone. Then he asked: 'Have you been told what I do?' I replied: 'No, only that you are a very successful businessman for your age.' He scoffed: 'If that means I make a lot of money for my firm, then it is true.' I asked: 'What is your position in it?' He said: 'I am one of the directors!'

Now I decided to unsettle him. So with calculated asperity I enquired: 'Surely you didn't start like that. You don't look to me one of the upper classes to have got there at the start.' He was totally unruffled and said: 'You are right. I am of humble origin, lower middle-class. I have made my way. But I married a beautiful rich young girl. We were at college together. I joined the civil service as a clerk, even though I got a First at Cambridge. It was my wife who coaxed me into resigning and joining this firm, where I started as a senior clerk seven years ago, and now am one of the directors. No one believes it, but I am convinced my *sickness* is due to that.' I said: 'Yes, I believe you all right.' He continued: 'Only I don't know, nor can I tell, why it took this route, and is threatening to be disastrous.' He paused. Then he changed the subject and asked: 'May I tell you a little about my three psychotherapists, so that we can avoid their mistakes?' I was reassured by that, and said: 'Do! And do not fear that I know them all, as you have been told.'

About his first analyst he was utterly scathing, but with typical English brevity and politeness. He said the analyst's room was shabby; had only a desk, two chairs, a couch and a bookcase with Freud, the *International Journal of Psycho-Analysis* and some paperbacks. I noted how particular he was in his observation of the *environment* he was in. He continued: 'The analyst told me I had been referred to him for analytic treatment, so will I take off my coat, lie down on the couch and say whatever comes to my mind. I felt that was an *outrageous demand*, since I didn't know him at all; but I did what he asked, because my wife was very distressed by my condition, and hoped I could be helped. He had kept me waiting twenty minutes. I lay down and was silent, as with you. The analyst said: "You are angry with me because I have kept you waiting. Your fantasy is I am doing naughty sexual things with my patients while you wait, like all children think when their parents are absent!" I muttered to myself silently: He is not only an idiot, but obscene as well. I kept going all the same for fifteen months. Fortunately he talked most of the time. I remember nothing of the rest of it, except sending him a cheque and saying I could not continue treatment with him. I felt my wife's dismay at this, so agreed to go to another analyst.' Again I noticed his *compliance*, but also one other element: his *authenticity* to himself. I had no idea what the latter entailed for him.

His attitude to his second analyst was quite different. He made a point of telling me the second analyst was an aristocrat like myself. I said: 'I know.' The trouble, he said, was that this analyst was too 'matey', and involved him in his social life, in order to relax him. That did not work either. Since things were not going well, his physician and his psychoanalyst arranged for a psychotherapeutic abreactive session, conducted by them both. He recalled nothing of it, but was sure they had tape-recorded it. He asked me whether I had been told about it, and I candidly replied yes, about the abreactive session, but *not* what had been said or happened. I emphasised that I had no wish to know about it. But I was sure it was not tape-recorded. I had noted how very paranoid he could be.

He left it at that. I agreed to take him into treatment three times a week. He quizzed: 'Not five times?' I replied: 'No, I do not want you to have the self-indulgent chance of rebutting and refusals five times a week. Three is all I would be able to take. You are free to refuse it.' He agreed, I noticed with relief, to that. He was a very well-paying patient, and we analysts are very hypocritical, like our patients, where money is concerned.

I shall report briefly from his 'first analysis' with me, which lasted some three years. I say 'briefly' because, in fact, there is very little I recall from that 'first analysis', as Mr Roberts always called it. When I look at my notes, there are only three 5″ x 8″ cards covering those three years. From the first year I record that the patient arrived punctually, took off his overcoat, then his jacket, and lay down on the couch, without any instructions from me. He pulled the blanket, at the end of the couch, over himself, even though the room was rather overheated, and lay with his hands clasped on his stomach, above the blanket. In my notes there is an unsaid thought: I nearly said to him, You haven't come here to be cremated. But remembering his remark about 'outrage', I desisted.

He must have told me some facts, because the notes state that he was born a first son to very young parents. His father was a clerk and his mother a nurse. When he was two-and-a-half years old his mother fell ill and was in hospital for some months. He was taken care of by his grandparents and did not recognise his mother when she returned. Personally he had no memory of it; it was part of the family story told to him. A brother was born, six years younger than himself. He mentioned *furtively*, and casually, being sadistic to his younger brother and making him destroy his toys, so that he would not be blamed himself. Otherwise it was a progressively successful childhood. His parents could not afford his education, but he had won scholarships all the way, and got to Cambridge University, where he passed the Tripos degree. He was not ambitious, and opted for the first job that came his way in the civil service. Fortunately it suited his obsessional character, and he got excellent apprenticeship in the use of exact and punctiliously accurate descriptive language. He married, and it was his wife who had noticed his talent and coaxed him to join a private firm, as I have already mentioned.

From the first year there is another note, stating that the patient is much less apathetic and has returned to work full-time; and I add: God alone knows why! I cannot take any credit for it. He says little and I even less. He never dreams, he says.

From the second year there is a note saying: I wonder why Mr Roberts keeps coming. He is working well. So far as I can tell, his family are flourishing. What surprises me is that in spite of silences he never bores me, or makes me feel like goading him. I let him be.

From the third year there is only one paragraph saying: Today, by mutual agreement, Mr Roberts has terminated his treatment. He is leaving for a two months' holiday by car to Europe, with all his family. I have told Mr Roberts that I could not have expected a better 'cure'. Never once in three years had I heard of him being with his wife and children, except at Christmas, either at his parents' house, or at home with his wife.

During the next three years I kept hearing of him, because his physician was the same as mine. Meantime I had been gravely ill with cancer, and had lost a lung by pneumonectomy, and half the larynx. It took two years and more of no work, and some eleven operations (because I developed secondaries) before I regained some of my voice, and could begin clinical work again. Meantime my professional morale had been sustained by one person only, J.-B. Pontalis, who kept affectionately coaxing and bullying me to write for *Nouvelle Revue de Psychanalyse*; he would publish even a page and a half by me. Such care and holding by a colleague of the same generation is, I believe, rare in the history of psychoanalysis; except for the friendship between Anna Freud and the American millionairess, Dorothy Burlingham.

Now I shall recount the second and last phase of Mr Roberts's analysis, on which this chapter is based. He must have heard from our mutual physician that I had fought back to living and working. I received a letter from him asking if he could come and have a consultation with me, but he did not want anyone to know about it so I should not reply to him. He was forewarning me that he would ring at such and such an hour on a given date and find out what I had decided. He rang, and I personally answered, giving him a date and time for the consultation.

The person who arrived for consultation was little different from the person who had left three years earlier, only rather more bald: the same style of dress, and carrying the usual plastic bag of food. I was determined not to repeat the last analysis, but I had no preconceived ideas as to how I should go about it, because I did not know what condition he was in. He was an expert at hiding all his affectivity, either behind compliance or apathetic depression.

He sat down and expressed his concern about what physical and mental sufferings I had gone through. I genuinely thanked him, but made a point of stressing that I was truly moved not only by his concern, but that of his wife and children, all of whom had asked after my health from my physician. I noticed he was rather perturbed by my mentioning his family.

When he came for his next session I took the initiative and told him, as soon as he had taken off his raincoat (it was early autumn): 'Mr Roberts, now you are going to sit in that chair, and talk to me, person to person.' He did exactly that, and flummoxed me by his opening remarks: 'Now I am one of the two chief directors of the company. I have made a mint of money in the last three years and have taken out a huge insurance policy. My wife has become a successful professional at her work. My children have done splendidly at school, and are going to their universities. So I think the best I can do for them and myself is to commit suicide. They will be richer and happier together, without me. You were right when you once said: "You thrive by your nuisance value to your family."' In fact, I could not recall ever having said that, but it sounded very much like something I could have said.

I was utterly lost as to how to respond. So I chose to call his bluff. I asked him: 'Since when have you been thinking about it?' He paused, then replied: 'For some seven months or so; and I have collected all the right medicines to do it properly and without failing.' I hit back: 'If that is true, I should have been attending your funeral months ago, and not be listening to you telling me this damnable yarn today. You really are both mean and cruel. I wonder whether I can help you, or even whether I want to. I am not a doctor, I have taken no Hippocratic oath, so I am under no obligation to save anyone against his wishes. It will be a pity if you kill yourself, because fathers often do not realise that, during their adolescence, their children *need* them to be there, and available *on demand*, as urgently and constantly as infants do their mothers. That is all I have to say. But I refuse to be an accomplice to your blackmailing complicity with yourself. I no longer have the strength or motivation of three years ago to devote energy, and my talent, to someone who wants to play games. I can refer you to someone else. Anyway, you know how to go about it effectively yourself. Thank you for coming. There are no fees for this consultation.'

I *acted*, and got up to end the consultation. For the first time, Mr Roberts burst into tears. So I sat down and said: 'Why do we not try it my way this time?' He sobbed: 'All right! How?' I said: 'I will see you once a week. But first I want to meet your wife and children. They could not be flourishing if you are the sort of *un*-relating parent and husband you have made yourself out to be.'

From that session onwards, everything changed. I invited them all to dinner, without telling them he was going to start a 'second analysis'. They were a handsome and joyous family. So the question I posed myself was: How has this come about when he is so *sick*?

When he came for his next session he was smirking; he had never even smiled before. So I teased him: 'What are you up to now?' He said:

'You have solved all my problems. Since the dinner my wife and children cannot stop talking of you. So you are their godfather now, and I can retire.'

I noted the use of the verb 'retire'. This man never spoke a word out of place: that was his professional talent, and his manner of speech in social life. So I jibed: 'Some relief, we have shifted from suicide to retirement. I never realised you were not only mean and cruel, but also lazy!' This piqued him. He said with some violence, very unusual for him: 'What do you know about working? You, with your peasants and staff in Pakistan; your butler, housekeeper, chauffeur and secretary here? When have you got up at six a.m. and made breakfast for your wife and each child in turn, all of whom wake up at different hours? And I take it to them. I even do the washing-up!'

This is exactly what I had been waiting for: the breakthrough to his authentic self. I will avoid using the words 'true self' (Winnicott, 1960a); 'true' and 'false' are at root adjectives loaded with religious connotations of damnation and beatitude. 'Authentic' is identifiable, as neither 'true' nor 'false' are. In the English language 'authentic' means: 'trustworthy, entitled to acceptance' (*Oxford English Dictionary*). So the question that posed itself now, clinically, for both of us, was how this man had become dislocated from *authenticity* to *compliance*, and to *outrage* (which he would attribute only to others!) in his maturational process from infancy to adolescence.

When Mr Roberts turned up for the third, once-weekly session, he started by demanding to come three times a week, saying he could now easily afford my exorbitant new fees. I told him bluntly that it was not a matter of money for me, as he well knew. After fighting death for two years and more, I no longer had either the motivation or the physical resources to meet the *demand* of three-times-a-week analysis. Now *I* make the demands, not my patients. If they cannot accept this, there are always other, very able analysts I can refer them to. He listened to me quietly and said: 'All right! So how do we go about it your way, as you suggested in my consultation three weeks ago?' I had forgotten what a cruel, obsessionally accurate way he had of hearing and memorising everything in his environment. I was lost for what to say. Then I decided to act on him and make him act as well. I use the verb 'act' because it is exactly what I did. Now it is very difficult to make an adult person/patient *act* in the analytic setting. Of course, in child analysis it is both normal and the idiom of clinical work: actions as play! I looked at him and asked: 'Please can you unclasp your hands. I fear you may fracture some finger.' It was a totally fatuous remark on my part, yet true to his physical stance of sitting and being.

With his customary compliance he unknotted his fingers and asked: 'What next?' 'Try breathing deeply, then hold your breath and let it go. It may relax you.' He smirked and asked: 'Have you been attending Dr Laing's lectures? He is teaching yoga breathing exercises since his return from some ashram in Sri Lanka, as a psychotherapeutic procedure.' I let it pass and stayed silent. Then he said: 'You know, Khan' (he had never before addressed me by name; I was *the other*, 'you'! – quite anonymous and impersonal) 'I remember everything from childhood to today, but it was the first analyst who, being so nosy and then saying absurd things which he called interpretations, made me clamp down and be silent.' I disregarded all that, and said: 'If you have remembered everything and kept the memory alive these thirty-five years and more, surely you can dose them in weekly instalments.' He was rather amused by that and smiled. Now I realised he had a sense of wit, not humour, and I could exploit that clinically.

He reminded me that his mother was a trained nurse, so she had been as caring (his word) as she was adamant about cleanliness and being *proper*. I did not quite understand what he meant by 'proper', but noted it as significant for future use: that he was a much-loved and tidy child by the age of two, and was shown off as such. What he still couldn't recall was his mother's absence from illness when he was two and a half. He had apparently asked to see her and was told that the doctors did not want children to visit their parents in hospital. They were considered a nuisance, he added. It is only the work of Dr Winnicott and Dr Bowlby that has changed all that, he told me. I said nothing, but sensed he needed a response. So I bantered, because I had said to myself that this time I was going to 'conduct' his analysis as if he was five years old: 'But you know, Johnny' (I deliberately used his Christian name for the first time, and in the manner one would talk to a child) 'no matter how tidy children are, they do have "accidents", as you English euphemistically call it.' He was rather startled and shuffled uncomfortably in his chair. It was the end of that session anyway. So we left with all issues suspended, which I knew was a most awesome predicament for him.

He rang during the week saying he must have another session that week. I said: 'All right, I can see you at nine o'clock tonight.' He arrived and was so tense and taut that I feared he would break. He said he ached all over, and I said: 'Yes, it is very painful. Take two aspirins. It helps.' I got up and brought him two aspirins and a glass of water. Again I had acted quite fatuously; but I knew I must *do* something for him. He quietly gulped the tablets and told the following story of his fifth birthday.

Evidently he had been a very popular child, because he remembered there were lots of children and parents at tea-time, when he was to blow out the five candles and cut his birthday cake. Whilst cutting the cake he farted! His mother had asked him to go to the lavatory before the guests came, and he had said he did not need to. As soon as he had farted (his phrase), he looked at his parents. His father was laughing, but his mother was grimly sombre. After everyone had left, she quietly told him he had done an *outrageous* thing, which was most *improper*, so he must go to bed. She brought him food later. At the time she was pregnant with her second child. He knew that. He was adamant that from that day on he lost all spontaneity, stayed quietly at home and read, instead of playing, as he used to before, with his friends. Unfortunately his mother was only too pleased how good his work reports were from the kindergarten teachers.

It was nearly eleven o'clock by the time he had told his story. He noticed I was utterly exhausted, and said: 'Shall I ask the housekeeper to put you to bed? I can help.' I thanked him, and said: 'Yes, please call the housekeeper. I am very tired. But thank you for trusting me. I have noted everything in my mind.' I left it at that, and he departed.

In the next session I knew he expected me to begin by saying something. I acted again, in words, and told him that, in my clinical experience of some thirty-five years now, one thing I am convinced about is that whenever a person makes a single act the cause and root of his later ailment, it is always an *alibi*, even though true to his *vécu*. What we have to try to find out is why one *act*, 'farting', became his *fatedness*. I was candid and said I had no answers at present, but I now had some clues to his *un*-relating and being *proper* with everyone, familially, professionally and socially. I did say at some point, because it is in my notes, what a pity it was that he did not see Winnicott when he was five. He had lost so much of the joyous personal fun in living all these decades. And I made sure to add: 'Thank God, you have not spoilt things for your family. They are really joyous due to you.'

When one sees a patient only once a week, each session takes on a strange urgency for both the patient and the psychotherapist. Yet the time in between passes too quickly for the analyst, but not for the patient. So one has to allow for not overloading the patient with anxiety or its counterpart – *demands*. To strike this balance of therapeutic alliance takes a lot of trust and strength in both patient and psychotherapist. It does not always work. With 'Johnny Roberts' it did. I deliberately changed the tempo in the clinical sessions, remembering he had had abreactive therapy. So we talked of what his hobbies were, a topic initiated by me.

I have reported that when 'Johnny Roberts' had returned for further psychotherapy I had somewhat rashly, and without premeditation, said to him: Let us try it *my* way! And that he now wanted to know what was to be 'my way'. For weeks I dodged answering him. Finally, in a session some months later, I said to him: 'Do you recall your mentioning Dr Winnicott and Dr Bowlby?' Now Winnicott had been my analyst, as I have said, and for at least two decades I had worked very closely with him, both as a clinician of children and editing all his writings from 1949 until his death in 1971. He had a real genius for child consultations, and he called his technique 'the squiggle game' (cf. Winnicott, 1971a). He would sit on the floor, fool around with the child, of any age from two years to thirteen-plus, and at some point take a piece of paper, shut his eyes, and randomly draw a 'squiggle' on the paper. He would then ask the child to make something of it: a bird or the shape of an object, perhaps. Then he would ask the child to draw a 'squiggle', and he would 'turn' it into something; and so gradually a sort of 'dialogue' would actualise between him and the child. I went on: 'Now my clinical problem with you has been – as I recall from the three years of your "first analysis" – and is, your tense over-earnestness and calculated brevity of narrative. It is only since you and your family came to dinner that I have begun to realise you have a sense of wit.'

He scowled and interrupted: 'And how is that going to help us?' I said: 'I am going to try and do "word-squiggling" with you, which will be quite different from your doing the *Times* crossword daily. That way, if we succeed, there will be a sort of *playing-space* in the sessions, instead of your edited reportage on yourself.' He challenged me: 'Try it!' Once again, he had the advantage of me. I paused and said: 'You know, when you told me about how your family had reacted to their dinner *chez moi*, you said: Now you can be their godfather, and I can retire. Now someone like you, who is so *very* particular in the usage of words, should have known better than to call me "godfather", because I am neither a Christian nor belong to the Mafia.' This put him in his place, and he admitted: 'All right, you score the first point. The *playing* is on!' On that note we parted for the Christmas break.

Now 'Johnny Roberts' talked. In his first session after the Christmas break, he started by saying: 'Thank you for refusing to come to Christmas lunch. My children insisted, so I let them invite you.' I quipped back instantly: 'I am not easily ingratiated. I come from a different culture and class.' I noted his growing aggressivity in speech. Then he told me how his young wife, after marriage, had taken a Cordon Bleu course in cooking. But after the first child was born, he found one excuse or another not to return home for dinner. So she gave up! He paused. I had noticed. I said, 'How well you have "habit-trained" your family! The concept of "habit-training" applies in the English language both to the lavatory-training of children and of pets. Your wife has accepted infrequent sexual intimacy, and your children have accommodated to you, according to their sex and nature. But you have certainly worked hard at it. Congratulations!'

He was very puzzled why I would not *interpret*, but shifted all conversation to ordinary drawing-room language. He tried his next trick: 'You know, since I married some twenty years ago, it was the first time I let my wife invite the grandparents from both sides, as well as my brother and family, for Christmas lunch. I got "pissed" before everyone arrived, so we had a great time.' He paused. So I bantered: 'My fee for achieving that is fifty pounds in cash!' He said: 'It is quite *outrageous!*' 'Well, if you don't want to pay it, go to someone else,' I teased. He would not let go, and hit back: 'This is what you call "playing-space": making money!' I was not lost for words either, and replied: 'In my clinical experience, with the *nouveau riche* middle-classes, no other metaphor works.' He laughed, for the second time, opened his purse and offered me fifty pounds in cash. I refused it, of course, saying: 'No, thank you. My father has taken care that I should never need to earn money.'

Time passed. Fortunately, during this period, 'Johnny Roberts' had a client who was being really outrageous to him. Nothing he did was ever right for his client. He complained bitterly about it. So one day, with deliberate naïveté, I asked him: 'How do you manage to provoke outrageousness in others? I myself have felt like saying quite outrageous things to you, but your compliant decency of behaviour has always hindered me!' He was pensive for a while. Then he left, as it was the end of the session. He missed the next few sessions because he caught flu, which was unusual for him.

I have a brief note on my cards saying: On his return Mr J.R. started by telling me how years ago in his 'first analysis' I had once asked: 'What goes on in that head of yours, since you talk with no one at home or work, and are alone by yourself over the weekends?' 'Well,' he said, 'I can tell you something now. Whilst I was in bed, I didn't even read or listen to the radio. Suddenly one day I realised that all the time there was a sort of cocktail-party chatter going on in the background of my head. I tried hard to catch something of what was being said, but never succeeded. Only twice I heard: "You dirty so-and-so" and "Behave yourself". Nothing else.' Then he paused.

I had been gathering data from his 'freer' conversation during the past months, and was just waiting to offer him my 'reconstruction' of what had actually been the cause of his 'clamping down' (as he had called it) after farting when cutting his birthday cake, at five years of age. So I said to him: 'I now have my own version of what happened in your childhood, which you have totally shut away, and which led you to the *outrageous* act of farting. But since we are at the end of the session I will tell you next time.' He accepted it quietly and left.

When he arrived for the next session, I warned him that what I was going to tell him, as to what *happened* in his infancy/childhood, could be utterly fictive, of course, but not nonsense. He must hear me out. I started to say (I quote from my notes): 'You know grandparents are always more indulgent than parents. You have experienced it with your own children. Now my reconstruction is: that you had been brought up as a "cot-baby", to use your phrase, clean and tidy, with lots of love and care by your nurse-mother. When she fell ill, and you were taken care of by your paternal grandparents – who, as you have told me, were even poorer than your parents – you slept with your grandmother, because they lived in only two rooms. It had been a treat for you to be cuddled and they did not mind how you messed around with food and your clothes. This is what I think happened. When your mother returned, you had to be *tidy* and *proper* again. It is then that you started to clamp down, but maturationally, your aggressivity got postponed until your brother was born, and you could take it out on him deviously.'

He listened with concentration. When I stopped he said: 'You really are diabolically uncanny!' It was the end of the session, and he left.

Unfortunately the very next day I was rung by a consultant from a National Health hospital and told that my elder brother had been taken there because he had had a severe heart attack. They had done what was necessary, but he was asking for me to come immediately, even though he had rung for the ambulance himself to go to hospital. I cancelled Mr Roberts's next appointment, telling him I had an emergency in my family, and did not know when I would be able to take patients again. I gave him the name of a colleague he could go to, if he needed, but told him I would be in touch with him.

When I arrived at the hospital my brother was comfortably in bed and said: 'You see I can handle everything!' Before going in, I had talked with the consultant who told me there were two choices: either to let him be and dose him with drugs, in which case he was bound to have another heart attack and die; or they could do 'traumatic therapy', which would certainly paralyse him in some way, but he would live for six months, no longer. Now another problem arose. My brother had been separated from his wife for two years, and he had named me as the 'first heir'. Legally it was rather a tricky situation. I consulted his wife and she was against 'traumatic therapy' but was willing to go along with whatever I decided. I told the consultant that I wanted my brother moved to a private clinic, and that I would take total responsibility for any mishaps. He agreed.

I told my brother that this hospital did not have the necessary equipment for his treatment, so he would have to be moved to another. He started to cry and asked: 'You will stay with me all the time, won't you!' I said: 'Yes!' He had been awarded the Military Cross as a young captain of twenty-one in the Second World War, and had been a most independent extroverted character all his life. Now he became totally dependent on me, demanding that I should stay with him all the time. We had him moved to a private clinic where I could sleep on a mattress in the same room. I had also rung my lung surgeon, who, in fact, did only heart surgery, and he agreed to take over. So all went well. On the fourth day my brother had his second heart attack and died peacefully.

I had by now informed all my patients of the situation and given each the name of the analyst I thought most suitable for them to consult, if in need. I said I should be away for six weeks or more. I went to my estates in Pakistan to make the grave for my brother in the ancestral graveyard, even though he was buried in England, and returned five weeks later. I am telling this because analysts rarely speak about events in their personal life that affect their work mutatively. The death of my brother had changed my whole outlook on life, and I knew my patients would sense it; so I told them as much. And it is not a question of transference or counter-transference, but actual real, *lived* life that makes our fatedness or destiny, and about which we are often somewhat devious, both with ourselves and others.

During the period of my brother's illness, 'Johnny Roberts' and his family kept in constant touch with me, asking what could they do. So on my return, the first patient I got in touch with and saw was Mr Roberts. I told him candidly that I was relieved my brother had had a short illness and died peacefully. It was very sad, but he had lived a full and happy life. So we could start where we left off. Mr Roberts said: 'Not today, next session.' I thanked him and agreed to it. That he was a person who really cared for others, I knew already, otherwise neither his family would be so thriving nor he be so successful in a business which involved public relations as essential to its success. But that he could *act* according to his feelings and show concern was quite a new experience for him. I decided to capitalise on it clinically. To use Balint's (1968) concept, it was a 'new beginning' for him (Khan, 1969).

In the next session Mr Roberts recounted how he had got drunk from sheer nervousness, expecting the whole family to lunch on Christmas Day. After the lunch, whilst the children were playing with their Christmas gifts, he had asked his mother whether she remembered his farting on his fifth birthday and being sent to bed. She had replied: 'Only too well, because you refused to go out for two weeks and did not go to school, and your father was furious with me for sending you to bed. You were a spiteful child,' she had added. Then he told her that he was having psychotherapy, and though he believed it was that *act* at the age of five which changed his whole character, his psychotherapist was equally convinced that this was an *alibi* for something that had been happening to him for a long time, especially since his mother's illness and absence. He made a point of stressing that his mother was taken aback and had said: 'Your psychotherapist is quite right,' and told him how everything had been fine with him until her illness. She had gone to her doctor because she could not conceive another child. He had referred her to a gynaecologist who performed a surgical investigation in hospital; but it all went wrong, and she had developed septicaemia and was away from home for three months. All this was quite sudden and his paternal grandparents had taken him into care.

When Johnny's mother returned from hospital (he had not been allowed to visit her) and saw him, she was both outraged and disgusted by the way his face was smudged with dirt and his clothes were equally dirty and unclean. She said nothing to the grandparents and quietly took him, washed him, and boiled clean all his clothes. Now he refused to sleep in his small bed and insisted on sleeping with her, as he had with his grandmother. It took her four months to make him clean and tidy again, and able to sleep separately. It was during this period that Johnny's school reports stated that he had become withdrawn, did not take part in games, and would read all the time. His mother tried hard to get him to play with his friends over the weekend, but he would shut himself in his room. Then she became pregnant and let him have his way, since he seemed quite happy reading books and collecting pebbles from the garden, and making little things by gluing them. This amused me, because when he had talked about his hobbies, he had spoken of driving *alone* to countryside flea-markets and buying silver items cheaply. For his eighteenth birthday he had asked for a book on silverware hallmarks. His other hobby was gardening, and only very recently he had bought a large house, with a big garden. He had not said anything about it. He jibed: 'I did not, fearing you would raise your fees again!' I laughed.

From now on, Mr Roberts was flooded with memories of how deviously spiteful he had been with his brother, but never overtly aggressive. And in his work it was the same: some of his colleagues were outraged because he deliberately omitted to do certain things. They could sense it, but could never pinpoint exactly what he had not done, so they raged. Yet, because of Mr Roberts's expertise, no client had ever left the firm.

Now the issues of aggression, spontaneity and playing occupied our work. And, of course, their reaction-formations: his meticulousness, *un*-relating (lack of mutuality), and devious spiteful acts. He wanted more frequent sessions, but I refused, saying I really could no longer work as hard as I used to.

Now I shall summarise the clinical work done during the last six months of Mr Roberts's 'second analysis', as I recall it from memory and my clinical notes. His mother had confirmed my reconstruction, so I now concentrated on establishing how all aggression in him had been slowly and cumulatively strangulated by his mother (cf Khan, 1963, 1964). She had loved and nurtured him; but all children *need* to be outrageously untidy and messy at times. Winnicott (1971a) has written most insightfully about this from his infant-child consultations. I told Mr Roberts that slowly the 'cumulative trauma' of his mother's caring, but inhibitive, attitude to his messy aggressiveness had turned him into a spiteful, deviously aggressive child, and on his fifth birthday he took his revenge by his outrageous farting. But after that, he had turned all aggression into obsessive reading, learning and *un*-relating. This made a great deal of sense to him, and he asked: 'Please help me to relate to my children.' I said: 'It is very simple. Since they know only too well your gamesmanship, why not ask them to help you with the gardening, when the weather is good? And do go with your wife and children to buy them clothes.' He replied: 'That is a jolly good idea' (a very English phrase).

I shall skip months of work and come to the only dream he reported in the whole of his psychotherapy:

He is walking in a street with a book in his hand. In front of him he sees a foreign girl in smudged white shorts, ankle socks and tennis shoes. He is excited and decides to walk fast, and as he passes her he accidentally (as it were) smacks her bottom with the book.

He woke up in a sweat. He said it was a nightmare, and added: 'You will say I am a pervert who gets sexy kicks from fantasies of beating women.'

I replied: 'You must stop putting your thoughts into my head. The dream, as I think of it, has as little to do with sex as the sauce one puts on the cooked Chateaubriand has to do with the meat. What you have obliterated from the dream-text (cf Pontalis, 1977) is the dreaming experience (cf Khan, 1976a). You mention that the girl's white shorts were smudged: that is exactly what your mother had been outraged by when she saw you on her return from hospital. So in the dream you perpetrate an outrageous act. But at least in your dreams you can be aggressive, as to wish and desire. That is real progress.'

It took us months to cover this clinical material. It was time for the summer break, and by mutual agreement we decided that Mr Roberts no longer needed psychotherapy. It is more than a year now since that time, and he and his family are thriving.

THEORETICAL AFTERTHOUGHTS

From the total psychotherapeutic treatment and care, holding and handling of this patient/person, I will single out three issues for discussion:

1. Winnicott has written extensively about his consultations with infants, children and their parents, especially mothers (1971a). I did not think that the 'good-enough mother' is *not* traumatic to the infant, so I wrote papers on cumulative trauma (1963, 1964). There are *too* 'good-enough mothers', who inhibit the infant/child's aggressivity by their obsessional over-care. This patient is one of such children.

'Johnny Roberts', as we have seen, had learned very early on to turn his aggressiveness into provocative and devious spitefulness, with his younger brother, and in adult life with his clients, as well as with his previous psychoanalysts. Now he had gone one step further and added outrageousness/outrage to his spitefulness. It never turned up in transference or counter-transference in the analytic situation; only in his corporeal stance of being so tense that I feared he would crack. I did not demand free associations. I confronted him person to person, when he had returned for his 'second analysis'. It turned everything upside down, for him and for me, as has already been seen. But first I want to mention a point suggested by Starobinski (1980) on Lautréamont. He used the concept of *outrance* to explicate the verbal 'outrages' by Lautréamont. I have advisedly chosen to use the concept of outrage/outrageousness, because *outrance* does not cover physical acts of violence. Marquis de Sade knew he was *outrageous* in his sexual habits and saw to it that he was imprisoned for most of his adult life, even though he had played a significant part in the French Revolution. My patient had also abstained from physical violence, sexually or otherwise; but he knew how to provoke outrage in *the other*. He did not succeed with me, because I had been a more outrageous person in my private life. I knew all the ruses of that affect, both in private life and professionally. I was a much cuddled infant/child, who grew up, very precociously, to speak seven languages, be a champion international rider and squash player. So he could not get the better of me.

From my clinical experience with perverts, borderline cases and drug addicts, I have come to the conclusion that the restriction of spontaneity in infant-/child-care results, in adolescence, in outrage/outrageousness; this stems from a devious affective ego-state which gathers cumulatively, and not all that unconsciously, in a person, and expresses itself in various ways which are erroneously labelled psychopathic character, narcissistic neurosis, etc. It is the clinical handling of such patients that is so difficult, because interpretation is an alibi the analyst uses to cover his incapacity to cope with the patient's conduct. The patient knows only too well how to exploit the analyst's technique to his advantage, with compliance, without reaching that authenticity which is his personal self. Such patients act in life what so-called neurotic patients either have fantasies or dreams about. When they can have fantasies or dreams, they are no longer dissociated in themselves.

2. It is believed by almost all analysts that every patient has the capacity for fantasy and dreaming. It took Winnicott (1984) to point out, from clinical experience:

In another more mature alternative to aggressive behaviour, the child dreams. In dreaming, destruction and killing are experienced in fantasy, and this dreaming is associated with any degree of excitement in the body, and is a real experience and not just an intellectual exercise. The child who can manage dreams is becoming ready for all kinds of playing, either alone or with other children. If the dream contains too much destruction or involves too severe a threat to sacred objects, or if chaos supervenes, then the child wakes screaming. Here the mother plays her part by being available and helping the child to wake from the nightmare so that external reality may play its reassuring part once more. This process of waking may take the child the best part of half an hour. The nightmare itself may be a strangely satisfactory experience for the child.

That the capacity for fantasy and dreaming are the end result of good environmental care (maternal and otherwise) sets specific tasks for the clinical *handling* and *holding* of patients who have suffered cumulative trauma from deficits in this maturational area of growth.

Holding is a function of the total analytic setting, whereas *handling* is largely an interpretative act, which analysts are usually adept at. Combining the two – especially in analyses of adults – involves putting up with the nuisance demands of patients, from telephone calls at all hours to getting into situations which compel hospitalisation. The latter rarely work beneficially; they only provide some respite for the analyst.

3. *Un*-relating my own clinical work, and my association with Winnicott when he did his 'squiggle-game' consultations, has taught me that there is a world of difference between infants/children who grow up being cuddled and sleeping either with their siblings or parents, and cot-reared children. The 'cot-bred' infant-child learns very early what *un*-relating is, even though every care is taken to make him comfortable and tidy. I have seen the aftermath of such upbringing, especially in the treatment of perverts and drug addicts. They (the latter) have a special gift or talent for what I call pretend-care, only to get rid of their 'victim' once he becomes dependent on them; they then search for the next victim. Now Mr Roberts was neither a pervert nor a drug addict; but he had mastered the art of being quietly spiteful, and provoking others to be *outrageous*. He spared only his family, and as I had said to him, I had no clue as to why. But I had added: 'Of course you have to be *dependent* in your *un*-relating way.' This thwarted him. He was furious, and said: 'You tricked me by inviting my family to dinner; otherwise you would never have found out about it.'

I was not lost for repartee. So I commented: 'You had me on for three years in what you call your "first analysis" with me, and others as well. So I called your bluff when you asked to have more psychotherapy. I know only too well that if a patient is *outrageously* demanding and *acts out*, the analyst is no less demanding, except that the analyst *acts out* through, and by, his *interpretative acts*. Now I do not do that. When I think a patient, as a person, needs me to *hold* him, by acting, i.e. *managing* his private life, I *act*; not always wisely, but never to my personal benefit.' He smiled again, and said: 'Little wonder they got rid of you from the British Psycho-Analytical

Society's teaching and training.' I said: 'I could not care a damn about it! I am sought after from all over the world. And even if I were not, I can return to my ancestral estates in Pakistan, make no mistake about it!'

[1984]

6

'Thoughts'

> ... L'amour cacherait la haine, la haine un amour
> fou ... La haine n'exige-t-elle pas la présence et la per-
> manence de son objet ... ?
>
> J.-B. PONTALIS ET AL (1986)

> L'homme n'est qu'un noeud de relations.
>
> SAINT-EXUPÉRY

In this chapter I shall present clinical material from the first three phases of the ongoing psychotherapy of a youth, to communicate how over-protective and over-caring mothering in early infancy and childhood can add up to a cumulative deprivation which distorts the emergent phase-adequate maturational processes of individuation and autonomy, and prevents the establishment of what Winnicott (1962) has conceptualised as the *I am* status in a child. It is this that forms the core of his selfhood and ensures a healthy psychosexual development, enabling him to weather the vicissitudes which every child has to face at the oedipal stage à la Freud (1905a), such as castration anxiety, and shifting attachment from the primary object (mother) to a relationship with her that can include others. Cumulative deprivation, on the other hand, results in a compliant, *as-if* character-formation, from which children try to gain autonomy and independence by exploiting the potential for the antisocial tendency – which is latently present in every person – throughout puberty and adolescence. They rarely succeed, hence the normal doldrums of adolescence (Winnicott, 1971b) are rendered pathogenic and traumatic. This leads to a regressive with-drawal from the attachment to, and dependence on, either the primary mother or her contemporary surrogates, and cripples growth towards a creative and functional adulthood. We analysts encounter it as a breakdown in that person. I shall detail how I handled it clinically, without the least intention on my part to instruct anyone else to follow the same approach.

A major feature of such a developmental arrest is conceptualised most aptly, in my estimation, by the terms 'love of hate' and 'hate of love'. Clinically it is imperative to distinguish between this experiential and relational predicament in the self-experiences – from masochism to sadism – which accrue from ego-id conflicts, and the admixtures from superego and ego-ideal structures which yield guilt and shame respectively. We have to be careful, in initiating the clinical relating with the person of a patient, that these metapsychological concepts do not stand in the way of our approaching the problems of the patient with an entirely open mind (Main, 1957). Of course, none of us escapes those adulterations of clinical naïveté which education invests us with, and which we learn to mask with analytical jargon. Here we are faced with a paradox.

The analytic ritualised clinical process cannot operate without masks, yet it has to transcend them in some ways. Each analyst gradually invents his own masks. The sterility in our work and thinking sets in when we use borrowed masks from others.

PHASE ONE

A psychiatrist (Dr X) wrote to me requesting an urgent consultation for a youth of twenty-two. He stated that he knew from reading my books that I did not like being sent long, detailed notes from the referring psychiatrist and/or physician. But a few facts, briefly told, might help me to decide whether I would agree to give even a single consultative appointment. He wrote that Benjamin (as I shall name him) came from a well-to-do professional middle-class family and lived with his parents. He had had a nervous breakdown eight months before, which prevented him from going to work. The family physician, who had medically taken care of Benjamin since the age of eleven, reported that all through his puberty and adolescence he was active and extroverted, with occasional bouts of eruptive moods, varying from excited hyperactivity to sudden withdrawal. A few days of rest and a mild sedative or antidepressant would usually restore him to himself, so, after his breakdown, the physician had advised total rest and prescribed an antidepressant. At the end of a month, however, there was little improvement. On the contrary, Benjamin seemed even more anxious and fretful. After talking to his mother, and with her agreement, the physician had sought psychotherapy for Benjamin. He had tried three psychotherapists, and the treatment had failed in each case after only a few sessions, because Benjamin could not tell his 'problem', although he was fully conscious of its nature and contents and knew it had caused all his mental crises since the age of eleven, including his breakdown eight months earlier. No matter how hard he tried, Benjamin could not talk about his 'thoughts', and they all blamed him for wilful nonco-operation. Dr X added that I should perhaps know that the three previous psychotherapists, from different schools of thought and practice, had written to Benjamin's physician giving what they considered to be the right diagnosis, and advising different methods of treatment according to their style of work. On one score they had all agreed: that his prognosis was very poor. Neither the physician nor Benjamin's mother shared this view, so the treatment would stop.

Then Benjamin had started to go to church, after a gap of some seven years, for solitary meditation. His mother, a devout Roman Catholic, considered it a healthy sign, but this did not work either and Benjamin was becoming progressively more withdrawn and apathetic, and saw no one except his parents, his steady girlfriend and his physician. It was then that the physician had referred Benjamin to Dr X, who had found him a pleasant and co-operative patient, except that, although he would mention his 'problem', he could not disclose its content. He attended regularly, but after two months Dr X, too, felt they were getting nowhere. He often combined individual therapy with group therapy in his practice, and in some twenty years this had always worked well. He thought that perhaps hearing other persons discuss their most intimate problems might encourage Benjamin to talk about his own. But unfortunately things went disastrously wrong, and after one session of group therapy Benjamin had completely collapsed. He would not get out of bed or see anyone except his parents and the physician; not even his girlfriend now. This caused grave concern in all, and Dr X was rung on a Sunday morning by the physician, telling him that Benjamin's condition had deteriorated dangerously; could he please come to the house immediately. He agreed and drove over.

Benjamin had rung Dr X on the previous Monday – three days after the group therapy session – to say that he would not be able to come that week because he had flu. Dr X emphasised that Benjamin, even though he was manipulative, rarely lied. When he saw him, Benjamin told Dr X, without rancour, that the group therapy session had intensified his 'problem'. It was at this point that Dr X called in the parents and the physician, and said, gently but firmly, that he really could do no more, even though Benjamin was direly in need of psychotherapeutic help. That he knew of a non-medical Pakistani psychoanalyst who was especially experienced in the clinical care and treatment of such conditions in young persons. If they all agreed, he would write to me and ask for a consultation. He was doubtful if I would have a vacancy for treatment, but at least I could advise him as to what sort of psychotherapeutic management and treatment could be helpful, and with whom. Lastly, he added, a new factor had emerged which, apart from Benjamin's illness, had to be dealt with urgently. His employers wanted to know how much longer they had to keep his job open and had stated bluntly that they could not do so for more than another three months. Dr X ended his letter by saying that he did not think Benjamin's prognosis was poor and believed that, given the right setting and treatment, he could recover. The family, he added, were both genial and co-operative, and as for medical coverage, if I agreed to take him into psychotherapy, both he and the physician would provide this, and be available for any help that I deemed necessary for Benjamin's treatment. Dr X gave me Benjamin's address and telephone number, and reiterated the necessity of my seeing him as soon as possible.

For me, clinically, it is imperative to have some idea, before I see a person in consultation, what routes he has travelled psycho-therapeutically. I am not particularly concerned to know beforehand what the illness is, or how grave it is. Knowing the routes a patient has travelled enables me to arrange, tentatively at least, the 'psychic space' (Stoller, 1985) that I preconceive would be facilitating and mutually convenient. I was rather impressed by the honesty and candour of Dr X's letter, so I asked my secretary to ring Benjamin and offer him a morning appointment the next day. Benjamin was expecting the call, agreed to come and arrived punctually.

My secretary had taken Benjamin to the consultation room. I gave him a few minutes to orientate himself to my clinical setting. When I came in, Benjamin got up, shook hands and told me his full name. To initiate the process clinically, I asked him how he would like to be addressed, and he politely replied: 'As Benjamin, please.' He did not ask how to address me. I was marking time to reorientate myself regarding Benjamin. The 22-year-old youth that I had vaguely anticipated meeting was quite different from the Benjamin who was standing in front of me. I walked to my chair and he sat down in his. I carefully but unobtrusively noted his style of dressing while we talked. He started by asking whether I had heard from Dr X; paused, and with a wry smile, corrected himself: 'Of course you have, otherwise how could you know my phone number? What I meant to ask was what has Dr X told you about me?'

I was still ridding myself of my preparatory preconceptions about him, so that I could see and experience him as he had *chosen* to present himself, physically and mentally. I felt certain that each of us had prepared himself as to how to deal with the other. So I parried his question to take more time to observe him, and asked whether he could please move from the chair he was sitting in to the one nearer my chair. He said: 'I am sorry,' and moved to the chair close to me. I noted that his apology had more the tone of shame than guilt, as if he had done something improper, so I quietened him by saying that as he could hear I have a hoarse and faint voice, and it does not travel well beyond a certain distance. He did not ask why my voice was hoarse and faint. Once he had made himself comfortable in the second chair, I told him briefly what Dr X had written to me. I stressed that all I knew about him was from Dr X's letter: namely, that he was twenty-two years old, had had a nervous breakdown some eight months ago, been to see three psychotherapists and none had succeeded in enabling him to tell what his 'problem' was. Then he had tried meditation, and when that didn't work, he had been referred to Dr X. I made no secret of the fact that – as Dr X had written quite frankly – during the two months he had been seeing Benjamin he felt he was getting nowhere with him, so had changed his psychotherapeutic tactics and asked Benjamin to come to group-analytic sessions as well. He had attended once and it had proved disastrous: it was as a result of his subsequent collapse into withdrawal and inertia that Dr X had written to me, asking me to give him a consultation urgently.

I had been watching Benjamin intently while talking to him, and realised he had noticed it. So he *was* perceptive, but he had listened with a bland expression. I paused. He said Dr X was a very kind and frank person but he had given the wrong impression of his behaviour, since his breakdown, on two counts. Firstly, Benjamin never went to any specialist from personal need or demand; he was sent by his doctor, with Mum's approval, to each one. Secondly, it was not that they had not succeeded in helping him to tell his 'problem', and what constituted it, but that each therapist was too eager to help and, when he could not, became accusative and impatient and would suggest different ways of dealing with Benjamin, ranging from sending him to a mental hospital to being treated at home by a social worker. Neither his mother nor his doctor would agree to any of their suggestions, so they would stop his treatment. Dr X was the exception. At this point Benjamin looked more frightened than anxious. I changed the subject and asked what Dr X had told him and his parents about me. He literally repeated what Dr X had written, but added that Dr X had told him and his parents that I was an aristocrat, and was famous as much for the quality of my work as for my style of living and dressing. He paused.

I changed the subject again. I was determined to keep the conversation between us alive, and not let it get too earnest, in order to establish the dynamic rhythm of what Freud (1940a) has called 'our common task'. So I remarked that since he had mentioned my style of living and dressing, he must have noticed that I had been keenly observing his style of dressing as well. He said yes, and asked why. I replied that it was rather atypical for a youth of his age in the mid-1980s. He said: 'How?' I answered that he was too well-groomed and dressed in a rather classical English style. Most youths today of his age, if they dress well, are rather exotic, and if they are a bit 'hippie' they dress with calculated untidiness and wear rather bizarre and colourful clothes. His were too tidy and gave no clue as to who was inhabiting them physically; they were rather impersonal, and a shade sombre. I suddenly noticed that his mood had changed, and he was fretting inside. So I eased it by a facetious remark: 'It is lightly snowing outside today so the roads are wet, yet your shoes are dry and shining, whilst your hair is damp.' He smiled and said: 'I was told by Dr X that, unlike most of your colleagues, you live in a very luxurious and expensively furnished flat. So before ringing the doorbell I took some tissues and wiped my shoes dry.' Saying all this had relaxed him. I noted that in spite of being 'folded in' on himself, he showed concern. An awkward pause now. I let him stew a bit. He asked: 'What would you like to know about me?' I replied: 'Today, nothing about your "problem", but it would help me if you could tell me a little about your family, home-life and how you have grown up.'

He was pensive. I sat back to listen to him. He started by saying that his had always been a pleasant home. His parents never squabbled, though they were totally different in character. Mum is very tidy, religious and devoted to her work. She ran a kindergarten when he was a child, and when they moved to the house where they live now, she went back to college for specialised training, and is now always preoccupied with child-care. His father is casual and takes things easy. They had moved house when he was eleven, and his dad had got a high-paying job which enabled him to send Benjamin's two brothers to college. His parents were very keen about education, though they had not forced any of the sons as to what subjects they should study. His three-years-older brother had finished college with a good degree, and now had a job in the City. He no longer lives at home with them, although he visits them every weekend. Benjamin's other brother, who is three years younger, is rather quiet, and a diligent student at college. He comes home during the holidays, but not for long, because he travels a lot in France and Greece as he is studying these languages.

Benjamin had always been quite different from both his brothers in that physically he grew up rather precariously, but he was strong and good at sports. At school he managed to pass his O- and A-levels, but did not go to university. He had never told anyone before, but this was because of his 'problem'. He was eighteen when he took his first job, as a clerk in a firm. His 'problem' had started when he was fifteen. Till then he was an extrovert and played rugby, had lots of friends, boys and girls, and had started to stay out late when they had moved to the new house. This had rather disconcerted his mum, but she did not interfere directly. But at the age of fifteen, he had acne and this changed everything. It was then that he began to withdraw from sports and social life. He felt *shamed* by his acne. During this period the problem started. He said he could tell me only this much about it: that it consists of very bizarre and macabre sexual 'thoughts', that have no relation to reality. He has never brooded over them. They are triggered off by any sort of perception, and once they start he cannot stop them. He paused and said: 'Please do not ask me any more about my "thoughts". I have

already told you more about my problem than to anyone else before.'
He became silent and I could sense he was tensely waiting for a
response from me.

I thought carefully and said: 'I am relieved you are not going to tell
me any more today. There will be plenty of time for you to share your
"thoughts" when we are relating mutually, and I will know you well
enough to be able to make some sense of them, and help you. If you spit
them out today, trying to please or oblige me, we shall get nowhere.' I
stopped. He leaned forward and asked in a rather excited way: 'Does
that mean you are going to take me on for treatment? Dr X was most
doubtful about that, and said as much.' I replied that I gave up treating
patients some fifteen years ago, but that I was willing to see him three
times a week and my fee would be so much per session. I asked: 'Can
you afford that?' He replied yes, Dr X had told him, and his parents,
that I was expensive. He felt he could work with me and that he needed
to, not only for his mental health but to get back to work as soon as
possible or he would lose his job, which was a very good one. He had
been with the company for nearly two years now.

I looked at my watch and realised we had been together for nearly
two hours, so I gave him an appointment for the following day and
brought the interview to an end by saying, 'I shall write a brief note to
Dr X to tell him that I have taken you into psychotherapeutic care. You
can inform your parents yourself.' We got up, shook hands, and he left.
Suddenly I felt exhausted. Evidently he had been more *demanding* than
I had registered. For future reference I jotted down: Diagnosis: a
precocious pervert *manqué*, and I added: I cannot figure out, from the
consultation, whether Benjamin's 'thoughts' are a variant of ego-
perversion or a sexual perversion. It was the next day that I dictated
extensive notes to my secretary, ending on a cautionary note to myself:
Do not let him get too trusting and 'intimate' too soon. Keep the
distance *relational* and live, and do not let it become a confessional
space (Freud, 1940a). After all, he was reared a Roman Catholic and
must know all the ruses of saying things without telling anything.

I have written about the first consultation in such detail, even at the
risk of it reading as superficial and banal, to indicate that how we
analysts initiate the clinical relating with the patient as a person, charts
the future course of the therapeutic encounters and the patient's
destiny, if we reach that far. It is my experience that analysts, especially

English and American, put more emphasis on how they have deciphered the unconscious phantasy, and its meaning, from the patient's overt verbal communications and behaviour, than on letting their clinical narrative speak for itself. Extreme examples of this are the writings of Melanie Klein, Herbert Rosenfeld and Hanna Segal. Winnicott's clinical narratives, especially of child consultations, are both unique and exceptional in this respect. Our French colleagues, when they write about their clinical work and techniques, may seem more authentic as to the verity of what they actually do, but it is largely a linguistic stance of communicating. Perhaps they give of their best in theoretical writing and conceptualising. My personal style of writing about my clinical encounters is quite different, in so far as I have no wish to enlighten or teach anyone, but to expand my own awareness of how I work clinically by 'sharing' it with my colleagues and readers. This endeavour to communicate with an invisible and non-present *other* frees me from using conceptual clichés from our metapsychology, and allows me to employ language as near to its ordinary usage as possible. For me, the analytic *écriture* does not constitute a hermeneutic mystique, and belongs to a very different order from the oral mutuality of shared converse, which is both more and less than discourse. None of us can ever shed his beginnings. I was reared in a non-literate, oral culture, hence my bias for sharing experiences, speechwise, rather than through predetermined and ordained conceptual *écriture*.

I have stated that I had dictated extensive notes from the consultation to my secretary. To make my style of clinical work intelligible to the reader, I must say here that I take notes in the first consultation, in the presence of the patient, while he is sitting, and with his permission, for two reasons: to prevent my attention from wandering whilst listening to the patient's material, and/or to create and establish a *psychic distance* between me and the patient. I regard this psychic distance as quite a different stance of clinical relating from what Stoller (1985) calls 'psychic space'. The latter I consider an achievement from clinical work with the patient, that is, if the clinical process achieves mutuality of converse and response. Of course it depends on the nature and gravity of the patient's illness, as well as on the analyst's skill and experience, as to how soon or late this 'psychic space' will actualise. Sometimes it does in the very first consultation, but I consider it necessary to ensure that the psychic distance is firmly and dynamically established first. I always take and retain the initiative.

To return to Benjamin. After ridding my head of the clutter of the consultation material, as I prepared to see him for his first session I had the following thoughts to guide my clinical handling and holding:

1. I asked myself why I had accepted him for psychotherapy and had given sessions for three consecutive days before the weekend. The only clues I had were that his predicament, 'thoughts', interested me. Perhaps a certain vanity that I might succeed where others had failed was a factor, too. I certainly considered him worth helping and felt I could learn from it. Furthermore, his 'misery' solicited help, in spite of his overt negativity (Freud, 1940a). Benjamin was a proud youth, and to seek help was for him a huge step towards health.

2. I didn't consider him the sick or difficult patient that my colleagues, with the exception of Dr X, had made him out to be. His recent invalided *vécu* gave one, I felt, a false impression of his potential to heal, and grow as a person, from being just *Mum's lad.*

3. I also felt he was more insightful and self-knowing than he had been given credit for. One remark of his during the consultation had vividly caught my attention: talking of his 'thoughts', he had said they *shamed* and *terrorised* him. He got no fun or pleasure from them, though I might find that hard to believe since they played such a big role, and occupied so much time, in his life at present. He had added, and this had deeply impressed me, that to feel guilt and pain (psychic) is a relief he could not find in himself. He merely suffered shame from his 'thoughts'.

4. Another reason why I had given him three consecutive sessions that week was, or so I persuaded myself, that if there was a time-lag, the little momentum of the clinical rapport we had achieved might get vitiated from a takeover by his 'thoughts'. This role of time-lag I had learned more from the analyses of children than of adults. Some children had to be seen twice a day because they could not hold the experience of the session across the time-lag (Winnicott, 1965).

5. I had the firm conviction that Benjamin's 'thoughts' were more

important for the self-protective role they played than for any possible meaning which his perverse fantasies, with their macabre contents, may have had for him. I had a hunch that the 'thoughts', in some weird way, created a *private space* for him which none could infringe upon, and which somewhere, in his relations with his mother and brothers, he had failed to find and establish.

6. Although Benjamin had admitted to two breakdowns, from his own account of himself I could identify four: the other two being the giving up of studying and not going to college, and when, at eleven years of age, he had not 'broken down' but 'broken out' (as from a prison) into defiant and extroverted hyperactivities, such as staying out late with friends, to the great chagrin of his mum.

7. Lastly, I considered the 'thoughts' were Benjamin's 'objective correlative' for the antisocial tendency in him, resulting from cumulative deprivations registered, but not experienced as such, in his early childhood. I am borrowing the concept from T. S. Eliot's essay on *Hamlet* (1918) where he writes: 'The only way of expressing emotion in the form of art is by finding an "objective correlative"; in other words, a set of objects, a situation, a chain of events which shall be the formula of that *particular* emotion, such that when the external facts, which must terminate in sensory experience, are given, the emotion is immediately evoked.' The clinical task, both for me and for Benjamin, was gradually to discover, and construct, this 'emotion' from the plethora of his 'thoughts'.

Of course it was one thing for me to think all this up. I had little doubt that feeding my thoughts to Benjamin would be quite another matter. I expected him to be compliant, without resistance or receptivity or reciprocity. Now we shall see how Benjamin dealt with me and my holding and management of his self-experiences, inside and outside the clinical setting. The dosage of holding and management was the crucial clinical task for me. He was a passive person, and could very easily 'hand over' to me the responsibility of personal initiative for purpose and action in his life. I was determined that he would not, and should not, become *Khan's lad* from being *Mum's lad*.

Furthermore, it would serve little purpose for him to achieve autonomy without a *me* – Benjamin – to fructify this autonomy. An *as-if* autonomy would be as wasteful, and as much a saboteur of creative personal living, as were his 'thoughts'. After all, he had indicated that these were 'autonomous', i.e., they were triggered off without his wish, will, or desires playing any role.

Benjamin arrived looking even more pale and anaemic than when he had come for the consultation. He also looked rattled and frenzied. He asked whether I would like him to lie on the couch, and I replied that I would prefer it if he could sit and talk, but should that prove too embarrassing for him, then he could lie down. I have no hard and fast rules about it. He smiled and said he now remembered another thing Dr X had said about me: that I was a maverick among analysts, and that is why, though I am famous, I am not very popular with my colleagues in London. I let it pass, and paused. He was getting increasingly uncomfortable but he did not fidget, except for continually readjusting his tie. I felt he was struggling to say something, but in measure, that is, not too much and not too little. At last he said that, on one score, he had withheld something essential at the consultation when telling me about his 'thoughts'. This had been shaming him, because I had been so straightforward with him. I teased him: 'You are not coming to a Roman Catholic confessional, and as I have already said, I dislike the *intimacy* of instant and compulsive telling about himself by anyone, be he an acquaintance or a patient. If it is a feature of his illness that he cannot be private with himself, it is my bias that I *must* stay private with myself and keep my distance.'

This rather foxed him. He recovered and said it was not a question of confessing with him, but of his *vows*. He asked me whether I knew anything about Roman Catholic Sunday-school lessons on religion. He was sent to attend them by his mum when he was six, and had kept it up until he was eleven. Then he had stopped going. The priests taught a lot about honouring the *vows* one made, and making 'vows' was one of their major tricks to rob one of all spontaneity. They led you to believe that one had only to make a vow for it to be fulfilled. Now Benjamin had made a vow, before he came to see me, that he would tell me about his 'thoughts', and their nature, though not their contents in detail. But he had omitted to tell me that they were cruel, vengeful, dirty, obscene and sadistic. He was not going to say any more about them today.

I felt he was being too solemn, so I teased him by asking: 'Is that all that has been bothering you since the consultation? Try and tell me something worthwhile.' He asked: 'For example?' I replied that one thing had puzzled me from his account of himself during the consultation: he had said he was a keen and very good rugby player at school. Yes, he hastily answered, but he had stopped playing rugby because of his 'thoughts'. In a pretend-angry voice I said: 'Damn your "thoughts", give me a chance to ask what I need to know.' I had deliberately avoided the use of the verb 'want', and continued: what had puzzled me was that he was so very lean, of medium height, and rather girlish-prim in his deportment. I was not being sarcastic, so, please, he should not take it wrong. Now I know nothing about rugby as a game, but I have had three very good rugby players as patients: two were six feet three inches tall and very strongly muscled, the third was stocky, of medium height, but all muscle and tussle. Benjamin said impatiently: 'I was exactly like the third one when I was fifteen. It is the "thoughts" that *infringe* upon all I do, or see, or say, that have made me so thin, as if from shame I want to become invisible.' The usage of the verb *infringe*, and what he had said about making himself invisible, not only struck me as insightful, but gave me hope about his future in psychotherapy and living. We rarely talk about the role of hope or dismay in us about our patients. I am not talking about counter-transference here.

As I prepared myself for our third clinical encounter, the last before a long weekend (because of a bank holiday on the Monday), I had to decide which of the dozen half-clues, that I had gleaned from Benjamin's verbal narrative and total behaviour in the analytic setting, I should focus on. Because of the three-day break, I wanted to end the session with a statement that could not be mistaken for an interpretation; and must throw some light on either the functions or the meaning of his 'thoughts'. So I said that when he had used the adjective 'dirty' for his 'thoughts', it was a euphemism for 'shitty'. He left walking rather perkily, not his usual style, as if some burden had lightened in him.

He returned the following Tuesday (fourth session) with a look of glee in his eyes, as if he had scored over someone. He spoke with a little more zest than before, and his idiom of speech was clear-cut and surprisingly apt and versatile for someone who had had no university education. He had told me he read a lot: novels, adventure stories and history books. I had noted that he always came with a book in his hand, as if it was his talisman against some unpredictable dread. He told me that walking home from his local tube station after the last session, for the first time he had noticed a pet shop, and it was open. The pet shop had always been there since they had come to the new house, but he had taken no notice of it before. This time he saw a beautiful black pup, playing with a squash ball, in the window. He went in and asked if the pup was for sale, and the man who owned the shop said yes, stating the price, which was quite expensive because it was a pedigree terrier pup. Benjamin said he would like to buy it and took out his chequebook to pay. The owner, however, hesitated and asked whether he lived in a flat or a house with some sort of a garden. Benjamin told him a house, with a large garden. The man explained that he had asked that question because terriers were small, active dogs, originally bred for hunting animals that live in burrows. They are fun as pets, but do not thrive in flats. They are not difficult to train, and on the whole are tidy dogs, but they do need exercise, and space to run around in; otherwise they develop all sorts of illnesses.

Benjamin said he could manage that. Then the owner gave him the name and address of the local vet who would tell him what injections were necessary, and when. He sold Benjamin the pup, the squash ball, and a bowl to drink from, and gave some basic instructions as to how to train him. When Benjamin arrived home with the pup warmly covered by his coat, and the bowl and ball, his father was sitting reading in the drawing room. He was very amused by Benjamin's new acquisition, but hastened to say: 'Well, son, how are you going to make your mum accept it?' Benjamin said he would keep and train the pup in his room, no matter how small the room was, feed and exercise it himself. They were still talking when his mum arrived home. She was at a loss as to how to react, but was soon issuing instructions about what needed to be done to train the pup and keep the house clean, tidy and unsmelly. Benjamin pointedly added: 'You see how Mum has already started to take over the care and training of the pup.' He had named it Stew, which I felt was both an apt and an ironic name for his surrogate self, remembering that, in slang, the word meant 'agitated state'.

I had not said a word so far. He paused and asked me whether he had been too extravagant in buying the puppy and whether he had done the right thing. I simply replied that, since he had paid for it, he could evidently afford it; as to the right or the wrong of it, all I could tell him was that this was the first positive act towards *self-cure* (Khan, 1974a). I paused, then very casually remarked that it was about time he started to take over some aspects of his mum's protective over-care of him. This he had now done by *adopting* (I chose the verb carefully) Stew, to train and look after; I went on to say that, though I could not be sure, my feeling was that he was going to correct some aspects and features of his mum's tactics of managing the family and the house. That if he had exploited his mum's ways to live a cocooned life at home, he had also paid for it, in so far as he had led a cramped and restricted life. That gradually even the spaces and activities he had opened up and started had begun to close in on him, and he had ended up by capitulating altogether to his mum, and had become *Mum's lad*, in her total care and protection. I considered that to be the primary purpose, and function, of his breakdowns. I continued: 'You have mentioned only two breakdowns: one eight months ago which led to your giving up going to work' – I stressed the act of 'going' – 'and the second when you stopped your psychotherapy with Dr X.' I hinted that I could sense in his developmental processes two more breakdowns before these, and I felt certain there was a fifth, much earlier in his childhood, which would not be too easy to decipher.

He had listened to what I was saying with a rigid impatience, as though I was 'infringing', to use his own phrase about his 'thoughts', on him and his internal psychic space. This was my first attempt at anything like an interpretation. He was over-sensitive and over-perceptive, so had got the message. The trouble with Benjamin was that every response was *over*-something, e.g. over-reactive, over-protective of self and others, etc. He defended himself by protesting that his last breakdown had been brought on by listening to a female member of Dr X's therapy group going on and on about her sexual life; whereas the other members of the group had harshly protested they had heard that stuff from her many times before, his own reaction had been quite different. The 'thoughts' had been triggered off and he had wanted to run out, but had not. Instead he had collapsed on reaching home. Though he felt *bad* about it, there was little he could do to change it.

I had noted his use of the adjective 'bad' in various contexts, where most persons would use the adjective 'guilty', and now told him as much. He asked anxiously: 'Do you really resent my getting Stew?' I replied that, on the contrary, I was rather pleased about it, and that I appreciated how hard it was for him to differentiate, and keep separately in focus, what I feel and how his mum responds or acts. He interjected that buying the puppy was the first thing he had ever done without consulting his mum. I refuted this by saying that his defiant bonhomie, and his somewhat antisocial camaraderie with his school-friends from the age of eleven – that had so disconcerted his mum because he had stayed out late – was his first gesture towards autonomy of personal living. It had been a fruitful respite for five years or so, even though it had ended in a breakdown which had taken the form of giving up sports and socialising.

Benjamin was peeved by what I had said, and again attributed it all to the infringements of his 'thoughts', adding, what had this to do with his poor mum? 'She can't help it, as Dad teases her often. She allows herself no respite from being over-tidy, over-busy and over-caring, all the time. Now that we, the sons, have grown up, she does it with the children she teaches.' I jibed: 'You surprise me. Since when have you grown up?' I terminated the session with that rather unpleasant remark. I did not want to coddle him. This was a calculated risk I was taking, just as a little earlier in this session I had drawn upon Winnicott's (1956) concept of 'antisocial tendency' to characterise the intent of Benjamin's changed conduct and relationship with his mum from the age of eleven.

The two weeks that followed were rather vapid, from the clinical point of view, though in spite of Benjamin's determined and sly defensive stance, a lot of life-material did get said by him, like his being over-concerned about Stew's well-being, especially his safety. Stew was a very active, playful pup, hard to keep restrained in the space of one room and a wooden cot which Benjamin and his girlfriend, Cathy, had made for Stew. I let it be. I am rarely the pacemaker for a patient, in spite of what Green (1976) has written about my work-style, although I do not tolerate clinical stasis easily. It does not matter to me in what area of a patient's life things are dynamic and mutative; they do not need to be so in the space of the clinical setting. I always keep my eyes and ears vigilantly perceptive as to how a patient is moving in life, and by this I do not necessarily mean in terms of acting or doing. 'Lying fallow' (Khan, 1977) and being clinically held and managed in regressive states in analysis are equally dynamic (cf. Little, 1985).

Regression to inertia in militant negative self-care, which is a negation of self-cure, is as damaging as it is wasteful of life. In Benjamin, such regressive moods were expressed through his 'thoughts', which Winnicott (1971c) conceptualises as fantasying, and which is the death of psychic life, causing a global arrest of developmental living, loving and hating. Self-cure is a concept I have introduced (1974a), and with which I believe each and all of us, in one way or another, are preoccupied at certain crucial stages of growth and change in our lives: at the oedipal stage, à la Freud (1905a), at puberty and adolescence, à la Erikson (1950), and at maturity, i.e., in our forties and fifties, if we reach there live and vibrant and are not corseted by those private rituals and habits that deny us the increment of experiences which only shared and mutual living with others can yield. This is especially true of the clinical work of therapists, where usage of conceptual dogma can replace empirical relating to a patient.

To return to Benjamin's fated existence so far, on one score I had no doubts at all: that his mum was as diligently over-caring as she was incapable of mutuality and playfulness. These features in her character had led to his 'love of hate' in childhood, awaiting, if not soliciting, damaging intrusions which he now called 'infringements' by his 'thoughts', which Winnicott (1960b) has labelled 'impingements', and which I believe lead to cumulative trauma, or to *cumulative deprivation*. I am stating the notion of cumulative deprivation for the first time here, and I rigorously differentiate it from the concept of deprivation as defined and used both by Winnicott (1984) and Bowlby (1969). In this context, even though I am anticipating from what accrued from later phases of clinical work with Benjamin, I want to postulate that I consider 'love of hate' in a child as resulting from his responses to the mother's (unconscious) hate of the child, which has the alibis of over-protection and over-care of that child. To anticipate further from later clinical understanding of Benjamin's 'thoughts' and vagaries of conduct, I am offering the hypothesis that during puberty and adolescence, there is an attempt to rectify these 'love of hate' attachments by the person, and to reverse the equation 'love of hate' to that of 'hate of love', which is equally damaging to living and growth.

I shall now curtail my clinical narrative and present only such material as is relevant to some understanding of my hypothesis that Benjamin's 'thoughts' had the intent and function of 'hate of love', which was his developmental and maturational gain as a move away from 'love of hate' resulting from his relation to his mum. Benjamin had arrived for his tenth session, that is, some three weeks after starting therapy with me, shaking and very frightened. For once he was also very late for his session. He eruptively told me, not his usual style, that he was late because of a terrible accident at home. Stew had grown rapidly, and was almost unmanageably playful, romping all over the house, no matter how hard Benjamin tried to keep him in his room, letting him go berserk only in the garden. That day, as Benjamin was getting ready to come to his session, Stew had sneaked out of his room, run into the sitting room and, after making a small puddle, had settled down in front of the fire. Benjamin was aghast at what Stew had done and instantly mopped up the puddle and cleaned the carpet with an antiseptic detergent, but it had left a wet patch on the carpet. He said most nervously and tautly: 'Mum will be home before I return, and God alone knows what she will do to poor Stew, because she will know immediately he has done it. I nearly did not come for the session today, but then thought you might be able to tell me some way how Stew could be protected from Mum's rage.' I kept quiet for a while and then said: 'You know, Benjamin, sometimes it is very curative to get the Other, be it a person or a pet, to do what one has never had the scope, space or possibility of doing oneself.' He looked rather dismayed, and said in a hippie, colloquial way that I could afford to be very cool and facetious about the terrible accident because I would not have to cope with his mum's rage. I laughed. He relaxed and said: 'Well, Dad and I will have to cope with whatever Mum gets up to. Most probably she will shampoo the whole carpet and it is a big one. So no TV tonight, and Dad will have to go to his room to read and relax. Dad works so hard and then to return to this . . . I feel very bad about it.' I left it at that and let him depart early.

Mum had done exactly what Benjamin had anticipated, to his dad's overt amusement. For the next two weeks the clinical material was mostly about soiling by children, and how Mum could tolerate that in other children but had taken every care to ensure that her sons did not make a mess of any sort. During these weeks, out of the blue and for the first time, Benjamin's older brother invited him to stay the whole weekend with him in his City flat, which he called his 'pad' as it had only one large room, a bathroom and a kitchenette. Cathy had agreed to take Stew to her home for the weekend and Mum, too, thought it was a good thing for Benjamin to go. He was rather taken aback by that. He went. His brother had put a mattress on the floor for him to sleep on. It was his first long, three-day weekend away from home in some twenty-three years. There he had a dream which he remembered. He always dreamt, he said, but never remembered his dreams. I interjected: 'It helps to have someone to tell them to.' He disregarded my remark, and continued that he would not be able to tell me the dream because his 'thoughts' had infringed upon it. I somewhat reassured him by saying: 'Benjamin, don't you think it is one step more towards health and getting back into living and working, that you have added a new psychic space to your self-experience, namely the dream-space? (Pontalis, 1972). Now "thoughts" will no longer happen exclusively in your head-space because of the availability of the dream-space. Surely that must be a relief.' He taunted me by saying I was very clever, and could get round everything. As a 'reward', however, he offered to tell me the dream:

He has returned home from his brother and rushes up to his room to see how Stew is doing. There is no Stew to be found, only shit everywhere.

He had woken up in terror and panic. He had rung Cathy to find out how Stew was, dreading that he had been run over and wounded. Cathy had answered sleepily, because it was five o'clock on a Sunday morning, and told him Stew was sleeping by her side, quite safe and peacefully. I stayed silent. He asked me what the dream meant. I should know, I was an analyst, he said. I replied, first, that it was hardly a dream, because I was sure he had this dread about Stew being run over by a car or a motor-cycle in the street, which is why he never took him out of the house for a walk. The garden was a safe place and the damage Stew did was only to Mum's plants and flowers. Second, I said I had a strong impression that the dream content had a *real* memory behind it, of something that had either happened in his childhood, or which he was told about. Benjamin was quite astonished and narrated a horrific story his elder brother had told him when he was six years old. His brother had read in the local paper that a man had raped a boy of five years of age, or even younger, cut off his genitals, strangled him, and smeared shit all over his body. The whole town was terrified by this happening, and the police were still looking for the rapist-killer (his word). Since hearing this story from his elder brother, Benjamin had become over-protective, like his mum, about his three-years-younger brother and made sure he fetched him from school himself. Mum would take him to the kindergarten, but she returned home too late to collect him. Benjamin paused thoughtfully. I waited to hear what else he had to say. He said it was very strange that it had never occurred to him that such a horrible thing could have happened to him, too, since he used to loiter outside his old house, which was on the edge of the city common, till quite late, even if it got dark, waiting for his mum to return. Dad would be with the younger brother inside the house. At this point I chose to give a third interpretation of his dream. Drawing upon the material from the session in which he had reported 'the terrible accident' at home, I said: 'Benjamin, talking about your mum's possible reactions to Stew making a mess on the carpet, you expressed dread about her rage regarding the mess. I think you were dreading more that she would shift from her over-protective care of Stew to hating him, which would kill him. That is certainly part of the dreaming experience, which stayed unacknowledged by you (Khan, 1976a). Your phone call to Cathy, asking how Stew was, and your dreaming that dream, when both you and Stew were safely out of reach from Mum's hate, confirms for me what I have "read" in the unstated dream-text.'

We covered a lot of ground, clinically, in the weeks following the dream, but most of that material is not relevant to the theme of this chapter. So I move forward several months to the last session before the Christmas break of thirteen days. Benjamin had arrived looking both apprehensive and concerned. He told me he had received a letter from the director of his firm, stating categorically that if he did not return to work on the second of January, he would be told to resign. He asked me: 'Do you think I can go back to work then?' I unhesitatingly answered: 'I see no reason why not, unless you make it into a *vow*, then you won't.' I acknowledged the risk entailed both for him and Stew, for different reasons. I stressed the fact that at the age of eleven, when he had moved to the new house, he had taken the risk of staying out late with his friends, and it had paid dividends. He had become strong physically, and good at sports. I added that I could not tell, as yet, why he had got such acute acne and was then invalided by his 'thoughts'. He asked: 'Don't you believe in physical illnesses?' I said I certainly did, but only up to a point; that from my clinical experience I knew acne to have very large psychic and emotional ingredients in its aetiology. What they were in his case, I should get to know only slowly. For the present, the important issue to talk about was how he could spend his Christmas break positively. He asked: 'Do you have any suggestions? Certainly both my brothers will come and Mum will undoubtedly find one or two young children to take care of at home, for one reason or another. So it will be a full house.' I thought carefully and said: 'You have told me your elder brother never stays at home, and your younger brother will certainly go abroad after Christmas. Then why don't you go over with Stew and stay at Cathy's house?' He said: 'That is a good idea, especially this year, because her parents are going abroad and she is coming to stay with us for Christmas.' I said I was available to him at home should he get into a mess with himself and at that point I ended the session, wished him a happy, uncaring Christmas, and thus we parted company.

PHASE TWO

Benjamin rang me on New Year's Day and told me he had decided to return to work the next day, so could I kindly change the times of his sessions. I said I could see him at 7.00 p.m. on Mondays, Wednesdays and Fridays. He accepted that and arrived punctually for his session, looking grey and exhausted, but not nervous or resentful. He said he had got through the day all right, and while waiting to come to the session, after work, had rung home to find out how Stew had fared. Dad had answered and said: 'As you can well imagine, son, Mum has taken care of everything.' Mum had talked to their neighbour, who was an elderly lady, living alone, and had someone to come every day to clean the house, buy and prepare the food; she was delighted to have Stew every weekday while Benjamin was at work. He said he didn't think he had told me that he lived a long way, some twenty miles, from my place, and an even longer distance from where he worked in the City, which was thirty miles away. But there was a direct nonstop tube-train from his district to where I lived and where he worked. Even so, he had had to get up at 7.00 a.m. that day. Mum had already got breakfast ready for him and the food for Stew. He had gulped his breakfast, spent fifteen minutes or more with Stew in the garden, and then rushed to catch the fast, direct tube-train at 8.00 a.m. This is why he was looking exhausted. Since Benjamin had never, as yet, talked about his work and the other persons there, I asked: 'How about things at work?' He said he was most surprised by how pleased everyone was to see him; even the director had sent for him to ask how he was, and to say that he was glad Benjamin was back and hoped he would stay well.

I was again marking time since I was not quite clear in my own self as to how to orientate his psychotherapy henceforth, in view of the rather sudden change in his life-style. I had thought a lot, since he had told me that he was returning to work, and three features stood out clearly, from what had been said between us and what had been happening at home and in my clinical space and setting:

1. There was a sharp and definite dissociation, in both his memories and activities, from infancy to the age of eleven, when the family had moved house, and his life since then. Except for remembering the story told by his brother when he was six, and his over-concern about his younger brother's safety until they moved house, Benjamin recalled very little from those early years. By contrast, he remembered everything vividly and exactly from the age of eleven onwards, even if he couldn't tell most of it. So the clinical task for me was to *construct* (Freud, 1937) the dominant and fateful aspects of his experiences from maternal over-care and the resultant stance of living in those years. I had surmised, from the little he had told me, that he had been a tidy and compliant infant and child. What was I to do: ask to see his mother because I needed to know about her relationship with him in those years, and his life at the kindergarten, which was run by her, and where all three sons had gone from the age of three to six years? I felt sure that unless I had a reliable knowledge of this, I would not be able to help Benjamin hold down his job. But I did not want to meet his mother because she would instantly trap me in her spider's web of over-care of Benjamin, which had engulfed Stew now, as well.

2. There was little doubt that Benjamin was very able and efficient at work, but he was clearly not indispensable to his employers. Also, at that time all companies, even the governmental institutions, were shedding staff because of the monstrous inflation in England. Yet Benjamin's job had been kept open for him to return to, even over such a long period as nearly a year. Furthermore, he had been paid his full salary for the first three months of absence, and half thereafter. In

addition, the company had paid, and would continue to pay, half his medical expenses (including psychotherapy, which was rare in England). The other half of his analytic fees was paid by his parents, who were fairly well-off now. So there must be some special qualities in Benjamin for him to receive such privileged treatment from his employers. What they were, I had no clue.

3. Except for mentioning his late nights out with his buddies, with none of whom he seemed to have become intimate friends, from eleven to fifteen years of age, I had heard nothing of any relationships at work. Cathy had been his only steady and intimate friend for the past two years, and the credit for that went to Cathy, who was Benjamin's age, came from a rich family, was an independent girl who worked hard, was good at sports, and had her parents' backing in everything she did. She had her own car and her parents were liberal. I have referred to Benjamin and Cathy as friends rather than as lovers because the little he had told me about his life, and their relationship, suggested that there was hardly any love or sex in it. He was deeply attached to her, and she alone stood up to his mother. She had her girlfriends, so was not dependent on Benjamin for company. She was really in love with him, but made no demands. She grasped the fact that he was an ill youth, and accepted him as such. In short, she was a most wholesome, uncomplicated and beautiful girl; Benjamin had shown me her photograph. Her parents had also accepted Benjamin unconditionally, and would leave the two alone, unlike his mother at his own house. Well, no girl is an angel, so there must be something in Benjamin that was so valuable that Cathy was willing to wait until he could share himself fully. What it was I did not know, and I do not think Benjamin did either. He had a strange capacity to live in a transparent *un*-knowing of himself, in spite of the haunting infringements of his 'thoughts' and his insights into their role in his relationships. He knew how to suffer himself without knowingly burdening anyone. This quality in him I had seen and experienced in our clinical relating. But all this gave no real insight into what had rendered him so sick, since childhood. My fear was that Benjamin might use returning to work as an operational alibi for shirking an authentic confrontation with himself.

Winnicott (1960a) has written, most perspicaciously and insightfully, about the dissociation between the 'true' and the 'false' self in a person. For myself, I have great misgivings about the usage of the adjectives 'true' and 'false', as mentioned earlier; and, when I was editing Winnicott's psychoanalytic writings, I had always questioned the verity and wisdom of their usage with him. However, neither of us had succeeded in finding any suitable alternatives. Personally, I prefer to use the adjective 'authentic' instead of 'true' and 'reactive' for 'false'.

As to the concept 'self', even that has gained currency only in the past two decades; and those two exigent pundits of *The Language of Psycho-Analysis* (1967), Laplanche and Pontalis, have not bestowed the status of a metapsychological concept on the nouns 'love', 'hate' and 'self' – which are clinically the source, as well as the raw material, of almost any psychotherapeutic work. One cannot find a more profound, sympathetic or comprehensive discussion of the concept of 'self' than in Pontalis's article 'The birth and recognition of self' (1975a), where even in his French text the English word 'self' is used, for the simple reason that there is no French equivalent.

In treating the predicament of a person like Benjamin, one cannot avoid or escape using the concept of 'self'. To substitute for it the metapsychological concept of 'the ego' is to curtail our clinical work, thinking and vision. For 'love of hate' and 'hate of love' are not the vicissitudes of ego-experiences and developmental functions, but are experiences that relate to and from the self, from its early beginnings to its adult status in and of a person. Even Erikson's (1959) concept of 'identity' is lacking in the scope and range covered by the concept of 'self'. Incidentally, Pontalis and Laplanche allow neither space nor use for the concept of 'identity': yet no treatment of an adolescent is viable without clinical exploration of the experiences of identity-formation.

Before I return to Benjamin and our work together, I would like to make one distinction explicit for the purposes of my clinical and theatrical narrative here. For me, 'love of hate' is *not* masochism, just as 'hate of love' is *not* sadism. The concepts of masochism and sadism belong to the psychosexual interplay of id and ego, ego-ideal and superego (Chasseguet-Smirgel, 1975), in the maturational and developmental processes of a person's growth, and though they are crucially significant in themselves, they constitute only a part of the total self-experience of a person.

Once Benjamin started to go to work, the concentration and momentum of the clinical work and relating dispersed and became patchy and random, for some five weeks oscillating between mere chatter about his external life in general and about Cathy and her parents in particular. One could have treated this as resistance and aggressive negativity, in so far as it rendered the clinical material generally nonsensical. I am of Bion's (1967) persuasion when he states: 'I never believe anything unless it is *non sense*.'

Benjamin had added two more experiental spaces to that of home-life and the analytic setting, namely that of the working-space and the sports club. There was a good sports club in his district, within a long walking distance from his house. He had become a member of it when he was eighteen, but had given it up when he was twenty, when his perverted sexual 'thoughts' had begun to intrude on anything spontaneous or enjoyable that he did, rendering it cruel or sadistic. This had led to an intolerable increment of feeling 'bad' (his word) and the consequent alienation, resulting from his gradual regressive refusal of friendship from others, that had restricted his life to Mum's protective over-care at home. An ironic fact to note here is that he had met Cathy at this club during his last weeks there. Cathy was a very sportive girl. At the end of his first week back at work, Benjamin had gone to the sports club with Cathy and renewed his membership. Even at some cost to the clinical situation, I was rather pleased that he had opened out towards life and external spaces, instead of fretting in his head-space.

I have said that my initial impression of Benjamin was that of a precocious pervert *manqué*. Chasseguet-Smirgel (1984) neatly describes 'perverse' ways of thinking as: 'Thinking that is the enemy'. I consider that this sort of thinking derives more from a sense of *sin*, leading to alienation, than from a sense of *guilt* (Menninger, 1973), and is more closely related to a pathological and precocious development of the ego-ideal than a severe superego (Khan, 1964). Though our clinical relating was diffused by Benjamin's new activities, I kept my private dossier of clues, from his spoken and unsaid account, alive in my memory. It is much more difficult, as well as treacherous, to remember in what contexts a patient has *not* talked about something than to record, memory-wise, the debris of the spoken data. Furthermore, I was convinced that with Benjamin it was well-nigh impossible to get material from actual memories of childhood, or from his mother's account of it, in order to truly decipher what had led to his 'love of hate' relationship between *them*. I am emphatically saying *them*: the love and hate being in both Benjamin and his mother, alternating in various contexts and roles and leading to the *as-if* type of character he had developed.

The difficulty in making sense of experiential data in an adult patient is that one cannot compel early recollections with ad hoc interpretations because, while these may convince us, and our patients accept them all too gratefully, this only repeats the complicity, in the here and now of the transference relating, which was experienced with the mother in infancy-childhood, and of which our patients would have been but haphazardly aware.

So the only clinical recourse left was *construction* which, being derived from the symbolic potential of Benjamin's otherwise high 'mentalised' (a word of my clinical coverage) narrative, would be both tentative and labile. I distinguish the psychic, the mental and the imaginative as qualitatively different from each other. All of de Sade's perverted writings are lacking in the psychic and imaginative dimensions, hence their ridiculous charades of cruelty that have no objective correlatives in reality. This is true of all pornographic writings, from de Sade to the 'confessional' letters in *Playboy* magazine (Khan, 1972). Hence, there is no love in de Sade's narratives of sexual or sensual relating and actions by his characters, only 'love of hate' by the victim and 'hate of love' by the perpetrators of those atrocities. The most telling example of this is de Sade's novel *Justine or Good Conduct Well Chastised* (originally called *Les Infortunes de la Vertu* but retitled to facilitate publication). Justine is the victim, her virtue being never to learn from her *vécu*, and thus she remains in a perpetual state of grace and innocence. In each episode she seeks 'protection' (which is, in fact, an unacknowledged complicity on her part), and over-care, from those who would not fail to sexually victimise her. This is her 'love of hate'.

Where Benjamin was concerned, I had noticed how he felt 'bad' when he had both enlarged the scope and breadth, as well as the amplitude of intensity, of his 'thoughts'. Fortunately for him, he never found an accomplice, and Cathy, once she came into his life, became his 'companion' but not his accomplice-keeper. The incidents and activities of these five weeks revealed the character of his relationship to his mother, to himself, and anyone he could feel for, and of others to him, and helped me to mutatively change my relating with him, clinically and otherwise.

It was towards the end of the second week that Cathy had come over to see the film *Lawrence of Arabia* on television. For a change he, Cathy, Mum and Dad were all watching television together. Mum could not sit still for more than a few minutes. She had to do something, for each and all of them, pour drinks or serve coffee, take away empty glasses and cups, offer snacks, etc. It was not possible for anyone to get deeply absorbed in the film. Dad and Benjamin said nothing, but Cathy could not take it any more. She got up and suggested to Benjamin that he should come and watch it on the television in her bedroom at home; unfortunately, the television with the large screen was not working that night. Benjamin, for the first time, left with Cathy without asking Mum or offering an apology. Since the film ended rather late and it was snowing, he stayed the night with her. They had breakfast together next morning and left for their respective jobs.

When Benjamin had finished telling me this, I do not know why, but I asked him to describe both Cathy's house and his. He told me, briefly and laconically, that Cathy's was a two-storeyed house, with a large sitting room, dining room and toilet on the ground floor and three bedrooms, all large ones, on the second floor. It was a tastefully furnished house. His own, he described as a large, three-storey house. The ground floor had a very big sitting room and a large kitchen, but no dining room as such, and a toilet. On the first floor was Dad's bedroom, which was also his study, Mum's room, where she slept and did all her leftover school work such as correcting essays, a guest room, and a bathroom. The third floor had three bedrooms – Benjamin's and those of his brothers – and another bathroom. His was the smallest room, in which there was a single bed, writing table and chair, a wardrobe with a full-size mirror and now, of course, Stew's wooden box as well. Hardly room to move around freely, and if Cathy or either of the brothers came into his room, one of them had to sit on the bed. So when Cathy came, they would sit or lie together on this narrow bed, and Mum was forever checking up on them under the guise of offering coffee and collecting the empty cups. No time was allowed for them to be intimate and relaxed, even in an ordinary way.

At this point I stopped him and asked if his brothers' rooms were larger. Benjamin said yes, and his older brother's room was the largest but he had not been using it for some years now, though a few of his belongings were still there. I told him, bluntly, that so long as he did not have a spacious room, private to himself, he would live fugitively, and peripatetically, for a few hours every day, either at work or at the sports club. I deliberately did not include Cathy's space, which was always available to him. I continued, rather vigorously, that I did not feel I could do much more for him clinically unless he changed his living space, and moved into his older brother's room, with the brother's consent, of course. He said his brother would consent, but Mum would not. I categorically asserted that he should ask her, and if she hedged or refused, he could tell her and his dad that I had asked him to move to another, bigger room. He was most nervous, and at first he tried to hedge and tarry, saying it needed new wallpaper, etc. I stayed adamant, and said that many of my young patients, from rich and upper-class families, had wallpapered their own bedrooms and studies. It made the room more *theirs*. I added, 'You are quite strong and are now body-building at the sports club, so you can do it.'

Benjamin arrived for the next session looking sheepish. To his utter surprise, Mum had agreed all too readily and given the necessary advice as to where to buy the paint, paper and brushes cheaply. He had hedged with her also, saying that he had no time during the week and that the paint shop was too crowded on Saturdays, and he could not stand crowds. So it would have to wait until the Easter break. However, he had returned home to find that Mum had measured the walls of the room, and bought quite a pleasant plain wallpaper and the necessary equipment to do the work. He told me this with a sly smile, because I had made two conditions for his asking for a larger room: one, that he should prepare it himself and furnish it with his own money; and two, that Stew should now sleep in the shed in the garden, where Benjamin could put a heater in cold weather. He remarked that when he had mentioned it to Cathy on the phone, she had said they could wallpaper the room together over the next weekend.

I had already noted the mother's tactics of adaptive complicity and manipulation, ensuring Benjamin's passivity and dependent attachment. I was sure he would start doing things to the room but would take a long time getting it finished, and this would provide me with ample data to 'construct' how he and his mother had colluded, from infancy and childhood, through that mutual complicity of relating which had led to his 'Divided Self' ('splitting' is the accepted analytical concept), and the resultant surrender to 'love of hate' in him that had expressed itself as compliance in childhood and, after his breakdowns, most noticeably in his robot-like style of dress (Ferenczi, 1932; Winnicott, 1960a).

I had suggested to Benjamin that he felt he had to inhabit his own body before he could become his own person (cf Winnicott, 1972), and that his sporting activities were a way of achieving this. It is significant to note that, having rejoined the sports club, he started with gymnastics, weight-lifting and squash before he could reach the capacity to play in competitive games again (Winnicott, 1971b). During this phase, his organised and calculated secretiveness had three features in so far as I could tell:

1. He was private, and could do what he pleased, and as little or as much as he wished and could manage.
2. Talking of playing squash, he explained that he was not playing a game *with* anyone yet. 'Not even Cathy, though she plays quite well for a girl' – I noticed the qualifying phrase. He was practising the angles of the services, and the long and double-sided drop shots. He had been the best squash player amongst his friends; amazing how quickly it had all come back to him. It was a very fast and tiring game, so fifteen minutes was enough. He did not have much time to spare now that he was working.

    I made a mental note of two facts: (a) he had very high expectations of performance from himself; (b) he must be a bad loser. He had to win the game. By playing alone, hard, both issues could be avoided. Here we see two different dispensations of aggression. In private play and practice, he was using aggression to strengthen and 'perfect' himself. In playing against a live opponent, overt aggression is entailed, which can and often does reach the point of 'hating' the opponent in order to meet the challenge and to win, and thus retain self-esteem. Only when a player can work up to this pitch of aggressiveness, can he give of his best. And, as Pontalis et al (1986) shrewdly and rhetorically ask: 'Hate – does it not demand permanence of its object?' Benjamin had the 'knowing' of that, but not its explicit conscious acceptance.
3. In my clinical assessment of the material from these weeks of sportive release and actualisation of the autonomous id-ego

functions, and establishing the core of an authentic personal selfhood, I had little doubt that Benjamin had a real dread of *destroying* his object (the opponent) in playing, which is quite different from defeating or being defeated. The latter two vagaries of 'playing' do not carry the intent to kill and destroy. Quite a few times, whilst talking of playing backgammon with Cathy, Benjamin remarked ruefully that the reason he lost the game so often was because he enjoyed 'killing' (his word for 'taking' her pieces), rather than playing to win. Similarly, by hitting the ball against the wall of the squash court as hard and as viciously as he desired, he could – at least in his fantasy – kill an opponent and then the play and the game would be over for good.

From the material of the third phase of Benjamin's analysis, by which time he could trust to tell me the contents of his 'thoughts' without fearing that even the telling of them would kill me (such is the lethal unconscious omnipotence of both love and hate), it became evident that these merely whetted his appetite for destroying the object and so were a sort of internal protective-shield to safeguard both the object and his own self from being killed and destroyed. Inter-personally and intra-psychically the hated object must be kept alive. So all the macabre cruelties, 'shitty' practices and sadistic intents of his sexual 'thoughts' were an outlet for that amplitude of hate and aggression that, in lived life, could endanger both him and the object.

From the second phase of Benjamin's psychotherapy, I shall single out one more event that proved most helpful for his future treatment. Cathy's father was the owner-director of a group of companies which flew tourists, at cheap rate, all over Europe. In winter it was skiing that attracted most tourists, especially the young ones. Cathy's parents were expert skiers, and she had been skiing since the age of six; as with all other sports, she both enjoyed it and was good at it. So in February, some nine weeks after Benjamin had started to work and play again, Cathy's father offered them free tickets and hotel accommodation *together* in an Austrian ski-resort for ten days. At first, Benjamin was both fearful and phobic. His reasoning was that he had never skied, and it would mean spending a lot of money on skiing clothes and equipment. I knew perfectly well that what daunted and frightened him was the long period of ten days of guaranteed togetherness and intimacy with Cathy. There would be no Mum around to *infringe* with her care-taking manoeuvres, and so his alibi that she was the spoilsport in every ongoing activity at home, or with Cathy, would become inoperative. I took a militant stand, and here was sponsored by his father, who offered to pay half the cost of his trip, clothes and all, and I said I would not charge my fees. Benjamin tried another ruse: he had been back at work for some nine weeks only, and to go away on holiday would be considered an irresponsible act on his part, and the director would not allow it. I said he could bargain: namely, that if they allowed him ten days' leave of absence now, he would work right through Easter and the two May bank holidays, when they were always short of staff. Furthermore, I told him he could use my name, and say that I considered it psychotherapeutically imperative, at this stage, for him to risk such a venture. I added, quite unabashedly, though not boastfully, that what I dictated as necessary from a clinical viewpoint, based on judgement and experience, had so far never been challenged by anyone. To his chagrin, even his mother stayed neutral and was helpful in getting him ready to leave for the skiing holiday, even though she did not positively sponsor the venture.

I noticed that Benjamin was not anxious or worried that he might hurt himself from lack of skill and experience in skiing. I felt he was more concerned that he would be in the young learners' group, whilst Cathy would romp at large with the adult and skilful skiers. Here, being shamed played a big role in Benjamin's anxiety. I reassured him by saying that it would surely be fun to be in the 'skiing kindergarten', starting to learn something fresh, from scratch, and personal initiative, and without any internal unstated demands marking his progress. That one enjoys most what one learns without any strings attached as to the results from the learning-performance. He and Cathy left quite happily together for their skiing escapade.

PHASE THREE

Benjamin had sent me a card from the ski resort to tell me that he and Cathy were enjoying the totally white and bare landscape, and that skiing was fun. This card was important to me for three reasons: I was relieved to know he had kept me alive as a *good* internal object; that he could begin to learn and try new experiences again (skiing); and that he had not surrendered to his 'thoughts' – his patent technique of splitting his ego, distancing himself from the loving object (Cathy in this case) – and so was *containing* his 'hate of love', intra-psychically as well as inter-personally. The reader may well ask: how did I draw such conclusions from some fifty words on a postcard? The fact is that Benjamin was one of those patients whom one rarely encounters in clinical work; because of their docile negativity, they are deemed unsuitable for analysis and the 'working alliance' a la Freud (1940a). They threaten us, often without our realising it, in our self-experience. Only a Ferenczi (1932) could take the sort of risks which the psychotherapy of such patients entails.

Benjamin's material from the second phase, most of it just fragmented memories, overt, covert and subliminal, was acutely registered by me, and had made me reorientate my thinking once again. I no longer considered the cumulative deprivation in him, from infancy-childhood, as entirely the result of traumatogenic exogenous behaviour by, and infringements from the character of, his mother. Even infants are not totally helpless and innocent victims of external 'maltreatment', be it severity in toilet-training or lack of touch and warmth from the mother, who in many ways is 'good-enough' (Winnicott, 1960a). Fairbairn (1944), who has made pertinent contributions in this area, has written:

It is the experience of libidinal frustration that calls forth the infant's aggression in relation to his libidinal object and this gives rise to a state of ambivalence . . . From the point of view of the infant himself, it is a case of his mother becoming an ambivalent object, i.e., an object that is both good and bad. Since it proves intolerable to him to have a good object which is also bad, he seeks to alleviate the situation by splitting the figure of his mother into two objects. Then, in so far as she satisfies him libidinally, she is a 'good' object, and, in so far as she fails him libidinally, she is a 'bad' object . . . he does his best to transfer the traumatic factor in the situation to the field of inner reality, within which he feels situations to be more under his own control. This means he internalises his mother as a 'bad' object . . . in my opinion, it is always the 'bad' object (i.e., at this stage the unsatisfying object) that is internalised in the first instance . . .

Ferenczi (1932) who, at the end of his life, opened up new vistas on the role of seduction, has postulated: '. . . the weak and undeveloped personality reacts to sudden unpleasure not by defence, but by anxiety-ridden identification and by introjection of the menacing person or aggressor'. Fairbairn goes on to hypothesise: '. . . in the internalisation of objects there is a measure of coercion, and it is not the satisfying object but the unsatisfying object the infant seeks to coerce . . . the essential "badness" of the unsatisfying object consists precisely in the fact that it combines allurement with frustration.'

Even though Laplanche and Pontalis (1967) give us a useful summary of the concept of 'object-relation(ship)', they disregard Fairbairn's contributions in this context. Fairbairn's emphasis on 'coercion' of the 'bad object' was most helpful to me in understanding the cruel and sadistic features in Benjamin's 'thoughts'. What Fairbairn conceptualises as the role of the libidinally satisfying and frustrating primary object, has been discussed in classical theory through the concept of 'seduction'. Pontalis and Laplanche give a detailed and lucidly itemised account of the vicissitudes of the 'seduction theory', both in Freud's writings and those of his followers, when *actual* exogenous 'sexual seductions' told by patients in their analyses were no longer credited as factual, but as *phantasies*, i.e., as psychic artefacts. Freud himself considered the revision of his seduction theory as a landmark that initiated his true psychological exploration of the patient's psychic reality, on a par with his insights adumbrated in *The Interpretation of Dreams* (1900) and *Three Essays on the Theory of Sexuality* (1905a). One cannot find a more detailed and enlightening discussion of the role of Freud's self-analysis in this discovery than that of Anzieu (1975). For a most insightful critique of the revision of the seduction theory, from an *actual* experience in childhood to fantasies later fabricated by patients, one has to read Masson (1984), editor-translator of *The Complete Letters of Sigmund Freud to Wilhelm Fliess*, 1887–1904 (1985). Masson spells out the duplicities, prevarications, accusations and hypocritical pseudo-acceptance of Ferenczi's (1932) paper by Freud, Eitingon, Jones et al with a relentless authenticity and factual documentation.

I had given up thinking of 'seduction' in infancy as an overtly cruel – sexual and aggressive – or deviously contrived act by an adult when I wrote my paper 'The concept of cumulative trauma' (1963), even though I was not fully aware of my rebuttal of the central role attributed to the seduction theory in both its variants, that is, as fact or phantasy, in the aetiology of neuroses, etc. Now I use the term 'seduction' in its ordinary Anglo-American definition: 'something that entices or influences by attraction or charm' (*Webster's Third International Dictionary*); 'an allurement to some course of action, seductiveness, seductive quality' (*Oxford English Dictionary*). And I consider 'seduction' as the primary nutrient in any mother-infant relationship (and it is mutual), releasing both the maturational and developmental processes in the infant-child which eventuate in those endopsychic structures that Freud (1940a) has conceptualised as the id, the ego, the superego and the ego-ideal.

In my clinical work with Benjamin I was also guided, in a creative way, by Paul Schilder's (1935) concept of the body-ego, and by the research and writings of Winnicott (1931, 1945, 1960a, 1972), Spitz (1959, 1962), Anzieu (1974, 1975, 1985) and Stoller (1985). 'Seduction' is no longer, in my clinical reckoning, an experience limited to body-orifices, breast and penis, but encompasses the myriad infinitesimal experiences of the infant's whole body-ego, both internal and external. That exogenous, traumatogenic experiences arising from the moods, character and handling of the mother, as well as such chance events as physical illness or deformity, can be fateful and distort both the maturational and developmental processes, is an inevitable hazard all of us have been exposed to and suffered from (cf Winnicott's [1971a] most moving account of his consultation with a child who did not speak English). It is either the grave intensity of one event (and I do not fully credit that) or – more likely – it is cumulative trauma, cumulative seduction and cumulative deprivation that play the mutative role in developmental arrest or its normal fructification.

I will conclude this case history with a resumé of some twenty-four weeks of clinical work with Benjamin, our longest period of working together, leading up to a long summer break, of which I had informed him at the start of his psychotherapy.

In the last session before Benjamin departed for his skiing holiday, I had noticed a pimple on his otherwise very smooth, soft face. I could not help relating it to his acne at fifteen, and to his first-ever separation for ten days from his mum *and* in the company of a girlfriend, who would be sharing his room. Benjamin returned from Austria barely tanned from exposure to sun and snow, since he had a fair skin, and his face was pimpled all over. To ease him into relating with me again, since he looked so taut, I asked good-humouredly: 'What in God's name have you been doing to your skin, Benjamin?' He told me he had consulted a doctor in Austria, who had said it was due to some allergy from the hot-house plants in his hotel room, and had prescribed tablets and a cream to use. He reassured me by adding: 'They will clear up soon.' 'Of course they will, Benjamin, now that you are back safely in Mum's care and keeping.' He changed the subject and said: 'Do you know what Mum has been up to, while I was away? She has wallpapered the whole room and got me a larger bed and an extra armchair.' He added sardonically: 'Mum certainly listens to you.' I hit back by saying: 'Of course she does, and would, because I have no vested interest in your room.'

I told him that what was more important for us to work on was the way he had left it to her to complete the job of furnishing the room. He shuffled in his chair uncomfortably, and changed the subject again, saying that, even in the overcrowded jumbo-jet where they were packed like sardines in a tin, he had not got frightened, nor did his 'thoughts' infringe upon him. That at the skiing resort Cathy was soon socialising with everyone, but this had not made him bashful (his word) or retreat into himself. In fact, he had enjoyed the company of boys much younger than himself in the learners' class. He laughed and said: 'We English behave so differently abroad. All the girls, including Cathy, did not wear bras when they dined and danced in the evenings.' He added, as it were, a footnote to this remark, to preserve his innocence: 'Girls can be as bawdy in their jokes as boys'; that he could not join in that sort of salacious bantering. Cathy had teased him all the time on this score, and each day would recount some 'dirty' joke she had heard while skiing.

From here we moved on to talk about how children touch themselves, and each other. He cut in with the information that not only had his mum not allowed pets in the house, because children catch allergies from them, but also that he and his brothers were not allowed to keep their hands in the pockets of their shorts, even when it was cold. I had learned, by now, that one tactic Benjamin always used to stop a topic that had emerged, by chance, and I had picked up to comment upon, was to give me a little more information, and then 'fold in' upon himself. I did not let him this time, and said I could not know about that; but what had stopped him touching himself when he was eleven years old and after? He did not like this sort of infringement, by conversation, on his head-space.

We battled it out during the following weeks. His one trick to avoid masturbation was to exhaust himself totally, through sports. His body was never relaxed and 'lying fallow' (Khan, 1977), thus providing that *potential space*, à la Winnicott (1971b), from where alone pleasurable autoerotic fantasies and experiences can be initiated. I told him as much, and moved on, in the following weeks, to show him how he had distributed aggression intra-psychically and inter-personally, first by turning it upon himself, and had become a passive, compliant child, safe from his mum's severity. Thus he had cultivated 'love of hate' in his relationship with his mother. I explicitly said that severity in a parent often masks hate; that this was the reason why the horrific story of sexual assault on, and murder of, a child had so obsessed him since hearing it from his brother. He was more identified with the 'rapist' than the raped one, hence his over-protective attitude towards his younger brother. During puberty and adolescence, his aggression was deployed in the service of a narcissistic ego-ideal, to make himself strong and perfect, hence his sense of shame, and not guilt, from feeling 'bad' because of his 'thoughts'.

Now he told me what had led to his breakdown eight months ago. He had overslept that day and had missed the 7.30 tube-train, which was rarely crowded. So he took the second direct nonstop train. It was packed, and he had to stand. Suddenly he saw a young Negress feeding her baby, with her bosom totally bared. That had triggered off the 'thoughts'. If he could have stopped the train, he would have done so, and got out. But he had to suffer it all, and no matter how hard he tried not to look, he found himself staring at the Negress's bosom and the baby sucking it. He again added a footnote: 'Dammit, both she and the baby were having a good time, whilst my head was hurting like hell with the "thoughts", getting more and more lewd, cruel, vicious and hurtful.' There was no pleasure in them for him, but he could not stop them. At last he had reached his station, but felt too exhausted to walk to the place where he worked. He rang his dad at his office and said he was suddenly feeling very ill. Dad had come over and fetched him, without asking any questions. He finished by saying: 'You know the rest of the story!' I said: 'Not quite, but we have shared enough for the time being.'

There were only four weeks left before the holidays during which period, because of being in my estate in Pakistan, I would not be accessible or available to Benjamin, so I decided during this time to 'consolidate' his initiative, from himself, towards active and positive living at home, at work and socially, and to stabilise his *trust* in me and *our* work together. He was still a very fragile youth, precariously establishing his *I am* selfhood and identity. There is no magical way of clinically achieving what one wishes for the patient, beyond the 'available' capacities in him or her *and oneself*, but I felt confident on one score: that in spite of his grave *sickness*, Benjamin had a high innate potential for growth and the necessary will to achieve the fruition of it.

When I encountered Benjamin after a break of four months, he looked fit and wholesome in himself. I was really surprised at how consistently he had sustained himself as an *evolving* independent youth, by his various activities during these months. It is not often we have patients like him in our practice, who, while they are very taxing and demanding, also extend our skill and enrich our vision. I really felt grateful to him for what he had achieved during the four months I had been away, not only for himself but for us both for future clinical work together.

[1986]

7
The Long Wait

PART ONE

And I pray that I may forget
These matters that with
    myself I too much discuss
Too much explain

T. S. ELIOT
Ash-Wednesday

Aisha was thirty-two years of age. She had been married twice; once by her father when she was barely seventeen, and ten years later by her uncle. Both these well-meaning characters were of noble, feudal, land-owning class in her culture. Her father was a gentle and quiet person. Her uncle was European-educated and very clever. She talked of both with reverent somnolent affection. She had no grudge against her husbands either. She had borne a daughter to her first husband, having become pregnant immediately after marriage. This husband had yanked her off to a large city, where he practised medicine. He had been educated in America and was smooth and clever. He had married her for status and soon got tired of her village-culture: too naïve and 'idiotic' for him. He started to *modernise* her (Aisha's phrase). She had to move out and into open society of vulgar promiscuous habits. He mocked her prudish bashfulness. When she had had her baby, he stopped her lactation with injections. She was already too thin, he said; breast-feeding would weaken her further. She had to go to college and learn proper colloquial English and French, and at home she was to speak the vernacular language, Urdu, and not the dialect of Punjabi from her ethnic region, which was Chanauti.

Aisha had been speaking to me in English. I requested: 'Can you please speak in your Punjabi dialect now?' She was surprised by my request. 'But would you understand it? You have lived thirty years in

London.' I smiled and said: 'All the more reason to hear your own idiom and voice. I will understand it all right. And when I don't, it won't shame me to ask you to help me out. Let us learn from each other and have some fun. Cures are in Allah's keeping and of his giving alone!'

This seemed to have a relaxing effect on Aisha. She sat back in the chair. 'Can I light a cigarette?' 'If you must,' I answered, 'but you know women from our class do not smoke in front of men, especially if they are older, as I am. It is mere nervous affront on your part to wish to smoke here.' She looked at me intently. I gently patted her head and said, in Punjabi: 'Your eyes are alive still, with a sense of propriety. Why betray them so fatuously?'

Aisha started to cry. I let her; then said, 'I think that was enough *dressage* for one morning.' I had deliberately chosen a word from horsemanship. She smiled and said, 'How do you know that?' 'What?' I asked. 'That I am a runaway, wayward mare. My father always says that of me.' All this was said in Chanauti idiom.

I gave Aisha an appointment three days later and said, 'Try to keep a bit of memory of today, as it has *happened* between us, here! Do not mentate it under (Khan, 1969b), with a superflow of useless thoughts; do not sell out to the London society either. And please keep yourself company, from time to time.' 'If I kill myself from "dreads"' (her word, in English) 'what then?' I thought a little and said, 'I don't think, Aisha, you will let go of me that easily. You haven't even tried me yet, so there will be little gain from defeating me at the very start.'

'You are the devil himself,' she said. 'Not "himself", my dear, but "itself",' I replied. 'The devil has no sentience of body; he is all spirit and malevolent mischief. Hence "itself". In life, distinctions are both necessary and healing.' She said, in her own Punjabi idiom again: 'Easy for you to prescribe them. Try it in my social and family circumstances.'

The sound of her voice stated the *other* side of her. Allah above knew whether this other side was beside Aisha, or in her, or above her. She felt uni-distant from everything. We parted on that note.

When she was gone I had a feeling of strange peacefulness, even a touch of joy to it. This young woman who had attempted eight suicides was not even remotely depressed or dismayed, in and from herself. I felt sure I could help her, and that she would let me.

When Aisha returned three days later, in the evening this time, she looked haggard, self-abused and tawdry. She was overdressed, by that little *much* which makes a woman's style scream with levities and depredations. I realised I had made a mistake. I felt sorry for 'the kid'. Yes, she had lost her femininity, and was just a 'kid', or *it*, now.

'This is when I want to kill myself,' she said. 'From loathing myself. Those eyes of mine in which you noticed, what was it you said, "propriety"? I told that word to all my five lovers this weekend and they all said, Yes, he is very clever, but in fact he hasn't been able to shake off his feudal hang-ups. One of them said he has met you, and that your arrogance is matched only by your loneliness. That you have no ordinary friends, only princesses and countesses and famous people. That you live in a gilded monastic cage. I told him how right he was. It is rather overwhelming to sit in your consultation room: thousands of books, Braques and Matisses for lithographs. Everything silver and posh. What do you do for fun? Do you never let your hair down? Don't you fuck around? You aren't that old yet!'

I had had enough of her bantering. She had obviously been ether-snorting that weekend and was high still, only more hollow, like a reed, today. She asked again, 'Do you never fuck around?' I decided to hit back and settle the account, so I said, 'Didn't any one of the five tell you that I am very lazy? I let women do the fucking for me.' 'Why women,' she asked, 'and not men?' 'Because in men potency has to be generated, and to open-across fucking-wise takes little mobilisation of resources in a woman. Women are inexhaustible unless they run into a psychopath, like your second husband. He fucked you into the beyond and has left you all spent and hollow. Quite sad to be you, once the ether has sneaked away, sleepy-wise. Why do you try to kill yourself, Aisha? Give them a little more time and they will do it to you, for you. Tonight is terrible for you, Aisha. Nature has barred the way. Wipe away that monkey-arse-scarlet from your lips, Aisha. If you cannot exploit the orifices, at least respect their quiescence. Mouth won't do what cunt alone can do. Want more brash obscenities, Aisha? I know plenty. I offer them gratis.'

Aisha began to cry. 'It won't work here either. I have flown eight thousand miles for this. *This!* I ask you.' 'Yes, Aisha, the pity is you have jet-flown those eight thousand miles. King Suntan took thirty years to ride and walk his way to Malerapa, from Peking to Lhasa.

When he arrived he was already cured of what he needed to know from Malerapa. The aged High Priest lay dying. The king approached him and put his face close to Malerapa's mouth. He could feel the soft cool breath, so faint. He felt he was all light. This was the greatest miracle. Much more than he had ever dreamt of. The last breaths of the ancient father-master-Malerapa had wafted all over his face. How could he preserve them for ever? He was in terrible pain: And Malerapa's faint voice was whispering, "You breathe for me now!"

'Well, Aisha, you have been fucking for me vengefully and mockingly this weekend. Now in the watershed of nature's ruses, breathe for me, and maybe you will learn to breathe for yourself, and then you shall know one is real and alive in one's solitudes alone. Accomplices are treacherous false coinage. Yes, do cry, Aisha. You need to cleanse yourself. Soap and water can't clean you. Only children can be washed clean and then smell clean. The adults only muddy the water, and stay polluted. Yes, Aisha, you are right when you mutter, "There is no mercy in you, Raja Sahb." What earthly use will mercy be to you? You will have killed both mercy and yourself. I don't need to die, Aisha. I have paid my dues for living-rights. Easy to collect death penalties from oneself. To let oneself live is the hard task. The bitter task. No groin-grease can ease your way to that. By the sweat of your brow shall you live, dear lady. Killing doesn't fructify into death that easily. Always get someone else to do it to you, for you. That mad howl in your eyes, Aisha! Let it out, or else it will devour you one day. Without killing you.'

'How you go on and on. Quite frightening. I feel I have come through. Your spate of words has cleansed my head of my thoughts. Your words are so distant and touching. I mean like touch, not like moving. I could sit bathed in your words. You never moralise. No permissions and no taboos. Where all things are equal one has to make someone unequal. That is the task you have set me. Do I get you right, my lovable Raja Sahb? You are not afraid to be loved. Psychiatrists and psychoanalysts are swaddled in phobias. I told you that I saw Dr X first. He was most condescending about you. Yes, he is Anna Freud's blue-eyed boy all right. Is he really an aristocrat? he asked me. I said: No, he is much more. He is beyond class-status! That upset Dr X. He warned me, you take liberties with patients. I pretended not to have understood. He said you were taken off training because of an affair with some patient. It is not done to mix with one's patients. But Khan makes his own rules. I said: Yes! he can afford to. Not many of us have that right of self-assertion. My father thinks Masud Khan is unique amongst the feudalists of our country. That was why my father agreed to pay all the costs for this treatment. He told my uncle: If Khan won't cure her, at least he will take the mickey out of whoring for her. Khan's father was the same. That will be respite enough for Aisha. And you have. I can never repeat last weekend. There will be no point to it. I have found that it's only when I get nothing from repeating, do I stop. I can never stop for good reasons. Yes! you need to rest now. Do I come tomorrow?' 'Yes, please, Aisha, same time, and don't be too hard on yourself!'

Aisha had stayed forty-five minutes longer than her session-time. Time had rushed past. She had talked in her native Punjabi dialect mixed with English and also some French today because she was not self-conscious. She speaks Chanauti Punjabi with a most impish accent and the choicest diction. I relished her speech. My Chakwali Punjabi is no match for the Chanauti accent and clipped phrasing. Her vocabulary is also much larger than mine. Not surprising since I have lived thirty-seven years in self-elected exile in London. No competition anyway. I am surprised at the freedom and spontaneity of my responses to Aisha. In some thirty-five years of clinical work in London, Paris, Rome, Berlin, Tübingen, Vienna, Alexandria, Israel, and all over the USA, I have never allowed such total and heedless headway to my thoughts, and speech, in a session with a patient. She is daughter and patient, both in turn and at once. A wayward mare to me. She senses and accepts it. So do I. There is no threat of 'intimacy' whatsoever! Why? Don't know. Only I am sure it is so. She has seduced – or rather *let them* seduce her – her dentist, her physician, her physiotherapist (in London), her legal counsel, the professor who taught her English and French when she was eighteen, the American and French consuls. She has let everyone fuck her: in London, at present, one most respected Member of Parliament (some twenty-eight years older than her), a famous international journalist, a British film actor four years her junior, the director of a theatre, a well-known Jewish art dealer (much older), even a lesbian women's lib lady. I have taken this information from the foolscap page she left on the couch. Yes, she shifted from lying on the couch to sitting facing me to talk, and back. Note she spoke English and French when sitting up and facing me; only when lying down did she speak in Urdu and Chanauti Punjabi.

Why am I so permissive with her? No one has ever talked with such bantering freedom with me. Not even socially. Our free use and abuse of the word 'fucking' is tell-tale. Is it because the word and the activity of 'fucking' are so utterly foreign to each of us, and our style, from traditions of upbringing, that we could deploy it so crassly this once? Interesting what she told me about Dr X. By reviling me he only diminishes himself. No, it is not possible for him to diminish himself. There is no room for shrinkage left in him.

Aisha says some profound and witty things, all so unbelaboured too. It is the genius of the speaking-culture she comes from. She recites Bullah Shah, Waris Shah, Baba Fareed with such pertinent ease. Yes, I had never heard of Shah Hussain before – a very poignant Punjabi mystic. She says she can sing and play tabla. Has many masculine traits in her most feminine personality! Rides well too, and daily, even in London. How elegantly she dresses; wears only hand-printed materials. Must have cost her husbands a mint. Serves them right. Wears mascara with distinction and style. So much beauty to her; if only she could inhabit it as a person. So much joy as well; but all of it is scattered and hidden. Her mystical pursuit is somewhat like Rimbaud's: derange the senses, desecrate and destroy your person, so that none can possess it! I don't know. Yes, Aisha is very mystical at root, and expansively so. So much chronic psychic anguish and pain in her. Bleaches her gaze and makes it, renders it, ashen-grey. Black eyes, swarthy skin, become her. Anyone reading this will say: Khan is in love with his patient. Not a jot. Impassioned aesthetic interest? Yes! In love? No!

In the after-images of the session I feel that all the rapid, heedless bantering was a front, *screening* something that is happening in her now (*was*, then). Neither of us could get to it. Just as well. It is the third time the phone has rung and rung. Hope it is not her. I must go to the appointed dinner tonight. She could be there. But she was not dressed for it. She knows how to dress herself. The privacies of the analytic space, and process, protected us both, from each other and ourselves. Freud's only new discovery: 'the psycho-analytic method' (1904). Shall tell of that another time. Privacy in the plural, as privacies. Must shake her off and dress and go to dinner. A pain, a happy pain, in me about Aisha tonight. How I let myself be taken over! A real talent that, almost a skill. Yes, Aisha has epiphanic lacings and nuances to her; like evening stretching into night-time. Enough! Enough, Khan!

Thus ends my scrawled notes from that night. In my files there is another note about Aisha, which I must have scribbled hurriedly next morning, breakfasting, before taking the first patient at 8.00 a.m. It reads: Aisha was there all right. Effulgent. She was in great form. Not the sullen, peeved woman of the last session. She was spacious, open, so well-spaced in her movements. Everyone gaped at her. She stayed with no one for long. After a brief joyous meeting, had left me alone. I was most impressed by her style of relating and hostessing. Real class she has, and is so immense, yet was faded at the edges. Exhausted, hence brittle. Could crack up any moment, I feared, and the same apprehension returned. I should not have left her alone over the weekend. Winnicott (cf 1945) would not have done. So difficult to consistently treat an adult patient as a four-year-old, pre-oedipal child. That is what Aisha is. Time will have to be held for her. I did it for that maddening girl. Must ask her how long her father envisages keeping her in London for treatment. It is costing the old man a huge sum. Useless my indulging quixotic generosity with Aisha. She will only waste it. She is rich. The fees are very stiff. Who in Pakistan has heard of being charged forty pounds for fifty minutes, five times a week? With Aisha, at and during certain stages, it might well have to be seven sessions a week. The old man must love her to fork out all that money without moaning or begrudging. Somewhere he feels responsible for having married her off at barely seventeen years of age; an overprotected girl cast on the high seas of Karachi.

It was with such thoughts that I started to prepare for Aisha's third session, at 4.30 that afternoon. She would be my first patient after siesta. Those are my best four hours for clinical work. It was not to be. At 4.00 p.m. my houseboy woke me up. Normally I wake at 4.15 p.m. He said that Sir William had been ringing since three o'clock. I took the phone. 'Khan speaking,' I said. 'I am glad you are awake, Khan. Things have got out of hand. Aisha started to bleed at 9.00 a.m. By midday her condition was critically worse. She was having a "natural miscarriage". You know what I mean.' 'I do not, Sir William. Please start again. You did not tell me Aisha was pregnant . . . nor did she.' 'She made me promise I wouldn't,' said Sir William irately, and added, 'She is four months' pregnant, and there is no telling whose baby it is. You know how she has been since she arrived just over four months ago. The best one could hope for was natural abortion. I had prescribed certain medicines. They worked. I have admitted her to a private ward in my hospital. Wait a moment.' I paused. Sir William was talking to someone. He returned to the phone and said, 'You'd better come over quick.' 'I can't,' I protested. Sir William snapped, 'Then are all your patients having miscarriages this afternoon? I am going to the hospital. Join me there: double-quick.'

I knew Aisha had a flair for dramatic happenings, but I didn't expect them to be of panoramic proportions. I was surprised she had kept her pregnancy from me, for she was a devoutly religious woman and it was not in her nature to be deceitful. I found, on arrival at the hospital, that her relatives had taken a whole room next to hers. This enraged me. It is always so with rich Pakistanis.

When I entered the room Aisha was lying very still, with her eyes closed, breathing in a quiet rhythm. Sir William, the staff nurse and the nurse on duty were busy attaching two bottles to Aisha's body, one to the left arm and the other to her right leg, just above the ankle. Sir William acknowledged my presence with the remark, 'So you have arrived, Khan. Jolly decent of you.' I refused to be teased by Sir William. I knew he enjoyed riling people. So I said, 'Do you know why I have come?' 'No, but you will tell me, won't you? Let me finish setting up the drips first. Aisha has lost too much blood, hence is light-headed. One drip feeds her blood, the other glucose. She has over-sweated too. She does do things extravagantly over-much. But she means well. Poor Aisha.'

I could sense the old fox was softening me up to get away with what he had decided to do. So I chose to surprise him. 'You know, Sir William, I would go along with you in fostering a natural abortion, should *you* decide that. But it is not you who has decided that. It is her bloody and soul-forsaken uncle who has decided it. And you know why? He is a creep and a coward. He got his high title through a series of mischances. He is no duke (in your class system). Just a commoner, who is more common than most commoners. He is terrified of Aisha's father's rage. And the old man can and does rage. Like with all cowards, the most expedient measure is the right and just measure. But it is not going to be so. With your help, Sir William, I am going to defeat Aisha's uncle's evil intents. Aisha is going to have her baby and joyfully rear it herself. Only then will she shake off her craziness, perverted habits, ether-snorting, near-alcoholism, compulsive fucking around. Self-dissatisfaction and degradations can stop only this way. There is no clinical way that I know of by which one can therapeutically blitzkrieg her demonic way of life at present. This pregnancy is a godsend for us and her, if only we can make the right use of it. Keep her in hospital for three weeks, till her system is cleansed of all sorts of poisonings. We can start afresh then.'

Sir William was gazing at me solemnly. When I stopped, he said, 'Bravo, Khan, the evangelist. "Rise from your sickbeds, all ye sinners of the world, and start afresh." Khan has sanctioned it now. He has said it, you do it. Well, Khan, I am all with you. The slight problem is how to tell it to the uncle. God! – like a bad play, here he is in person. Be gentle with him, Khan, don't frighten him over-much.' I snarled under my breath, 'You and your over-muches.'

He greeted the uncle with proper ceremony. The uncle, a little taken aback to find me there, said, 'Ah, Khan, how very kind of you to come personally. Aisha is not too ill, I am sure.' 'No! No,' I replied, 'she still lives. A lot can be taken out of her yet.' 'What are you hinting at, Khan?' 'Oh, just the shapeless foetus inside Aisha. You know it is still there?' 'Really!' 'Oh yes, very much so: and healthy, too. Ask Sir William.' He looked at Sir William and started to say, 'I thought –' 'Please let us not start telling lies at this critical juncture. It is not that "you thought" but that "you wished".' 'Don't forget, Khan, I am her uncle and she is my responsibility in this town.' 'You mean your crass irresponsibility, sir. No, Aisha is going to have her baby, God willing.' 'You don't mean it?' 'Of course I do.' 'You know her father will kill her, himself, when he knows of this, and if he doesn't, someone in the clan will. They couldn't take the disgrace of it.' 'No, sir. You are wrong on that score. They can, you can't. It puts your nose out of joint for good and all.' 'All right, if you want it that way. I can't and won't.' 'Fortunately that is not my problem, sir. Please leave the room. Aisha is waking up.' 'I do not take orders.' 'Since when, sir, is it not in your nature to take orders? There is a great economy in that, I tell you. You don't have to use judgement or will. Don't fret, please.' 'What if I don't?' 'You will, sir, you will. Turn round, and walk out, like a brave man who has just made a most difficult decision. Yes, please shut the door behind you.'

When the uncle had left, Sir William gasped, 'Really Khan, what you get away with! And all the time. Do you remember Caroline, and your saying to her brother: Your Royal Highness, I recommend to you very strongly that you go next door and get drunk while the physician checks whether the brain has been affected by the overdose or not. There's a good lad. Don't strain to cry, your Royal Highness. No one could have stopped and saved Caroline from this. It had to happen once. Thank God it has, and not irretrievably. You know, Khan, he always remembers with gratitude that you were so thoughtful and caring about him. Well, Aisha is awake. Hello, you rogue, how are you feeling?'

Aisha asked in a very faint voice, 'Do I still have my pregnancy?' 'Yes, Aisha, and it is for keeps.' 'My uncle –' and she faded out. I winked at Sir William and he winked back at me. We were united in our intents and endeavours. Aisha came to again. She strained to say, 'And the money –' I shook my head and said, 'Aisha, don't think of that now. My father has left me enough money for six generations of friends. I shall pay if your father won't. But he will. Anyway, I am going to squeeze your uncle for the hospital expenses.' A faint glimmer of mischievous intent showed in her eyes. She lapsed into silence again.

I stayed till midnight, some seven hours. Aisha had been hallucinating off and on: drug and alcohol withdrawal symptoms. With little else to do I decided to note down the odd sentences that she spoke fitfully, each coherent in itself. Here is what I recorded during that stretch of some five hours:

I didn't know home was so beautiful until I left it [said in sections of three words at a time] . . . Habib [first husband] was such a fool. Knew it too but couldn't face it . . . Ami [Mother] had been good to Ubu [Father] until her abortion . . . Raja Sahb is right, fucking kills the soul and not the body . . . I used to pray with such relish . . . My daughter must not suffer like me . . . Ishaq [second husband] not even sex crazy. He is just plain crazy and stupid . . . The English cannot fuck even. They mess around. Just that . . . I love flowers in my hair. They smell natural . . . I have harmed only myself. That is my only virtue . . . Walking barefoot is the secret . . . Rain brings out the fertile pregnant smells from the earth. I am only roused when Shabeena [her daughter] hugs me passionately, impatiently . . . If I die my horse will be unconscionably sad . . . I enrage Shabeena often because then she glows with beauty like drunken roses . . . I cannot stand the poet in me. Too much responsibility. Shall gift it to Raja Sahb.

He collects talents . . . Sir William fancies Khan. They are such thieves
together . . . My brother is so vain that he forgets to be proud . . . My father
has always loved me with his ears . . . This is why I speak Chanauti so
beautifully . . . Dare I wake up tomorrow and collect my scattered person . . .

Well, I had Aisha moved to another private hospital after three days.
She found her uncle's abject crawling to her more galling than his evil
machinations. After three weeks Aisha was considered fit enough to try
living in the outside world. I arranged for her to share a small flat with
an Indian Hindu woman of her own age, Prem, who was a widow and
had a son of ten years old. They took to each other. Aisha was a good
cook. Sometimes I ate with them both, never with Aisha alone; she
didn't want it either. Things were progressing fine and at the right pace.
Then Aisha had a dream. A bird had been fluttering in her room. She
failed to guide it out of the window. It collapsed from fluttering against
the walls. She had been literally howling. Prem had come in and shaken
her awake.

Aisha was still dazed when she came to her session some twelve
hours later. She told me the dream and offered to give some
associations. I said gently: 'Please don't, Aisha. You aren't – weren't –
ready for the dream. Some extraneous factor has triggered it off. We
will keep it in our care till we are ready to experience it.' She said she
knew what the 'extraneous factor' was: 'Ishaq is in town and is staying
with my uncle. Sir William rang to tell me this.' At the end of the session
I told her: 'Today is Friday, Aisha, and you are going to stay with a
friend of mine this long weekend, because I have to be in Paris. Pack
and come here at 8.30 this evening. I shall feed you and my driver will
take you to Felicity. You have met Felicity.' 'Yes, I have.' 'I will collect
you personally on my way back on Monday after dinner.'

So Aisha went to the countryside and I to Paris. This was our first
brief respite from each other since her treatment started. When I
returned, Sir William called on me and said, 'We have to start thinking
about her confinement.' 'Have you any plans?' Sir William said, 'No,
and that bothers me. She shouldn't have the baby in hospital. Too very
different from her first confinement. We shouldn't test her over-much.'
I talked about it with Aisha. Couldn't see any positive route out. Then
out of the blue, Miriam, a friend of mine, returned from Abyssinia and
came to stay with me for a few days on her way home to Vienna.

Miriam was three years older than Aisha but was unmarried. Aisha and Miriam took to each other. Miriam invited Aisha to stay with her in Vienna until the baby was due. Sir William knew a gynaecologist of international repute there. He contacted him and then Aisha was all set to leave with Miriam. There was just the problem of money. I gave her two thousand pounds as a gift for the baby and appointed myself the godfather.

Four weeks later Miriam rang me from Vienna, at 3.00 a.m., to tell me that labour pains had started. I took an early plane and was at Aisha's side by two o'clock, accompanied by Sir William. At 7.00 p.m. Aisha gave birth to a yapping, healthy, seven-pound baby. I returned to London after a week and Aisha followed with her baby son a month later.

Aisha had been in London some six weeks when her father sent a message that he had had a massive heart attack. He wanted to see his grandson. Aisha flew to her ancestral home with her son, Ijaz Masud, when he was ten weeks old. She was seen off at Heathrow Airport by her uncle, her brother and sister-in-law, Sir William and Prem, the Hindu lady. I didn't go. I hate taking leave and saying goodbyes. Aisha and her son had come to dinner the evening before. Just as she was leaving, Aisha gave me a cheque for three thousand five hundred pounds. Her father had sent it for me. She asked if she owed me more. I said, 'No, thank you.' Then she asked, 'Do you remember my dream?' 'Yes, I do, and I shall make sense of it to you when we meet again in Pakistan.'

So ended one of the most extraordinary relationships of my life. Of course, it didn't end. But henceforth Aisha and I were different to, and with, each other. The 'long wait' had fructified into our relationship. Aisha's new life was rooted in her person and not in any long wait. If what I have said about her has given the impression of a rather irresponsible person, then I have not been fair to her. Aisha was in many ways more responsible than most patients I see from European cultures, and she was always, deep down, true to her own self; one cannot ask more of any person, including oneself.

I have left out of my clinical account the role of religion in Aisha's life and daily relationships. Here my need is to convey to my readers the feel and rhythm of the clinical work we did together. The rest can wait. Not a long wait, I hope.

PART TWO

Up and down, this way, that way, what the dickens are
you playing at? We're not getting anywhere.

ARISTOPHANES *The Birds*

Waiting is in the very nature of man. Since time immemorial man has
either waited for, or waited upon, someone: a deity, a god, a beloved.
Some transcend this bondage and wait upon themselves: the mystics.
Even so, the mystics wait *upon*. The riddling and the paradoxes of
waiting constitute some of the noblest creations of the human mind
and soul. All voyagers negotiate waiting. Baudelaire (1975) and
Cavafy (1975) verify it. Waiting is the core experience of any person
who seeks to make his own tools for experiencing others and himself.
Wait, the long wait, can be health and it can be sickness. He who waits,
finds. Unwaiting guarantees unfinding. The American craze for
package-tour, berserk, resourceless wandering is the result of not
waiting. Programmed voyaging is both arid and wasteful.

We cannot talk of waiting without talking of death – with a small 'd'.
Use capital 'D', and one is done for: Death, that most singular
experience that no human has yet lived. Folks die and are dead. But
death is infinite. The most macabre and weird grimaces have been
painted of death; yet death is beyond all imaginings. Human beings
cannot imagine what has not been in the lived experience of anyone.
We concoct living images and declare that they have the semblance of
death. Not so. They are elaborate lies of the living about dying and
death. Death stays silently, sentiently, invisible. Waiting involves us
with intimations of death, or so we think. As to the interlacing of
waiting and death, a most poignant and explicit statement of it is by
Freud in his correspondence with his fiancée, Martha Bernays (Freud,
1960). His was a long wait. And he lived it with all the terrors he could
invest it with. He bemoaned his waiting for the little princess Marty.
He capered into absurd, heroic antics, Don Quixote-wise: a novel he
wanted Marty to read, in spite of its ribald humour. His jealousies
made him ill, again and again. He berated Marty relentlessly. He

would be abject one day and the supreme lover, the man of the future, the next. Haunted, Freud lived his waiting, haunting. All the time he knew Marty was an excuse. He was waiting on himself, to achieve himself. Can we forget, ever, the waiting of Oedipus the King? A waiting he plans for himself; and watches unfold with a harrowed and harrowing impetuous zeal. He postpones, at the same time as he expedites, the course of waiting to its end. Even his end doesn't terminate his waiting. Not while in Athens. There is the long journey of the blinded Oedipus, awaiting exile ahead. Only by cursing does he assuage the hunger of his waiting and can he find death. Then we hear no more of him. We track back to another long wait: Antigone's! Death consumes so many through the instrumentality of the long, vigilant wait.

There are Hamlet and King Lear to instruct us further in the labyrinthine mazes of waiting. Hamlet cheats, but cheating itself becomes the catching trap of waiting. What a long route he takes before Laertes rescues him from the long wait. Then he hands the torch of waiting to Horatio. 'Absent thee from felicity awhile,' he exhorts with candour, explicit and exact for once. And Lear advises himself, 'O that way madness lies; let me shun that; no more of that.' Even in madness Lear seeks balance. Hamlet risks his own. There is no care in Hamlet. Lear knows, even as he goes mad. He awakens holding death in Cordelia in his arms. His heart cannot break. His frame does. Life is lost, but not the will. Lear does not submit: 'Never, now or never, never, never.'

My theoretical narrative has no pretension to being either reasoned, scholarly or consecutive. I shall present in rapid juxtapositions the various guises and spaces of waiting. I hope that each reader will collate them into a unity that suits and nourishes his particular and peculiar bias, and/or need. None should be pontifically instructed in this context. To do so is to sin against the Holy Ghost. We write to share, and not to indoctrinate. Each and every reader is vulnerable to the extent that he or she is receptive. We are changed from taking, only by that which has no intentions to enlighten and/or educate. Education is best undertaken by the individual himself, of himself. Resentments are the just reward of all tutorings of others. We learn from company and not from exhortations. The more we impose upon an expectant and receptive mind, the more we push it into the absences of waiting.

If suspense is the positive stance in waiting, then absence is its negative counterpart. Hamlet – with his compulsion to instruct always and every-wise: Ophelia first, then the Players, and lastly Horatio – is absence personified! That is his true ailment. He nurtures it and never once does he seek to be free of it. Yes, for a fleeting moment, by the grave, when he meditates on death. But not for long. Soon his words lose any sense of awe, and sermonise instead. Not letting himself feel anything, without the lacing and sauce of thoughts, Hamlet is suspended in that most cruel stance: forever dying. 'Man delights not me – nor woman neither . . .' He doesn't renounce anything because he can never commit himself to any thing, any purpose, or any person. He is always around everything, forever waiting! – with a dagger, to kill Polonius, or with scathing words, the Queen his mother. He dispenses away the lives of Rosencrantz and Guildenstern to rid himself of their embarrassing and intrusive presences. That they have orders to have him made short shrift of, Hamlet recalls only as an afterthought. The ailment of Hamlet is paradigmatic of the most pernicious form of illness accruing from the long wait. And that is why *Hamlet* as a play is unsatisfactory as drama and poetry. It is static, at the core, as well as in its nefarious skirmishes with reality and others. Because Hamlet cannot change, he devastates all and sundry. He is a killjoy of immense talent and genius. Eliot (1918) was right in his criticism of *Hamlet* insofar as it lacks vital 'objective correlatives'. But Eliot was wrong insofar as he expected Hamlet to be either a redeemer or to be himself redeemable.

Hamlet is a character in a play. Hamlet cannot sense a spurious loss of grace, as Eliot's piety prescribed for Hamlet. Hamlet is beyond redemption and saving, simply because Hamlet has no referrents outside himself, and even his 'inside' is the inside of the head-space, the space inside the cranium. How many lies cascade down one thought alone: a king, infinite space, eggshell, bad dreams! Hamlet has bad dreams! Some put-on that is! On seeing his father's ghost he searches for his tablets: 'Oh God, I could be bounded in a nutshell and count myself a king of infinite space, were it not that I have bad dreams . . . meet it is I set it down' (an aphorism obliterates the message and purpose of the ghost's visitation) 'that one may smile, and smile, and be a villain.' Really, Prince Hamlet! Is there no room for anyone with you? How wretchedly lonely you are and all of you mere mentation! The most awesomely wretched and lonely character in all literature. You rebut even pity. You writhe in the contortions of the little-ease, of your own perverted manufacture. Winnicott (1971c) has also written about the terrible fate of those who live in and from the head-space.

A certain reckless disregard of method and mentations is what had 'saved' Aisha. Watching and witnessing herself play Russian roulette with her chances in daily life, gave her maddening outrageousness a certain dignity. At core, Aisha was everything that Prince Hamlet could never be. After she had seen Laurence Olivier's *Hamlet* (the film), her dismissive comment was very telling. She had said: 'Hamlet is an unwomaned male youth.' I had been surprised, not only by her grasp of Prince Hamlet's truth, but by her capacity to phrase it so neatly, and so put it out of court. Everything sticks to Prince Hamlet. Aisha shook off everything. I often wondered why she had surrendered vast acreages of her person to others. She was not a compliant character. She was fearlessly wilful. She wasn't a masochist either. When her second husband, in drunken rage, had fractured her left forearm, she had settled the account with him by saying to her father, unabashedly: 'Erection never fails him, but it doesn't extend him either. Hence, his violence.' So she had persuaded her father not to punish her husband. The husband came from the urban civil service classes, a hybrid clutter of nobodies in our culture. Nothing could have so castrated him than to credit him with mere erectile potency. Phallus doesn't have any traditions; not even in the ancient Greeks. Phallus and waiting and death are consentient. I have discussed this issue at length in the five case histories I present in *Alienation in Perversions* (1979).

I have a feeling that Jacques Lacan (1966) had the knowing of that. But his writings are so untameable, like the phallus itself, that one can get little thinking joy out of them. Lacan was essentially menopausal in sensibility, hence his Hamletian conjugations and prevarications of *the lack* and *desire*! The *symbolic* perpetually quarrelling with the *real*, each equally discontented in his hands. Lacan's *language* was never *les paroles*! This is how he sabotaged his creative thrust and potential. He hypnotised his audiences because he couldn't enter their souls and hearts. He, like Prince Hamlet, and Freud himself, is 'the lonely began'. The three of them are sterile therapeutically. Each instructs and can stand no reciprocity of refusal. Hence, in the end, all three are living in a climate of refusals. In drama, Prince Hamlet can litter his absences and refusals with the *killed* others! In life, Freud and Lacan lived in splendid heroic isolation of their own boasting and flaunting. Both were nurtured by their Antigone-daughters. Freud didn't have to kill his son-in-law because Anna-Antigone had spared him that task. But Freud had killed enough heirs for one lifetime. Lacan had killed far fewer, but these he had really killed. No metaphors for him in this context. Thou shalt be killed so that I may thrive, was Lacan's persuasion. He had the courage of the deed. Most noble and remarkable that. Once ritualised, and particularly by manipulation of language, all was permitted for Lacan. Not so for Freud, who stammered with the hallowed Judaic interdiction on murder. He had to reason his murders into pious, righteous deeds. Lacan doesn't seem to demand self-immolation, as Freud certainly did. The 'training regime' for analysis is soul-immolation for sure. Its pundits have elaborate circumcision rules and rituals. Collectors of prepuces, they fatten themselves on others' anguish. It ablates all phallic assertiveness. Freud's 'Societies' make sad 'academies'. Lacan, like Samson of yore, pulled the whole edifice on their heads before he died.

Let us look at some other variants of suspense and waiting. In modern literature there is no sharper, more vivid portrayal of waiting than in Eliot's verse-play, *Murder in the Cathedral* (1935). The chorus awaiting the Archbishop's arrival is composed of women only. The opening verses set the pith and pitch of the tautness of this play:

> Here let us stand, close by the cathedral. Here let us wait.

So the vigil is set. But this has been a long vigil: seven years, we are told! Only *now* the waiting has taken on a new task:

> . . . Some presage of an act
> Which our eyes are compelled to witness, has forced our feet
> Towards the cathedral. We are forced to bear witness.

This is an excessive demand – the demand from waiting and suspense – and a new responsibility: '. . . to bear witness'. The old women, already exhausted from seven years' waiting tending vigil, want no share of the new burden. They repeat what has been their wont:

> The New Year waits, destiny waits for the coming.

Yes, they know of that. The words have become ritualised in their thoughts; they have merely a sedative soporific effect now. Habit has evened out the sharp edges of intent waiting. They try to render the *new* task into one of habit:

> For us, the poor, there is no action,
> But only to wait and to witness.

So they are reassured by their own litany of words and phrases. The Priests have come, and banter with their thoughts. They talk themselves into a pretend:

> Let us therefore rejoice . . .

This put-on gaiety of mood is shaken by the perseverating old women:

> Here is no continuing city, here is no abiding stay . . .
> We do not wish anything to happen.

Now the suspense of waiting has changed into the taut confrontations of demand and counter-demand. In this climate no autonomy is possible for anyone: whether of the collective group or a wilful individual stand. The chorus gains in its conviction through speaking together. We have here perhaps the most heroic and noble twelve verses, written and spoken, since Milton's *Paradise Lost*:

> But now a great fear is upon us, a fear not of one but of many,
> A fear like birth and death, when we see birth and death alone
> In a void apart. We
> Are afraid in a fear which we cannot know, which we cannot face, which
>   none understands,
> And our hearts are torn from us, our brains unskinned like the layers of
>   an onion, our selves are lost lost
> In a final fear which none understands. O Thomas Archbishop,
> O Thomas our Lord, leave us and leave us be, in our humble and
>   tarnished frame of existence, leave us; do not ask us
> To stand to the doom on the house, the doom on the Archbishop, the
>   doom on the world.
> Archbishop, secure and assured of your fate, unaffrayed among the
>   shades, do you realise what you ask, do you realise what it means
> To the small folk drawn into the pattern of fate, the small folk who live
>   among small things,

> The strain on the brain of the small folk who stand to the doom of the
> house, the doom of their lord, the doom of the world?
> O Thomas, Archbishop, leave us, leave us . . .

Yes, Eliot has caught the ever-proliferating and harassed anguish of
the last thirty-six years of European man and cultures. A few years,
later, W. H. Auden (1936) was to versify it thus:

> . . . Someone must pay for
> Our loss of happiness,
> our happiness itself.

There are no remedies. To see the dire predicament with a clarity of
words is the only true relief possible now. But the Priests, besotted with
their holy unrealistic catechisms, have no patience or respect for the
sifted wisdom of the old women. They rebuke them thus:

> What a way to talk at such a juncture!
> You are foolish, immodest and babbling women.

The fatuous arrogance and superiority of the Priests is betrayed by the
inept use of one adjective: 'immodest'. There can be no question 'at
such a juncture' of modest or immodest. One realises, most painfully,
that it is the Priests who are out of touch with reality. It is they who will
unwittingly lend furtherance to that disaster, which will be the murder
of Becket . . .

Let us reconsider what new elements have been added to our
cartography of the terrains of waiting and suspense. The individual, in
these spaces of waiting and suspense, has to programme himself, no
matter how feebly. There is a task – to bear witness – that cannot be
escaped or shirked. Isn't that why Aisha had sought analytic therapy?
The chemically drugged absences from being her own person no longer
assuaged her. Fucking around was little help also. She had to risk
discovering the full measure and extent of *disillusionment* (Milner,
1969). Yes, waiting postpones disillusionment and Aisha had said so,
mentating in the slough of despondency. A person has to hurt himself
to awaken to the truth, there is no future outside the present. All
illusion is cussed self-betrayal. Aisha had asked, 'Then what is there left
to do? You are taking away everything, straw by straw. "The wayward
mare" will soon be starved to death.' She had added, with considerable
irritating wit, 'Anyway I won't have to attempt suicide again. You

would have done all for me.' I had told her, 'The "all" is the give-away. One cannot do all, even by way of dosing death by starvation.'

As I write, I think afresh about divesting a person, clinically, of the 'love of created things'. I had put this young woman through an ordeal of total stress. Was reducing Aisha to such absolute resourcelessness necessary? Most, if not all, of my colleagues would say I had behaved in an outrageously haughty way; that this had more to do with Khan's temperament than with the patient's need. I do not have to defend myself. Yet to my reader I owe some explanation. If *waiting* and *suspense* are positive spaces and *absence* is the vitiating negative agent, then I had to find a way of being there, around her, when I was not there. Renunciations and 'measured' deprivations kept her aware of me. She could feel it was I, Khan, who had plunged her into sheer bereftness of body-experiences and stopped her social harloting. Never once did I say to Aisha, 'Do not do this, or behave thus and thus.' My austere image was her companion. She was alone, but not lonely. Loneliness and absence are two faces of the same coin. Together they mask disillusionment. Even Freud had cheated on this score. Religions of others' making were their illusion, not his! (Freud, 1927). From loving me, Aisha would reach to loving herself, and then to sharing that self-love with someone. That was my audacious programme and it worked. I do not recommend it to any other clinician.

I have described in some ten case histories (Khan 1974, 1983) how I have battled with myself to help patients like Aisha take on the struggle to be their own persons, in their own hands. I had not started Aisha's treatment from naïve good faith; I brought to it some thirty-five years of hard struggle. I had no illusions as to the task I set – for both of us. The imperative was: I had no personal need or desire to save a patient or heal a patient. I do not think of results: gains and losses. I am engrossed with the planning of a strategy that the patient and I can elaborate and execute, step by step. I have not done another case like Aisha, before or since her. She was exceptional in every sense. 'Folded in' upon herself, she had harboured an immense self, all of some thirty-two years. Ours was a confluence of riches, in every sense of the word. Hers had been a long wait. We strove together, helping each other's morale when low. At the end, neither of us felt a loss or a void from the absence of the other. I meet her once or twice every time I go to my country. We know we share a past: an intense and immense past.

And now we have become affectionate acquaintances. Her son and daughter love me and stay with me at my home in Pakistan. She lives and pursues a life of her own. When her father died recently, I was fortunately in Pakistan and able to attend the funeral. I stayed the night in his vast mansion. Aisha had been very sad, but she had not needed to lean on me.

I shall end with some thoughts on the themes of waiting and disillusionment in Freud's writings. An obvious point to note is Freud's dosage of his own person to the patient. The physician who used to be available to his patients, as they needed him (Freud, 1895), had gradually put himself out of their reach. Militantly so, after he had written 'the psycho-analytic method' (1904). Even Dora's case was differently handled. He imposed 'deprivations' on his patients to compel 'transference-love' from them (Freud, 1915a). A rather sick programme, I regret to say. Today I see it for what it is worth after its outrageous inhuman demands. The patient is victimised in every respect. Lie down, do not touch me with your eyes, demanded Professor Doctor Sigmund Freud. Use only words to tell of yourself. Do not seek to know me. The game is played one-sidedly. So the spaces of waiting start to emerge, expand, and swallow up the patient. You must tell me everything, Freud demanded. You have surrendered all rights to privacy. And I shall goad you with interpretations. All will become clear. All what? the patients asked. The 'what' is the task, Freud told them. Let us sort out the *hows* to this unknowable *what*.

Here Freud made his true discoveries. Here our debt to him is beyond measuring. He had the moral and emotional strength to pursue the *how* in all its myriad paths and by-ways. He was indefatigable. Verily so. Few of his followers have his guts and strength. This is where Jung had collapsed in himself. Jung became a *collector* of images, archetypes and other bric-à-brac of human cultures. Freud stayed strictly a taskmaster, to himself and to his patients. If Freud imposed the long wait on his patients, he also had the charity and compassion to companion them all the way. He forgave his patients more than any of them ever forgave him, especially when they were his students – Stekel, Adler, Rank, etc.

Freud's had been a haunted life; only at the end did he find true love in his Antigone-Anna. Freud died a man in grace. How many of his followers reach that far, and find in some other the love they desire and need? Freud's end is his greatest virtue. He died a loved father by his exceptional daughter. Destiny had claimed Freud to itself. Thus!

[1987]

Afterword

The seven persons who feature in this book were all very well versed in what it took to live *with* others and *from* others. Each one of them would exploit, as it suited his or her wish, whim or need, and let him or herself be exploited. So I ask myself what else they had in common – apart from the fact that they all made demands on my person – whether they were homosexual, like Bill and Mr Luis, or absent from themselves, like Benjamin, or resourcelessly promiscuous, like Aisha. Rightly or wrongly, I have come to the conclusion that another characteristic shared by all seven patients was that they could not relate to themselves. Each of them found his/her person and body insufferable or disgusting, in spite of evidence from experience that they were cherished by others, both physically and emotionally. They all had a very poor notion of, as well as capacity for, playing with themselves in a pleasurable and private manner. Of course, I am referring to what we call autoerotism or masturbation. It was this insufficiency in them *vis-à-vis* their relation to their own self and body which made them very needy of some accomplice to actualise and fructify for themselves a physical, sensual experience.

The reader will be inclined to think of these patients as patently masochistic characters. In so far as I understand the concept of masochism (Khan, 1976b), this involves one person suffering in the hands of another person and deviously enjoying his pain. In this sense of the term, none of these persons were masochistic. In their transgressions, they enjoyed hurting only *from themselves*. For them, being hurt and taken advantage of by others was a relief from their fantasies, in which they tortured themselves with beratings and humiliations. Clinically, it was very painful to witness their self- inflicted suffering.

Analysts and psychotherapists do not readily admit their aversion to being put upon by stresses not of their own making. Coming from a different culture than most of my colleagues, and from a family background with a tradition of care at all costs, I am not perturbed by such demands. I like to think this is why I succeeded in helping these patients to find their own way, as none of their previous analysts had been able to do. I do not believe it was because I was wiser, or better, than my colleagues, but *humbler*, and prepared to enter into a relationship of mutual sharing, in which analyst and patient gradually establish a rapport whereupon they can begin to learn from each other and thrive. Those who can take this risk will earn the same benefits, both clinically and personally, that I have done.

Another point in common with these patients was that, while they rarely complained of being depressed, I noticed that weeks at a time would pass in which they in fact did nothing. They sank into apathy. They would cover up their inertia during these apathetic periods by such statements as: 'I don't feel up to it these days'; 'What the hell! It is not that urgent, is it? It can wait'; 'They don't work as hard as I do, so I have the right to do nothing for a week or two.' I also noticed that these apathetic stretches of time would often reach a climax with the patient committing an irresponsible or inappropriate action, and I came to realise that it was a build-up of over-anxiety that had led to their 'eruptive acts'. The cycle completed, they would return to their normal, and usually productive, professional and family lives.

To my knowledge, apathy is an affect that has not been widely explored in psychoanalytic writings. It is quite different from depression. A person who is depressed possesses an awareness of, and distance from, his depressive feelings and state; he can admit that he is depressed, feel sorry for himself, and try to make others an accomplice to his depression. The person in a state of apathy, on the other hand, has no conscious awareness that he is apathetic. Furthermore, unlike depression, apathy is a global affective state. It envelops the whole person, and there is little distance left between the observing ego and the experiencing self. Another characteristic of the apathetic state is that the person feels totally 'impersonal' to himself, hence there is a certain clarity in the patient's self-narrative at such times. The quiet and controlled tone can all too easily mislead one into believing that the patient is doing well, until he suddenly confronts one with another of his eruptive acts. The most moving and pathetic example of this is the conduct of Bill when, at the height of his career, he picked up a youth and was imprisoned for it.

A further interesting, although clinically negative, aspect of the apathetic state in these patients was that, at such times, they either did not dream or did not remember dreaming; and, if they dreamt, it was the same repetitive, inconsequential dream, from which they would wake exhausted – 'so washed out', as one of them put it, that it took all morning to pull himself together. When they did not dream, they would wake up feeling not so much exhausted as desolate.

It was the management of such states that perhaps constituted the most clinically demanding aspect of the treatment of these patients. I consider myself lucky that they somehow found in themselves the affection and trust to allow me to guide them through their periods of apathy and eruptive actions.

Having lived and worked in London for forty years, I have learned that self-exile is quite different from being an *émigré*. I did not have to fabricate a new identity as a British citizen and, while I am open to learn from the culture in which I have been living, the tenacious hold that my own roots and culture have on me has strongly influenced my way of working. My patients came to me with some knowledge of my background from various sources, and because of the way I work they also found out more about me as a person than is generally the case within the parameters of the analytic situation. For I do not subscribe to the traditional school of thought which regards anonymity on the part of the analyst – *not* being known to the patient – as the prerequisite for a productive analysis. Our patients have their own ways of finding out about us, and, besides, in training analysis we continually encounter our analysands in non-clinical situations. It is my experience that letting myself be known to my patients, in a certain measure, 'neutralises' the situation in a positive way; whereas the assumed anonymity of most analysts can provoke unnecessary infantile attachments and attitudes in the patient which analysts then interpret as the patient's transference. And whereas my clinical approach creates its own demands for both analyst and patient, it also facilitates that mutual sharing which is fundamental to my way of working.

Most patients come to us with clear-cut reasons for seeking analysis. We analysts tend to regard these with a certain suspicion, and to interpret them as some sort of defence in the patient against his true, hidden wishes. I have learned to take the patient at his word, and not be shamed if I am proved wrong; for this can often suggest different ways of looking at the patient's present and future, and it may also help to enlarge our perspective on the patient's past. Despite being trained clinicians in one school or another, we are as handicapped by our prejudices as are our patients by their own conduct or misconduct.

Analytic sessions are such private experiences between two persons that a third has no scope to 'sit in' and learn, as is the case in most other areas of medical practice. In his clinical work, therefore, the analyst draws upon the writings of his colleagues – which he assimilates according to his particular need and style – and I should like to acknowledge my own indebtedness to psychoanalytic literature in this respect. I also wish to express my gratitude to the patients who appear in this book; not only have they extended my range of human experience, but what they have taught me has made me able to help others better who have come into my care – or so I think.

[1987]

Chronological Bibliography

1984 'Prisons'. Published as 'Fate-neurosis, false self and destiny' in *Winnicott Studies: The Journal of the Squiggle Foundation*, 1, and in French as 'Prisons' in *Nouvelle Revue de Psychanalyse*, 30 (1984).

1984 'Outrage, Compliance and Authenticity'. Published in French as 'L'outrage' in *Nouvelle Revue de Psychanalyse*, 31 (1984) and in *Contemporary Psychoanalysis*, 22 (1986).

1986 'Thoughts'. Published in French as 'Pensées' in *Nouvelle Revue de Psychanalyse*, 31 (1986) and in German as 'Gedanken: Von der Liebe zum Hass zum Hass auf die Liebe' in *Psychoanalyse Heute* (1987).

1987 'The Long Wait'. Published in *Psychotherapies*, 3 (1987) and in *Normal Magazine* (1987).

References

Anzieu, D. (1974). 'Skin ego'. In *Psychoanalysis in France*, ed. S. Lebovici and D. Widlöcher (New York: Int. Univ. Press, 1980).

(1975). *Freud's Self-Analysis* (London: Hogarth Press; New York: Int. Univ. Press, 1986).

(1985). *Le Moi-Peau* (Paris: Dunod).

Auden, W. H. (1936). 'Detective Story'. In *Collected Poems* (London: Faber, 1976).

Balint, M. (1968). *The Basic Fault: Therapeutic Aspects of Regression* (London: Tavistock; New York: Brunner-Mazel, 1979).

Baudelaire, C. P. *Selected Poems* (Harmondsworth: Penguin, 1975).

Beckett, S. (1958). *The Endgame* (London: Faber).

Bion, W. R. (1967). *Second Thoughts: Selected Papers on Psycho-Analysis* (London: Heinemann Medical, 1967; New York: Aronson, 1984).

Bowlby, J. (1960). 'Ethology and the development of object relations'. *Int. J. Psycho-Anal.*, 41.

(1969). *Attachment and Loss*, Vol. 1, 'Attachment' (London: Hogarth Press; New York: Basic Books).

Brierley, M. (1937). 'Affects in theory and practice'. In *Trends in Psycho-Analysis* (London: Hogarth Press, 1951).

Cavafy, C. P. (1975). *Collected Poems* (London: Chatto & Windus).

Chasseguet-Smirgel, J. (1975). *The Ego-Ideal: A Psychoanalytic Essay on the Malady of the Ideal* (London: Free Association Books; New York: Norton, 1985).

(1984). *Creativity and Perversion* (London: Free Association Books; New York: Norton).

Clark, R. W. (1980). *Freud: The Man and the Cause* (London: Jonathan Cape/ Weidenfeld; New York: Random House).

Eliot, T. S. (1918). 'On Hamlet'. In *Selected Essays, 1917–32* (London: Faber, 1932; New York: Harcourt Brace, 1950).

(1935). *Murder in the Cathedral*. In *The Complete Poems and Plays of T. S. Eliot* (London: Faber, 1969).

Erikson, E. H. (1950). *Childhood and Society* (London: Paladin, 1977; New York: W. W. Norton, 1963).

(1959). *Identity and the Life Cycle*. In *Psychological Issues* (New York: Int. Univ. Press).

Fairbairn, W. R. D. (1944). 'Endopsychic structure considered in terms of object-relationships'. In *Psychoanalytic Studies of the Personality* (London: Tavistock, 1952; New York: Routledge, 1966).

Ferenczi, S. (1932). 'Confusion of tongues between adults and the child'. In Ferenczi, 1955, and Masson, 1984.

(1955). *Final Contributions to the Problems and Methods of Psycho-Analysis* (London: Hogarth Press).

Freud, S. (1895). *Studies on Hysteria. Standard Ed.,** 2.

(1900). *The Interpretation of Dreams. Standard Ed.*, 4 and 5.

(1904). 'Freud's psycho-analytic method'. *Standard Ed.*, 7.

(1905a). *Three Essays on the Theory of Sexuality. Standard Ed.*, 7.

(1905b). 'Fragment of an analysis of a case of hysteria'. *Standard Ed.*, 7.

(1912). 'Recommendations to physicians practising psycho-analysis'. *Standard Ed.*, 12.

(1915a). 'Observations on transference-love'. *Standard Ed.*, 14.

(1915b). 'The unconscious'. *Standard Ed.*, 14.

(1920). 'Memorandum on the electrical treatment of war neurotics'. *Standard Ed.*, 17.

(1927). *The Future of an Illusion. Standard Ed.*, 21.

(1937). 'Constructions in analysis'. *Standard Ed.*, 23.

(1904a). *An Outline of Psycho-Analysis. Standard Ed.*, 23.

(1904b). 'Splitting of the ego in the process of defence'. *Standard Ed.*, 23.

(1960). Letters to Martha Bernays. In *Letters, 1873–1939*, ed. E. L. Freud (London: Hogarth Press, 1960; New York: Basic Books, 1961).

(1985). *The Complete Letters of Sigmund Freud to Wilhelm Fliess, 1887–1904.* Trans. and ed. by J. M. Masson (Cambridge, Mass.: The Belknap Press of Harvard Univ. Press).

Green, A. (1973). *Le Discours Vivant* (Paris: Presses Universitaires de France).

(1975). 'Sexualisation and its economy'. In *Psychoanalysis in France*, ed. S. Lebovici and D. Widlöcher (New York: Int. Univ. Press, 1980).

(1976). 'L'autre et l'expérience du soi'. Introduction to Khan, 1974a, French edition: *Le soi caché.*

Hartmann, H. (1939). *Ego Psychology and the Problem of Adaptation* (London: Hogarth Press; New York: Int. Univ. Press, 1958).

Khan, M. M. R. (1955). 'The homosexual nursing of self and object'. Published in Dutch in *Inval*, Inhould 1, 1969.

(1963). 'The concept of cumulative trauma'. In *The Psychoanalytic Study of the Child*, 18; Khan, 1974a.

(1964). 'Ego distortion, cumulative trauma and the role of reconstruction in the analytic situation'. In Khan, 1974a.

(1965). 'Foreskin fetishism and its relation to ego-pathology in a male homosexual'. Part I of 'Fetish as negation of the self', Khan, 1979.

The Standard Edition of the Complete Psychological Works of Sigmund Freud, published in 24 volumes (London: Hogarth Press; New York: W. W. Norton).

(1969a). 'On the clinical provision of frustrations, recognitions and failures in the analytic situation'. In *Int. J. Psycho-Anal.*, 50.

(1969b). 'Vicissitudes of being, knowing and experiencing in the therapeutic situation'. In Khan, 1974a.

(1970). 'Le fétichisme comme negation du soi'. *Nouvelle Revue de Psychanalyse*. Part II of 'Fetish as negation of the self', Khan, 1979.

(1972). 'Pornography and the politics of rage and subversion'. In *The Case Against Pornography*, ed. D. Holbrook (London: Stacey, 1972); Khan, 1979.

(1973). 'The beginnings and fruition of the self – an essay on D. W. Winnicott'. In *Scientific Foundations of Paediatrics*, ed. J. Davis and J. Dobbing (London: Heinemann, 1981).

(1974a). *The Privacy of the Self* (London: Hogarth Press; New York: Int. Univ. Press).

(1974b). 'Freud and the crises of psychotherapeutic responsibility'. In Khan, 1983.

(1976a). 'Beyond the dreaming experience'. In Khan, 1983.

(1976b). 'From masochism to psychic pain'. In Khan, 1979.

(1977). 'On lying fallow'. In Khan, 1983.

(1979). *Alienation in Perversions* (London: Hogarth Press; New York: Int. Univ. Press, 1980).

(1982). 'The empty-headed'. In Khan, 1983.

(1983). *Hidden Selves: Between Theory and Practice in Psychoanalysis* (London: Hogarth Press; New York: Int. Univ. Press).

Lacan, J. (1966). *Écrits: A Selection* (London: Tavistock; New York: W. W. Norton, 1982).

(1973). *The Four Fundamental Concepts of Psycho-Analysis* (London: Hogarth Press, 1977).

Laplanche, J. & Pontalis, J.-B. (1967, Eng. trans. 1973). *The Language of Psycho-Analysis* (London: Hogarth Press; New York: W. W. Norton).

Little, M. I. (1985). 'Winnicott working in areas where psychotic anxieties predominate a personal record'. In *Free Associations*, 3 (London: Free Association Books).

Main, T. F. (1957). 'The ailment'. *Brit. J. Med. Psychol.*, 30.

Mannoni, M. (1985). *Un savoir qui ne se sait pas. L'expérience analytique* (Paris: Denoel).

Masson, J. M. (1984). *Freud. The Assault on Truth. Freud's Suppression of the Seduction Theory* (London: Faber; New York: Farrar, Straus).

Menninger, K. (1973). *Whatever Became of Sin?* (New York: Dutton, Hawthorn Books).

Milner, M. (1969). *The Hands of the Living God: An Account of a Psychoanalytical Treatment* (London: Hogarth Press; New York: Int. Univ. Press).

Pontalis, J.-B. (1972). 'Between dream as object and the dream-text'. In Pontalis, 1977.

(1975a). 'The birth and recognition of self'. In Pontalis, 1977.

(1975b). 'Trouver, accuellir, reconnaître l'absent'. Preface to Winnicott, 1971b, French edition: *Jeu et réalité*.

(1977, Eng. trans. 1981). *Frontiers in Psychoanalysis: Between the Dream and Psychic Pain* (London: Hogarth Press; New York: Int. Univ. Press).

(1986). 'Argument' for *Nouvelle Revue de Psychanalyse*, 33.

de Sade, Marquis. *Justine or Good Conduct Well Chastised* (New York: Grove Press, 1965).

Schilder, P. (1935). *The Image and Appearance of the Human Body* (London: Kegan Paul).

Smirnoff, V. (1980). 'The fetishistic transaction'. In *Psychoanalysis in France*, ed. S. Lebovici and D. Widlöcher (New York: Int. Univ. Press).

Spitz, R. A. (1959). *A Genetic Field Theory of Ego Formation* (New York: Int. Univ. Press, 1962).

(1962). 'Autoerotism re-examined: the role of early sexual behaviour patterns in personality formation'. In *The Psychoanalytic Study of the Child*, 17.

Starobinski, J. (1980). '. . . Alterius spectare laborem' (*Maldorer sur le rivage*). *Le Nouveau Commerce*, Cahier 45–46 (Paris).

Stoller, R. J. (1985). *Observing the Erotic Imagination* (New Haven, Conn.: Yale Univ. Press).

Strachey, J. & A. (1986). *Bloomsbury/Freud: The Letters of James and Alix Strachey, 1924–25*, ed. P. Meisel and W. Kendrick (London: Chatto & Windus; New York: Basic Books).

Winnicott, D. W. (1931). *Clinical Notes on Disorders of Childhood* (London: Heinemann Medical).

(1945). 'Primitive emotional development'. In Winnicott, 1975.

(1949). 'Birth memories, birth trauma and anxiety'. In Winnicott, 1975.

(1952). 'Anxiety associated with insecurity'. In Winnicott, 1975.

(1956). 'The antisocial tendency'. In Winnicott, 1975.

(1958). 'The capacity to be alone'. In Winnicott, 1965.

(1959/64). 'Classification: Is there a psycho-analytic contribution to psychiatric classification?'. In Winnicott, 1965.

(1960a). 'Ego distortion in terms of True and False Self'. In Winnicott, 1965.

(1960b). 'The theory of the parent-infant relationship'. In Winnicott, 1965.

(1962). 'Ego integration in child development'. In Winnicott, 1965.

(1963a). 'The development of the capacity for concern'. In Winnicott, 1965.

(1963b). 'Dependence in infant-care, in child-care, and in the psycho-analytic setting'. In Winnicott, 1965.

(1965). *The Maturational Processes and the Facilitating Environment* (London: Hogarth Press; New York: Int. Univ. Press).

(1969). 'The use of an object and relating through identifications'. In Winnicott, 1971b.

(1971a). *Therapeutic Consultations in Child Psychiatry* (London: Hogarth Press; New York: Basic Books).

(1971b). *Playing and Reality* (London: Tavistock; New York: Basic Books).

(1971c). 'Dreaming, fantasying and living: a case-history describing a primary dissociation'. In Winnicott, 1971b.

(1972). 'Basis for self in body'. *Int. J. Child Psychotherapy*, 1.

(1975). *Through Paediatrics to Psycho-Analysis* (London: Hogarth Press, 1975; New York: Basic Books, 1978).

(1984). *Deprivation and Delinquency* (London: Tavistock).

Index